Michael Booth is a journalist and food writer who contributes regularly to numerous British and overseas magazines, and has written for all of the UK's broadsheet newspapers.

EAT, PRAY, EAT

Terminally disappointed, and regularly the worse for wine, Michael Booth needed to change his lifestyle. Instead, he travels with his wife and two young children to the Indian subcontinent to write the definitive book on Indian food. From Delhi to Amritsar and the Taj Mahal, they meet the locals, sampling their different cuisines along the way. In Rajasthan they dine like maharajas before heading for Mumbai and the slums of Dharavi. But Booth's plan is derailed when his metaphysical, middle-aged malaise spirals deeper. Fortunately, his wife enrols Michael in a yoga bootcamp, and he is helped by a meditation guru to find equanimity and equilibrium. But can he ever regain his balance, overcome his addictions and face up to life as a husband and father?

MICHAEL BOOTH

EAT, PRAY, EAT

*One Man's Accidental Search for
Equanimity, Equilibrium and Enlightenment*

Complete and Unabridged

CHARNWOOD
Leicester

First published in Great Britain in 2011 by
Jonathan Cape
The Random House Group Limited
London

First Charnwood Edition
published 2012
by arrangement with
The Random House Group Limited
London

British Library CIP Data

Booth, Michael.
    Eat, pray, eat : one man's accidental search for
equanimity, equilibrium and enlightenment.
    1. Booth, Michael- -Travel- -India. 2. Spiritual
biography. 3. India- -Description and travel.
    4. Pranayama. 5. Food habits- -India. 6. Cooking,
India. 7. Large type books.
    I. Title
    915.4'04532–dc23

    ISBN 978–1–4448–1297–8

Published by
F. A. Thorpe (Publishing)
Anstey, Leicestershire

Set by Words & Graphics Ltd.
Anstey, Leicestershire
Printed and bound in Great Britain by
T. J. International Ltd., Padstow, Cornwall

This book is printed on acid-free paper

To all those approaching or past middle age, confronting their dispiriting physical decline; plagued by a gnawing sense of mortality; and frittering their time away on distractions, regrets, and very expensive kitchenware . . . everywhere.

And Lissen. Who is, thankfully, none of these things. Apart from middle-aged.

Preface

This book was originally intended to be a straightforward culinary travelogue, of a kind I have written before. I would journey around India, gently unearthing interesting regional recipes, meeting people who were passionate about food, and then conjure illuminating insights into their lives, their country and its history — a kind of culinary social anthropology. That was what I told my publisher, a kind, trusting, generous man who, perhaps because he is used to dealing with proper writers of eminent status, neither expected nor deserved to be presented with what follows.

You see, thanks largely to the intervention of my wife, this book instead turned out to be about what happens when a spiritually bankrupt, cracked-up, burnt-out, disappointed, gluttonous, low-functioning alcoholic father of two is confronted by the humanity, insanity and wisdom of the Indian subcontinent. Although, I should add, there was also a fair amount of eating along the way.

1

The Permanent Necessity of Distraction for the Psychological Equanimity of Mankind

> And then, ten years this side of forty-nine, I suddenly realised that I had prematurely cracked.
>
> F. Scott Fitzgerald, *The Crack-Up*

'Once you discount the various comforting, delusional myths to which some of our species subscribe — God, heaven, Father Christmas, Shanghai, and so on — everything we think, do, wish for or say is motivated by one of two fundamental imperatives: the need to reproduce, or the — I'd say, more pressing — need to distract from the horror of our own mortality. And, frankly, we might as well lump the sex stuff in with all that too and be done with it, because sex is just another distraction, isn't it?'

'Michael, don't you mean 'Shangri-La'? Shanghai does actually exist.'

'Oh, yeah, right, Shangri-La. That's what I meant.'

'So, how do you distract yourself?'

In answer to my friend's question, I sweep my arm around the room, taking in the empty wine bottles on the dresser behind me, the clean-scraped dessert bowls in front of us and the sink stacked with pots and pans.

'Food. I think about food, I read about food, I write about food, I eat food. You run marathons. You — ' I point, at this late hour a little vaguely, in the direction of the other dinner guests. 'You have your endearingly childlike fixation with football. You have your weird Bob Dylan obsession. And you buy every single shiny white plastic gizmo that Steve Jobs can come up with, regardless of its function or form.'

It had taken me almost forty years to fine-tune my grand theory of the Permanent Necessity of Distraction for the Psychological Equanimity of Mankind (although, as yet, it does not seem to have generated all that much buzz in philosophical circles), and I genuinely believed it. On this occasion I had chosen to share my insight with friends who were — fortunately — accustomed enough to my drunken sermons not to take it personally or, in all likelihood, to be listening in the first place.

'I can see that, if you don't have any spiritual belief, like you, life becomes kind of empty, but I see a flaw in your particular distraction,' said Jesper, the Apple Mac addict.

'What's that?'

'Well, the thing you have chosen to distract yourself with is probably going to kill you sooner rather than later.'

'And it'll be a lonely, sad, forgotten, constipated end, if your weekend in Rome is anything to go by,' added the marathon runner, laughing.

My wife, Lissen, and I had just been to Rome

2

without our two young sons, Asger, eight, and Emil, six, to mark our tenth wedding anniversary. Lissen had arranged the trip as a surprise, and I was thrilled. In the days leading up to our departure I scanned food websites, blogs and guidebooks to plan a comprehensive itinerary of gelaterias, pasticcerias, trattorias and wine bars, and on landing that first afternoon we pinballed across the city ticking them off my list.

This wasn't what Lissen had in mind, she told me, after the third pistachio ice cream of the day (pistachio is the best litmus for assessing a good gelateria, so, naturally, you have to try that before getting stuck into the other flavours. You can dismiss out of hand any places that colour their pistachio bright green. These people are not serious about their ice cream. They are making ice cream for children. Real pistachio ice cream should be a pale, almost browny-green, and preferably made from nuts harvested from the groves around the city of Bronte in north-eastern Sicily).

'Hmm, I see,' I reflected . . . inspiration!

'Why don't we split up for the rest of the day — you go off and see the churches and stuff, and I'll carry on to that cake shop with the cannoli I told you about on the flight — and we can meet back at the hotel before going out for dinner? I've booked us at two places. One of them has a Michelin star, but if we don't fancy that there's another less formal . . .'

'Michael, we are in Rome. We are alone. Today is our wedding anniversary. And you are suggesting we split up?'

3

It seemed the logical solution. Apparently it wasn't. For the next ten minutes, halfway up the Spanish Steps and at a volume that could have woken Keats, Lissen detailed the flaws in my plan. In the end I kind of got what she meant but, more to the point, I felt wretched that I had upset her so.

This was by no means an isolated incident on the path towards the lonely, loveless, indigestion-plagued demise predicted by my friend. I offer more examples here, not in any — almost certainly futile, but still worth a try — 'love me, I'm stupid' ploy, but to illustrate just how out of kilter my life had become, how fatally distracted my appetites had rendered me. Christmas is usually a bit of a flashpoint, too, for instance.

When you live a life of untrammelled gustatory self-indulgence; when you see nothing wrong in eating *foie gras* on an ordinary weekday; spend at least an hour a day and usually much more preparing the evening meal; and are pleasantly inebriated at least three times a week, upping the ante for Christmas is a challenge.

On the Christmas in question, I had bought a free-range goose, which I wanted to debone and then stuff with a deboned duck, rolling the two together in a kind of ballotine, and serve with a reduction of a stock made from the two birds' bones. It was an elaborate and technically challenging dish; pretentious and fussy and not something I would ordinarily make on a week-day. There would be *pommes purée* to accompany it, made according to the instructions I'd once been given when working in the kitchens of the

Michelin starred L'Atelier du Joël Robuchon in Paris — the flesh of fresh-baked potatoes arduously ground through a ricer and blended with an entire pack of butter; home-made red cabbage; various other trimmings; and individual chocolate soufflés with clementine sorbet for dessert. And then there were the chocolates I was making for the coffee, and a starter to prepare . . .

Lissen, though not especially religious, does feel that one should attend church on certain days of the year, primarily Christmas. I, on the other hand, don't believe there is any day on which church attendance is either necessary or desirable, and I certainly didn't have time to sit in a draughty, over-lit hall, singing about donkeys and listening to a second-rate theology graduate in a dress tell me how to live my life. There were carrots to *brunoise*, *bouquets garnis* to tie.

We had a fearful row. Apparently, I was placing the needs of my stomach above those of my family's spiritual nourishment. Lissen may even at one point have blurted, 'It's only food!' There were threats of non-cooperation regarding the washing up and so on, all of it ending with me huffing and sighing my way through most of the service, but leaving early having 'forgotten' to turn down the oven.

While we are on the subject of church, there was also the time I was caught eating the tiniest of nibbles, just the corner of one piece of a bar of Amedei Toscano Black 66 Extra Dark from my pocket during a funeral we were attending. It was Lissen's *farmor*'s, or grandmother's, funeral, but it was just a nibble. And she was really, really old, but it seems this was inappropriate behaviour.

At this stage, I might as well also ask the jury to take into account the 400 euros I was discovered to have blown on a surreptitious solo dinner at Guy Savoy, an exquisite, classical, three-star restaurant in Paris, just a week or so after I had vetoed a new sofa as un-affordable (although I would still argue that, if you consider the quality of produce and the man-hours that went into those fifteen courses, the meal was far better value and of more lasting consequence than any sofa could ever be); the £50 bottles of white Châteauneuf; the £400 countertop ice cream machine; and the fifty-mile round trip to buy some fresh curry leaves, crucial for an Indian dish I wanted to make.

We had recently moved from the centre of a city to the remote countryside, many, many miles from the nearest Indian restaurant or Asian food store; many, many miles from nori seaweed, fresh lemongrass, and couverture chocolate; from a decent selection of Burgundies; from fresh mangosteens and waiters who scrape your linen tablecloth between courses; from well-stocked deli counters, artisanal butchers and pistachio macarons — far from all the things I held dear in life.

Until this awful rupture in my life, I had eaten Indian restaurant food, on average, once a week for the last three decades of my life. Aloo bindi, saag paneer, chapattis, dhansaks, baltis and bhajis were a fundamental element of my diet

6

and without that tin foil coffin of dense, tangy, mouth-burning slop on a Friday night, I grew fidgety and morbid.

The reality was that we could no longer afford to live in the city. For the previous ten years we had supplemented our income by borrowing against our home, as many had, but with the economic armageddon of 2008 the music had stopped on that little game, and we'd been left scrabbling for a chair. Meanwhile, though the cost of living had risen, the rates offered by magazines and newspapers to freelance journalists had long been etched in granite. I was being paid precisely the same as when I started out as a journalist in the late nineties. In fact, many of the publications I wrote for had actually cut their rates; meanwhile the great, wild frontier of the internet was about as lucrative for a professional writer as a parish newsletter.

I don't mean this to sound like a whine. I made a reasonable living, akin to a fairly experienced teacher, albeit without the dignity that comes from making a lasting contribution to the betterment of society. And, of course, I have only myself, my poor choices, and, ultimately, one must conclude, my various deficiencies of character and talent to blame for my stunted career. When I had started out, naturally I'd had lofty ambitions to make a name as a writer but, though I'd had cover stories, picture bylines and — the most glittering prize of all — picture biographies on the contributors pages of national magazines (oh, how we journalists fret over those thumbnail portraits which most readers probably flick past wondering why they allowed ugly people into a glossy magazine), mine wasn't a name on which a newspaper purchase decision ever rested and, even after ten years, when I rang a new commissioning editor it was only a fifty-fifty chance he or she would have the first clue who I was. Having to break down editors' doors when, deep down, you feel that they should be beating a path to your door can be spirit sapping at the best of times. With your fortieth birthday looming, that kind of thing can weigh even more heavily; even minor snubs and career setbacks (the loss of a regular column; watching an editor steal an idea I had pitched) were affecting me disproportionately. I would fret over the nuances of an editor's hastily written email for hours trying to gauge whether they were being deliber-ately terse, or simply too busy for niceties and, of course, any actual, justified criticism had the power to lay me low for days. Whatever happened to the notion of mellowing with age? If anything, I was getting more angry, more resentful, more bitter. It wasn't pretty, and I am far from proud.

I wasn't clinically depressed — I would never try to dignify my behaviour or cheapen such a diagnosis by claiming that — I was just really, really unhappy, mired in a listless malaise, mostly of my own making, increasingly preoccupied by petty grievances and penny pinching.

To those with a salaried job, a temperamental boss, a dreary commute and a predictable career path, working for yourself must sound blissful. Certainly, those of my friends with grown-up employment had no tolerance whatsoever for my grumbling, and I do know that autonomy in one's life and work has been cited as one of the cornerstones of happiness. But autonomy brings with it a whole other set of stresses and strains, particularly if, like me, you have the self-control of a safari-park baboon in an airport long-stay car park, as a result of which working from home usually ends up with you eating every sugary or fatty substance you can find in the house during the course of a slow morning, and frittering entire days on non-work activities before realising, in my case usually around five-thirty in the afternoon, that you have achieved precisely nothing (other than finding the answer to what *did* actually happen to Terence Trent d'Arby).

It didn't help that my concentration was shot to smithereens. I made Asger's goldfish look like an air-traffic controller. It appeared that my synapses had either been scorched to buggery by the increasingly fragmented, frenetic nature of the modern communications I consumed intravenously, or simply withered with age. Scientists who know about this kind of thing say the internet is literally changing the way our brains work, weakening our prefrontal cortexes, turning us all into ADHD hummingbirds. They say that modern media and technology have created an environment of constant alarm or emergency: that flicking through television channels, for example, puts one on a high alert akin to Neanderthal man wandering through the jungle on the lookout for lurking things with sabre teeth. Every time you change channels or browser addresses, whenever a new email lands in your in-box, or your phone pings with an SMS, your brain is forced to readjust to what it perceives subliminally as a new environment or threat: you are on the sofa with Oprah one minute, in the outback with poisonous spiders another, waiting for your numbers to come up on the lottery the next, being asked whether that piece of work you promised yesterday is ready yet, and so on. No wonder that for many of us it all can be much to cope with; that our brains slowly subside under the ceaseless slurry of information.

The result, for me at least, was that engaging with anything for longer than a few minutes became impossible. Out of a usual working day of eight hours, I would estimate I spent thirty minutes to an hour on paid work. The rest was spent listening in on other, more successful journalists' Twitter conversations and feeling bitter that they were all friends with each other, were being invited to more literary festivals than me, and given more exciting commissions. Or, aimlessly revisiting blogs I had already visited that week in the vain hope of finding a new post about what the blogger had made for dinner the previous evening. Or checking all my email accounts. Or checking the Amazon ranking for all my books in turn, and those of my rivals or friends, then feeling dejected at the disparity between the figures. Or googling my name and/or the names of my books to see what — if anything — had been said about them recently. Or, looking at Friends Reunited in the (vain, it turns out) hope that the lives of the people I went to school with might be marginally more pitiful than mine. After all, as everyone knows, if you are spending time on Friends Reunited you are, by definition, a total lose — Oh.

The highlight of my day was picking the kids up from school and watching *Shaun the Sheep* with them when we got home, which was no way to earn a living. Actually, the highlight of my day if I am really honest, was the slow dissolve afforded by a bottle of Pinot Noir while making dinner at about six o'clock.

It is the fate of the failed to end their days surrounded by fields, far from a decent fromagerie. Apparently the local school was good, the kids could have a bedroom each, and there was also something about the air being cleaner, but my life as I had known it was over. I began to retreat within myself, brooding on my looming middle age, and how and why all my dreams had ended here amid endless industrial arable land without a Michelin star for miles.

One afternoon, I watched a nature documentary about the Siberian salamander, a singularly unappealing amphibian distinguished only by its ability to bury itself in permafrost and remain, essentially, frozen for several years at a time. Sometimes I felt that's what I wanted to do. Other times, I felt that's exactly what I was doing, out here, amid the muddy fields surrounded by people called Ted with tatty wax jackets and battered Subarus.

Where did it all go wrong? I wondered one day as I sat down on the side of the bed to put my socks on, my stomach having now reached a size where I was no longer able to do this standing up. (What next? Wearing my trousers up under my armpits, Peter Ustinov-style? Joining the local madrigal society? Gout?) Those of us who grew up in the eighties were indoctrinated with a belief that anything was possible, that we could achieve the most fanciful of dreams, that we deserved them, were *owed* them. Glittering success, wealth, fame and shoulder pads big enough to bear the complete works of Jackie Collins like improbable epaulettes — all these were your birthright, assuming you were ambitious and arrogant enough to grasp your destiny. Somehow, though, my life had turned out to be defined by a notable absence of penthouse apartments, Savile Row suits and costly timepieces. Instead, if I were to curate an exhibition of my life, prime exhibits would include a rusty Toyota, some IKEA shelving and box wine. I had a permanent overdraft, a wardrobe by Primark, and an escalating frequency of traumatic dental emergencies — the reality of life at the fag end of one's fourth decade.

If you have ever had the misfortune to be involved in a serious car accident you will be familiar with the sense, a second or two before impact, of how time slows down — all the better, I suspect, to sadistically present you with its inevitable consequences. Well, approaching forty takes those pre-impact seconds and elongates them to at least eighteen months.

'Up until you're forty, it's all 'Hello, hello, hello' to life and experiences,' one friend who had just passed that milestone moaned to me. 'Then from that day onwards, it's basically just 'Goodbye, goodbye, goodbye''. Forty. How could I possibly be about to turn forty? I can remember hearing of the death of John Lennon, and though realising it was sad, also feeling that, at forty, he had had a reasonable innings. But here I was about to enter the realm of the living dead myself, redundant, surplus to society's interest or requirements.

Middle age became a self-fulfilling prophecy: the closer it loomed, the more middle aged I became. I started reading the gardening pages, and found Radio 2 increasingly tolerable. I was irascible for much of the time. Anything could set me off: impolite driving; the use of the word 'impact' as a verb; the cost of electric toothbrush heads; people starting every sentence with 'Yeah, no . . .' I was cracking up. Slowly, sadly, laboriously collapsing in on myself — although, at the time I was sure nobody, not even Lissen, had noticed.

As a distraction (see?) from my career ennui, rural displacement and alarming physical decline (a lone but determined hair sprouting from my left ear; involuntary groans whenever I attempted egress from squashy sofas; a haemorrhoid the size of a horse chestnut), I embarked on various ambitious projects to make my own Indian food at home. But the results were a wan imitation. I could never get the sauces to thicken properly, the flavours didn't sparkle and zing like they did in good Indian restaurants. I thought — misguidedly, as I would discover — that ghee was simply clarified butter, and couldn't understand why my versions of my favourite dishes lacked the rich mouth feel and satisfying heft of the restaurant versions. Oh, what was the point?

Having children should, of course, have brought purpose, focus and joy into my life. Asger and Emil brought limitless amounts of the latter: they were in that golden age zone when your children actually quite like you, want to spend time with you, and are developing enough of a sense of humour to laugh at the same things as you — armpit farts, Gene Wilder movies, air drumming to 'Won't Get Fooled Again'. But the birth of one's children also very clearly marks the point at which your life is no longer just about you. Instead, it becomes, initially, about making sure their heads don't loll off; then it's about spooning mush into their tiny mouths; holding them up when they try to walk; getting them ready for school; making sure they make the most of the lessons school has to teach them; then it's about running a taxi service to ferry them to karate, swimming and guitar lessons; and, I imagine quite soon, to discos, parties and picking them up from the police station on a Friday night. At this fearful rate, it'll be wedding speech and goodbye for ever before I've had time to properly get to know them.

Again, this responsibility, and the displacement of one's focus from the purely solipsistic, should be a good thing, the final step to maturation as a well-rounded human being, but as a chronic narcissist, for me this development was tainted with regret at never achieving the goals I had set out for myself as a young man. Time had officially run out. Societal pressure insisted I now dedicate myself to my children's goals, not my own, but I still felt I had unfinished business.

The trouble was, for much of the time, instead of forging an upward career path, I would simply sit staring into the middle distance thinking about rectal cancer; fretting about a persistent mouth ulcer; contemplating my financial situation and how my family would cope if I fell seriously ill; and wondering who would turn up to my funeral and just how distraught they would be on a scale of one to ten. I was dogged by constant tiredness — exacerbated by hangovers — and the wearying guilt of a to-do list that never got done, and in truth never had a hope of ever getting done (loose electrical wiring is only dangerous if you touch it, right?).

So, it appeared I now had three things in common with one of my literary heroes, F. Scott Fitzgerald, when he wrote one of my favourite books, *The Crack-Up*: I was thirty-nine; it did appear that I had, in some way, cracked; and, thirdly, I had found in alcohol my perfect self-medication plan. (It was, of course, a shame that I didn't also possess an era-defining gift for rendering the frailties of my peers in unbearably poignant poetic novels of soaring grace yet intense economy, but you can't have everything.) And, though, looking back, the telltale signs of my own, far less tragi-romantic emotional fissures should have been all too apparent, neither did I share Fitzgerald's self-awareness regarding my own, dreary — I suppose at the time it felt inevitable — disintegration. Others

15

had spotted it, though.

'I've seen this before in men your age, and let me tell you,' a doctor I met at a party told me after we had been chatting about our lives for a while and he, presumably, had noted how many glasses of red wine I had guzzled during the conversation. 'If your life continues like this, something will break. It is not a question of if, but when you will have a breakdown.'

Lissen, also of course concerned, had suggested both yoga and meditation as lassos to a man up to his waist in quicksand. I point blank refused to participate in anything requiring either a fitness centre or the burning of joss sticks but as a compromise, for a while, and as an alternative, I am ashamed to say I did seek some kind of answer in self-help and pseudo-spiritual books. I read them all. *Awaken the Giant Within, The Seven Habits of Highly Effective People, How to Get More Done in Less Time, How to Have What You Want and Want What You Have* — trite, cloying, axiomatic, simplistic and useless, the lot of them. This was shampoo bottle philosophy — 'Because you're worth it!', 'Act how you want to feel!', 'Sing in the morning!' — all of it apparently addressed to an audience of brain-damaged Pollyannas. They said so very little to me about my life, for some reason usually in seven simple rules: I should learn to dance, they advised. Why not try laughter therapy? I should write self-affirming messages to myself on Post-its and leave them around the house, and so on. But my idea of therapy was reading a book, alone, with a bottle to hand. Or sleeping. Was that wrong?

A familiar refrain of the happiness gurus is, 'Be true to yourself'. But having mostly defined myself by my ambitions and my career, the truth was, as these had withered, I had very little notion of who remained. Others talked about God or the Universal Spirit, which was a non-starter as far as I was concerned, but most seemed content to regurgitate the same truisms over and over: set goals, think positively, count your blessings, learn to appreciate the little things in life, smell the roses, live in the now, kick your habits, join a club, floss.

One of the books was written by a man called Chuck Spezzano. I mean, *honestly*.

Another best-selling happiness book I read was by a French psychiatrist, François Lelord. *Hector and the Search for Happiness* is one of several *faux naïf* parables of the genre, in this case about a Panglossian shrink who travels the world trying to find out what makes people happy or not ('Over two million copies sold worldwide', according to the cover. As if that is any kind of recommendation — people slow down to look at car crashes, don't they?).

Along the way, Hector draws up a list of happiness 'lessons'. They include:

No. 8b: Unhappiness is being separated from people you love

and,

No. 10: Happiness is doing a job you love.

17

Well I'll be.

In an interview I read with Lelord he claimed: 'Some people are gifted for happiness. You can see it even in babies . . . It is like being good at maths, music or sport — you are born with happiness abilities, but after that you need to practise it.' People are born with a default happiness setting — which can be anything from 'clinically depressed' to 'joyful' — he said, and can only temporarily deviate from that according to external influences.

Though I am rarely separated from the people I love, and do a job I quite like (albeit with not quite the success I might have envisaged), it seems unlikely that I was born with a gift for happiness. My default setting lies more towards the Eeyore end of the spectrum.

One of the few books I read which did speak to me, Christopher Hamilton's *Middle Age*, had such an irredeemably dour message that it was all I could do to stop myself hastening off to bake my head as I turned the last page.

As we approach middle age, Hamilton writes, 'there is the cold presence of death . . . the body shows itself profoundly vulnerable to natural processes over which it has little or no control . . . the skull starts to stare out at us as we look in the mirror . . . It is, in fact, as if death is already inside one . . . '

Now we are talking.

By middle age, Hamilton continues, you will have realised how shitty the world is, how nice guys don't finish first, that your grand plans will come to nothing, 'that arrogance and conceit are often the requirements for success and prestige; and that goodness is usually largely held in place not by genuine virtue but by fear and anxiety'.

He quotes Maxim Gorky's Ryumin: 'And the older you get, the more you become aware of the filth, the banality, the mediocrity, the injustice that surrounds us . . . '

And to think, Gorky hadn't even *seen* daytime television.

Hamilton blames our Western culture of entitlement and attention-seeking for most of the ills of modern society: 'There is the need to be acknowledged as an individual. In its extreme form this becomes a craving for celebrity, the desire to be noticed, not just now and then by a few, but to be bathed always in warm glow of recognition, admiration, envy and desire.'

Did I mention that I was once interviewed on the *Today* programme, by the way?

★   ★   ★

One day, after I had spent an hour or so making a chicken tikka masala that was actually worse than the sugary industrial gloop you buy in jars, Lissen came into the kitchen, poured herself the last glass from the bottle of wine on the table, and sat down opposite me.

'Michael, this isn't working,' she said, looking down at the glass of wine, her fingers twisting the stem. My stomach plummeted. Were we really having this conversation? Surely things weren't that bad. I wasn't at all prepared for this.

'I think we need to get away,' she said.

'What . . . from each other, you mean?' Sometimes it did occur to me that Lissen might grow tired of me, eventually.

'Eh?' She looked up. 'No. All of us. You just look so tired. I can't remember when I last saw you look really happy. I am sick of these conversations we have about your drinking. You know how I feel about it, but you still do it. It's out of control. You're drinking way too much. I've been thinking about this a lot. I think we need a break, I think you need to get out of your rut, get away from your routine. I think it's the only way to sort this out. Why don't we go to India?'

'India? Are you serious? Take the kids to India? Are you mad?' I snorted. 'Think of the traffic, and the food bugs, and the poverty, and the heat, and the insects, the diseases, the malaria . . . ' Then I paused. A switch flicked in my head. Somewhere a voice whispered, 'Just think of the seekh kebabs, Michael . . . '

As if reading my mind — and, frankly, it wouldn't have required great psychic powers on her part — Lissen continued:

'I am completely serious. But there would be a condition. This would not — and I can't tell you how much I mean this — this would *not* just be one of your food tours. I am not traipsing around restaurants and food shops for three months.'

'Three months?'

'Yes, well, I don't think there's any point going all that way to sit on a beach for a fortnight, do you? Look, I am not thinking of this as a holiday.

20

There are some things I want you to experience first hand, some things I think can help you. If we don't sort things out soon, this family isn't going to function for much longer.'

What did she mean? Was it what I thought she meant?

'It would be good for all of us to open our eyes a little to how the less well off in the world live, wouldn't it?' Lissen continued. 'I'm not asking you to go to India and not eat, and maybe you can write some pieces while you are there, but if we come too, then we have to have an agreement. The deal is: I decide the general overall itinerary — where we go, how long we spend in each place . . . '

That sounded fair. Lissen had been to India in her twenties and often talked fondly about her time there. And, at least I wouldn't have the bother.

'And I get to plan every other day once we are there.'

I put my glass down. I knew exactly what she had in mind here: all kinds of spiritual shit. Temples and ashrams and people with matted hair and Maori tattoos. Joss sticks, yoga, vegetarians and hemp. Tie-dye, toe-rings, baggy cotton draw-string trousers, eyebrow piercings, crystal pendants, 'healing', chakras and organic pulses. Lissen had shown these kind of leanings before. She once roped me into an alternative therapy weekend in the woods close to East Grinstead where I had been instructed by a white witch to walk around pretending to be a balloon. The hot shame of this had seared itself into my cerebral cortex, a memory never to be erased, but India presented a whole new world of kundalini-chakra-chi balderdash to endure.

So, on the one hand, I had a vision of having to sit cross-legged in a cloud of sandalwood smoke holding my thumbs and forefingers together and chanting 'om'. On the other, were the dhosa, the fiery biryanis, tender koftas, soft, chewy chapattis . . .

'Okay, let's do it,' I said.

Lissen had a small amount of money saved which, she said, she hadn't told me about because it was her 'escape pod from you'. I took this in the spirit of openness in which it was offered, and tried not to think too much more about it. I said that I could perhaps find some articles to write while we were out there and talk to my agent about maybe getting a food book out of the trip.

We broke the news to Asger and Emil, nervous about how they would react to the prospect of being taken away from their new friends and home. But we pretty much had them at, 'the policemen ride elephants'.

We spoke to the teachers and head teacher at the school. Once we had made clear the educational nature of the trip — that we weren't going to sit on a beach in Goa for three months; that we would take in the great historical sights of northern India as well as travel extensively in the south — and agreed to take a heavy programme of schoolwork with us, they accepted.

Over the next week or so, while I began systematically buying up all the supplies of antibacterial hand gel within a twenty-mile radius, Lissen began plotting our three months in the subcontinent. Peering over her shoulder as she sat at her computer, I would offer helpful suggestions, which were mostly waved away.

Lissen's eventual plan went like this: we would fly to Delhi and spend the first month travelling, initially to Amritsar (where I imagined she would want to spend some time at the Golden Temple, but I had also heard they were expert deep-fryers and made the best lassi in India), and then through Rajasthan. A stay in Mumbai would be the jumping-off point for the next month spent travelling through Kerala and Tamil Nadu in the south. For our last month, I had suggested continuing over to the east coast, to Pondicherry, where there was an interesting historical culinary tradition with French influences, as well, of course, as Madras, famous for its spice blends. But that last four weeks' itinerary remained vague right up until our departure.

'I'll take care of it,' said Lissen. 'Don't worry about that.' Then she gave a little smile, just the slightest of smirks.

2

Primates, Partition, and Parabolas of Piss

Six months passed between the original decision to travel to India and our actual departure, a hiatus largely determined by awaiting the window of tolerable weather and reasonable prices which old India hands told us lasted from mid-January to mid-March. Any earlier, and you hit the peak holiday season when hotel rates and crowds are at their height, any later and you fry in the intolerable summer heat.

The six months gave us a decent amount of time to get ready but, for Asger, it also allowed time for anxieties to manifest.

'Do they all still have bows and arrows?'

'Who?'

'The Indians.'

I explained the misunderstanding.

'So, what, they have guns?'

To Emil, who asked, 'Will I still be able to see my friends?' I had to explain that his friends would be four thousand miles away but that we could skype them. 'You know, when you talk through the computer and can see the other person.' He looked at me as if I had taken leave of my senses.

In terms of fomenting fear and anxiety, the Discovery Channel had a great deal to answer for. We saw one absolutely horrifying documentary about a man in Mysore whom locals call to remove king cobras from their bathroom cupboards, and another about the threat to local villages in Bengal from man-eating tigers.

'Will they give us one of their guns?' asked Asger.

'What for?'

'For the snakes. They have snakes in their houses.'

'No, they don't give out guns, and there aren't really snakes everywhere like that.'

'What will we do if a tiger comes?'

'Distract him with jazz hands.'

I was nervous about the snakes. I read up on the threat online. That was a mistake.

'The King Cobra is the world's largest and most formidable venomous snake,' said one website. 'A bite from one can kill an adult elephant in less than three hours.' Over twenty thousand people a year die from snakebites in India,' it continued, adding that India also happens to be home to the world's second most venomous snake, the Krait, which 'has a tendency to seek shelter in sleeping bags, boots and tents'.

Then, of course, there were the spiders. I am a lifelong, card-carrying arachnophobe and have paid a couple of — stressful, yet ultimately unsuccessful — visits to psychologists over the years to try to deal with what I consider to be a completely rational fear of spiders. (They know I am afraid of them. Why else do they always come haring towards me at full speed?) Perusing the internet one carefree morning, I found a blog written by a Staffordshire family about their three-week tour of northern India. It mostly focused on the various lavatories with which they had become intimately acquainted, but in one photograph taken in some godforsaken guest-house in Chandigarh my eye was riveted to a gigantic spider clamped to the tiles beside the toilet roll holder. It was the size of a fruit bowl. I added the website to my bookmarks and, during the day, returned to it every half-hour or so, daring myself to touch the screen.

Other dangers which kept me awake at night, and surfing the internet wide-eyed by day, included: being stricken with exotic stomach infections (one family friend picked up a bug while visiting Mumbai four years ago and still suffers from the consequences of having half of his stomach removed in the subsequent treatment); dying in a horribly mangled car wreck (nearly 100,000 die in traffic accidents there every year: do not google 'Indian road traffic accidents'); terrorist attack (the Mumbai attacks, in which over 170 people died, had taken place just over a year earlier); malaria (up to 40,000 people are believed to die from malaria in India each year); and child abduction (no reason to believe India is more risky than anywhere else, but still, well, you know).

Another symptom of middle age of which you might care to be forewarned is that, just at the very moment in your life when you come to accumulate the most stuff — white goods, nasal hair clippers, children — you are also cursed with a keener sense of what you have to lose, which is why anxieties and fears, sometimes real but more usually imagined, increase exponentially.

'I have never met anyone as afraid of life as you are, Michael,' Lissen remarked to me one evening as I prepared small name, address and telephone labels and distributed them in the pockets of Asger's and Emil's clothing.

'It's not fear,' I said. 'It's preparedness. I've been thinking about these tracking devices you can have implanted under your children's skin. They are quite expensive, but I think they could be a good idea . . . '

From time to time I would try to probe more into Lissen's side of the itinerary. What was she planning? What kind of spiritual flim-flam would she be subjecting me to? What did she hope to get out of the trip? But she was tight-lipped, talking vaguely about trying to open my eyes to how lucky I was, helping me to 'find some balance' and, more ominously, curbing my drinking and 'getting fitter'. How was a trip around India going to make me fitter?

Finally, after a series of visits to the doctor for injections had made pincushions of our upper arms; after countless rows about what we could and couldn't fit in our rucksacks; after intense fretting over visas, footwear, sunblock, the right clothing and which antibiotics and stomach remedies to take; we found ourselves walking through the arrivals hall at Delhi Airport at six o'clock one January morning to the sound of Christmas carols playing over the tannoy.

As the customs official slowly turned the pages

of my passport and spent a few minutes getting his stamp in order, I gave everyone a precautionary squirt of antibacterial hand gel and turned on my mobile phone. It chirruped with an automatic message welcoming me to India and giving me the British embassy number for who to call in the event of an emergency. Even my mobile phone, it seemed, took it for granted we would get into trouble.

Inside our taxi on the way to our hotel, buzzing with the excitement of being in a very foreign land on a whole new continent, we wiped the mist from the windows, only to find that the mist was outside. It was an unexpected, cold, damp white blanket which we would get to know well over the first fortnight of our journey; fog is apparently common in northern India in January, bringing temperatures to almost freezing and disrupting air traffic, yet mentioned in no guidebooks. So much for preparedness.

From what we could see of it, Delhi appeared to be one great post-apocalyptic building site. The roadsides were lined with rubble, mounds of corrugated iron, and endless 'Work in progress' and 'Streetscaping' signs, though there was little evidence of any actual work. I spotted an outdoor storage area filled with stacks of asbestos sheets (luckily, strict safety precautions had been observed: someone had written a sign on a bit of card saying, 'Asbestos'). It was difficult to tell whether this disarray was on account of the impending Commonwealth Games, or simply Delhi's default state (hindsight revealed the answer to be 'both'). Everywhere people were huddled around piles of burning rubbish. Stray dogs — lean, urine-coloured curs — lay curled on the warm embers of these litter pyres. Sprawling camps of plastic and cardboard lurked among roadside shrubbery. And wherever you looked there were parabolas of piss as men stood or, worse, crouched, with their backs to the road relieving themselves. You soon learned not to look too closely at anyone loitering in the shadows.

Emil gave an excited yelp. 'Monkey! Monkey! Monkey!' He had spotted a troop of rhesus macaques rummaging through a pile of the kind of flimsy plastic bags with which India turned out to be almost entirely carpeted. They were a cheering sight.

Perhaps if I hadn't read so much about Infosys, the state-of-the-art call centres or India's role as an economic powerhouse among the emerging 'BRIC' countries, I might have been better prepared for a country whose capital resembled a Victorian-era London slum, but the popular narrative of modern India is a persuasive and appealing one. Delhi, though, had the feel of a place abandoned, lacking any controlling authority, its people devoid of a sense of civic society.

'I wonder, do you think God might actually be dead?' I said, staring out from our sixth-floor hotel room at the stagnant rubble which surrounded us. 'I mean, let's say for a minute he actually once existed and did create the universe, what if the sheer effort of it all was too much for him and that great burst of energy sort of conked him out?'

'Mummy! Daddy says God is dead,' cried Emil who, having spent some formative months at a Catholic primary school in Paris, tends to have a more conservative theological perspective on such things. I realise that blurting my thoughts out like that in front of my children won't win me any parenting awards, but I think I might be on to something. It would definitely explain the sense I often have of life on earth as some kind of rampant, unsupervised experiment and it also negates the need for the slightly unconvincing 'spontaneous creation' theory propounded by militant atheists to explain the birth of the universe.

We decided to hit the streets, so left our hotel and headed for Connaught Place, one of New Delhi's main hubs and the location of Palika Bazar, where we hoped to stock up on a few travel essentials. Asger had lost a crucial Pokémon figure and, as she always seems to do on arrival in a new city, Lissen needed to buy thermal underwear. Emil was now on the hunt for some undefined monkey-themed merchandise.

Leaving the calm of our hotel lobby we were finally about to see, hear and smell India, in all its unfiltered, unfettered glory. Emil gripped my hand tightly as we were met with a cacophony of car horns and two-stroke engines, and a wall of alien smells, few of them pleasant. I don't want to sound like some foppish eighteenth-century Grand Tourist fluttering a nosegay in front of my nostrils and prone to swoons, but at this early stage, unacclimatised as we were, it was all rather challenging. We were instantly accosted by people trying to show us the way to places we didn't want to go.

'You want shopping mall, sir? Follow me.'

'You staying at that hotel? Hey, I work there, let me show you the way.'

'Currency? Currency?'

'You want ladies, mister? Ladies?'

I stalked ahead briskly staring straight ahead, only to find that the rest of my small clan had already accumulated a carnival of shoe polishers, souvenir sellers and one man operating a wobble of ostrich string puppets.

Connaught Place, when we were finally able to shed our entourage and find it, turned out to be a cluster of concentric ring roads filled with a crazy carousel of *Wacky Races* traffic: battered auto-rickshaws; yellow and black Fiat taxis old enough to have ferried Nehru to assignations with Edwina Mountbatten; and buses which looked like they'd been cobbled together from tin drums formerly the property of an especially energetic steel band.

Stupidly, we actually attempted to cross this free-for-all, making several aborted runs into the motorised melée, before retreating back, shaken. Finally, we spotted other pedestrians disappearing down a subway to the bazaar in an island in the centre of the ring roads.

Once in the bazaar itself, I had my first lesson in Indian street smarts. A passer-by pointed out a splat of bird shit on my right shoe. There wasn't a bird in the sky but by an extraordinary coincidence there was a shoe cleaner to hand. I

31

paid him grudgingly. Lord knows what substance had been artfully splatted on my shoe, but whoever had done it — and my money is on that helpful passer-by — they had at least been charitable enough to avoid my trousers. (Thinking about it, the whole incident was uncannily reminiscent of the corporate business model of most of the telecommunications companies I've ever had dealings with: they shit on you, then charge you to clear up the mess.)

Lissen and Emil had gone off to explore another part of the market, leaving Asger with me. As the man crouched by my feet wiping the last of his faux bird poo from my shoe, I looked round to see where he was. Asger is both more outgoing and more tolerant of irritations than his younger brother, but that's a fatal combination when dealing with the street hawkers of Delhi. I finally caught sight of him, surrounded by a cluster of shoe shiners, postcard salesmen and ear-wax cleaners, reaching him just in time to intercept a man brandishing a rusty piece of wire which he was about to use to probe Asger's left ear.

After I had doused Asger in antibacterial hand gel, we returned to our hotel room where we spent the rest of the afternoon watching Bollywood gossip shows, with their breathy, excitable bulletins detailing which actress had snubbed which former lover on the red carpets of Mumbai. Apparently two actors called Salman Khan and Shahrukh Khan were engaged in a long-running feud the intensity of which made that of the Campbell and MacDonald clans look like a toddlers' squabble. I hadn't a clue who these people were, but I was hooked.

★ ★ ★

That evening, I was in charge of the itinerary and had arranged to meet one of Delhi's top food writers, Sourish Bhattacharyya, of the *Mail Today* newspaper, a recently launched Indian version of Britain's *Daily Mail* aimed at the country's burgeoning middle class.

Sourish was a jovial, balding man in his late forties, whose sizeable girth betrayed a professional life spent at Delhi's better tables. On his recommendation we met at the Embassy Restaurant near to our hotel.

'This is as old as India itself,' he said as we settled down to our table in the spacious, chintzy dining room filled with the enjoyable hubbub of Indian families at table. 'The family who started it came from the Punjab after Partition. They had an Embassy Restaurant in Karachi, and when they finally made it to Delhi they opened another.'

This 'Midnight's Restaurant' is today one of the most venerable in Delhi; among other claims to culinary posterity, its owners introduced ice cream to India in 1948. Its decor was a little careworn but it served truly majestic Punjabi cuisine — rich, deeply tasty, and aromatic. The gravies, particularly the one accompanying my butter chicken, had a striking umami tang, like the crust that congeals around the top of the ketchup bottle (in a good way), while the meats had the succulence and lightly charred flavour that can only come from a pukka tandoor oven.

Before leaving for India, experts had told me that the food I would eat there would be nothing like the Indian food I was used to in the UK, but though they were of an infinitely superior quality and had far more nuanced, vivacious flavours, the dishes we ate at Embassy were at least recognisable.

'Well, of course,' said Sourish. 'The food you know as Indian is really a mix of Punjabi and Bangladeshi food. They were the people who were most affected by Partition, the ones who, if they at all could, left India and ended up in your country.'

The historian Lizzie Collingham describes this extraordinarily successful, cultural-culinary invasion in *Curry: A Tale of Cooks and Conquerors*, explaining how the post-Partition Punjabi — and, to an even greater extent East Bengali — diasporas of the late forties and fifties brought 'curry' to Britain. There were already Indian restaurants in Britain by the early nineteenth century: the first cropped up to serve the nabobs — retirees of the Anglo-Indian community — around Portman Square in London, but it was this mid-twentieth-century wave of immigration which disseminated curry across the British Isles.

We all tucked into chicken malai tikka (a creamy chicken dish), chicken pakora (deep fried in chickpea flour batter), Amritsari fish (river sole cooked with gram flour, carom seeds and a special masala) and seekh kebabs (pounded lamb, mixed with herbs and spices and formed around a metal skewer). 'There are two main kinds of Punjabi cuisine. There is frontier food, from Peshawar, which is chunky, not so spicy, with fatty mutton. It's very simple, with garlic and salt marinades. But this is the creamy, dairy-heavy Punjabi food, with a Persian influence. They will use perhaps thirty to forty different types of spice in the masala.'

Masala — the toasted, ground spice mix elemental to much Indian cooking — is the single most daunting element of so many Indian recipes, with all those quarter-teaspoons of this and half-teaspoons of that. 'I know,' said Sourish. 'But you don't need to worry.' He turned to greet an older man wearing a dark, three-piece suit. 'This is Sunil Malhotra, the owner of the Embassy. We were just talking about Indian recipes. Michael here can't quite cope with measuring all the ingredients.'

'Ah,' chuckled Mr Malhotra. 'Don't worry about measuring. We don't. In India nothing is precise. Nothing is measured. We just use our fingers.' He pinched his thumb and first two fingers together. Sensing the conversation was moving inexorably towards food, Lissen — who likes food, but sensibly doesn't take it much beyond actual eating — made her excuses and headed off for an early night back to the hotel with the kids, who had nibbled tentatively at most of the dishes, but devoured the sweet, billowing clouds of naan bread (setting the pattern for many of their meals during the trip).

I asked Mr Malhotra the secret of the breads,

35

the best naans I had ever tasted. 'Come, I'll show you,' he said, heading off to the kitchens. There, in a fearsomely hot, dark kitchen straight from the Middle Ages, were the twin tandoor ovens, the pride of the Embassy.

'Nothing cooks meat as good as a tandoor,' explained Sourish, who had joined us. 'You can get it so hot, but the meat always stays moist and tender.'

The ovens reached up to 300 degrees centigrade, Mr Malhotra explained, and the tandoor post is the toughest in the Indian kitchen because of that. Three scrawny men, their hair wet with sweat, flicked floppy frisbees of dough in and out of the ovens with great skill. 'My cooks have to stand right over them all night. We instruct them they have to drink lime juice with salt and sugar all through the evening.' The best type of tandoor is a clay one buried in the ground, he explained, then come the clay ovens above ground (the type they used at the Embassy), and then, for home use, metal tandoors, which are commonly available throughout northern India and, increasingly, as regional Indian dishes go pan-subcontinental, in the south too.

We returned to the table, and Sourish ordered another bottle of the surprisingly drinkable Sula Vineyards Sauvignon Blanc. Wine-making is a recent development in India, and Sula, a Californian-inspired operation founded in 1997 a hundred miles north-east of Mumbai, is the market leader. We finished our second bottle along with two Embassy Puddings, proudly brought to our table by Mr Malhotra. 'A *Charlotte* with

36

an Indian touch!' he said, setting the fruit-soaked sponges down in front of us.

Our conversation turned to Partition, the seismic mass migration of Hindus from what is now Pakistan to India, and of Hindustan's Muslims in the other direction. It affected over 14 million people. Up to a million people are thought to have died as a result, while countless more endured unimaginable hardship, first during the migration itself, and then in attempting to forge new lives in what was, for many, enforced exile in a foreign land. Some call it India's holocaust, and all of it — the atheist feels obliged to point out — prompted by the mutual intolerance of two groups of people towards each other's religious dogmas. And, for all the turmoil and unthinkable suffering, India still boasts the third largest Muslim population in the world after Indonesia and Pakistan, along with a powerful Hindu fundamentalist movement doing its best to make their existence a misery.

But Mr Malhotra had a more upbeat, revisionist take on Partition, one I had never even considered before: 'Yes, it was a bad time,' he said. 'But just think how big India would be today if it hadn't been divided! I don't think about the bad times — even at the time we just could not go into them. There were children, mothers, we had to rebuild and start again, or else what?'

Personally, if my family had been forced to leave its hereditary home, seen its hard-earned property taken over by its most hated enemy, and been made to rebuild its shattered existence in a foreign place where it wasn't really welcome, I might feel a little differently about matters. Most likely, I would have curled myself up into a ball and hoped it would all go away. It occurred to me that Mr Malhotra was the living embodiment of the trite, 'think positive' approach recommended by so many of my self-help books. Hearing him recount his family's experiences and explain, without any apparent resentfulness, how their attitude to their new life in Delhi had been born from a sheer survival imperative, the rationale behind the triteness struck me quite powerfully. The victims of Partition, at least the ones who survived, simply had to find the tiny scraps of potential in their situation, they had to believe the next day would bring a minuscule, incremental improvement on the one which had preceded it, and that, in the long term, their dreams would ultimately flourish in new soil, whether it be the bloodstained earth of India, or the hostile hinterland of the British Midlands.

Sourish and I ended the evening at one of his favourite bars, the Gem Bar, a rough, narrow second-floor room off Paharganj, a grubby, knackered street popular with backpackers. We drank potent and, frankly, vile White Monk rum until the early hours. As we said our unsteady goodbyes, Sourish promised to take me to his favourite Rajasthani restaurant the next day.

'Well, what do *you* think?' said Lissen when I asked if this would fit in with her plans when we woke the next morning.

'You're not really going to enforce this alternate

day itinerary business, are you?' I asked.

Her look, which could have frozen a marauding tiger at fifty paces, was all the answer I required. It appeared I must brace myself for some spiritual tourism.

3

Bye Bahá'í

In his novel, *White Tiger*, Aravind Adiga describes Delhi as 'the capital of not one but two countries — two Indias — the Light and the Darkness both flow into Delhi'. But so, too, are there light and dark Delhis, New and Old. Old Delhi's decrepitude was stupefying. They say the city you see today is — at the latest count — the fourteenth incarnation of a major settlement here and it looks like it. Its buildings were virtually all in a state of parlous disrepair, even the recent ones — especially the recent ones — which seemed to have been built from some type of easy-crumble, hard-to-clean meringue. Meanwhile, New Delhi's broad avenues, named after the likes of Simón Bolívar and Tolstoy (a testament to India's communist past and Cold War links with Russia), along with its sterile lawns and Lutyens' architecture, seemed to exist in complete denial of their rambunctious neighbour.

Life for most residents of Delhi — at least, the ones who lived their lives in public, there are doubtless Delhi-ites with sufficient wealth to insulate themselves from the torrent of everyday life — seemed to be coloured various shades of wretched. I watched my young sons from the corner of my eye as they took it all in during our

40

drive through the city the next morning. They didn't seem that perturbed, actually. It wasn't that they didn't notice the poverty; more as if they were trying to figure out exactly what it was they were looking at. They simply lacked the cognitive tools, the experiential references, to interpret what they were seeing.

At traffic lights close to India House a small homeless girl cartwheeled across the street and rapped on the rear window of our car where Emil was sitting. I was in the front passenger seat but could see him in the rear-view mirror to my left. He smiled at her, and waved. She pulled a face as if to say, 'Can't you give me something, just a little money or some food?' cupping her hands together. Lissen was talking to Rashed, our guide and driver, but I saw Emil reach over to a plastic bag we had brought with us containing some snacks and water for the day. He held it up, mouthing, 'What? You mean this?'

I nudged Rashed to hold the electric window up. We had been told there was a risk that traffic-light beggars had accomplices in tow who might use an open window to grab more than the few rupees customarily offered to them. Emil kept jabbing the button, mystified at its malfunction and gesturing apologetically to the girl, who scowled angrily. The lights changed, we drove away, and I felt awful on both their parts. I was not only thwarting my son's generous intentions and depriving a needy child of some food, but it seemed I had already switched to my default setting of wary unease. I was pulling up the drawbridge on India.

41

I looked over at some of the gigantic billboards which envelop most of the city's crossroads. If advertising is an accurate mirror of a society, then India's adverts did not reflect a nation entirely at ease with itself either. In one, a fat child was stuffing his face with a candy bar while sitting at his school desk. Children in Indian ads always seem to be on the porky side and are usually wearing glasses, presumably both signifiers of aspirational wealth and education. The candy bar, the ad claimed, helped him to study. Next to it was one of the ubiquitous ads for skin-whitener masquerading as a 'sun protector', touting reams of flaky pseudo-science. But the most implausible billboards featured computer-generated images of forthcoming apartment blocks — invariably bright pastel colours, with spacious balconies and residents picnicking on perfectly tended lawns. They might as well have been pictures of a Mars colony.

We were en route to the first stop on Lissen's spiritual itinerary for the day, the Bahá'í Mandir, or 'temple'. 'I think this might be a religion even you approve of, Michael,' she said as we arrived at the temple's immaculate grounds. I would have liked to argue, but my knowledge of the Bahá'í faith was scanty.

'Isn't it an Islamic sect?' I asked.

'No, it is 'a humanitarian religion which prides itself on being open to all',' she read from a guidebook. ''The temple is the last of seven built around the world, each of them nine-sided, and built to welcome people of all faiths to pray together in worship of the creator of the

42

universe.' Now, even you can't argue with that.'

'Hmm, 'creator of the universe', you say . . . might have a bit of a schism there already, I'm afraid,' I said. 'So where are the other temples?'

'Panama,' began Lissen. 'Wilmette in the US, Western Samoa and Kampala.'

'Only the best addresses then,' I said. 'This is clearly a religion looking to be taken seriously.'

We walked through the temple grounds with its closely trimmed lawns, towards a cathedral-sized, white, concrete water lily. Teenage American missionaries in Gap sweaters and white sneakers guarded the entrances to the 'lily', shushing the Indian visitors as they entered, and lending the place a cultish atmosphere. These were that peculiar breed of earnest American kid, with perfect teeth, a slightly forced, upbeat manner, and the IQ of a cheeseburger. They shushed Asger, who was singing the theme tune to *Harry Potter* and casting spells with a stick.

Inside, it was odd to be in a place of worship with no focal point — no altar or pulpit, just pews arranged in a semicircle. Lissen had long given up playing advocate for any religion, but she explained that the Bahá'í faith is supposedly the rationalist's choice, seeking equality, international peace, human rights and so forth. Also on the plus side, there is no old, angry dude in a dress at the top of its hierarchy. But its golden age was the sixties and seventies; today, there are thought to be only about five million followers around the world, and it seems to have slipped

43

from the religious Premier League.

On the wall of a small museum on the other side of the park there was a summary of the Bahá'í faith's tenets, none of which — aside from the weird bit about an auxiliary language — you could really argue with:

The oneness of Mankind.
Independent investigation of Truth.
Equality of men and women.
Elimination of prejudice of all kinds.
Universal Peace.
The common foundation of all religions.
The adoption of a universal auxiliary language.
The abolition of extremes of wealth and poverty.
The founding of a World Tribunal to adjudicate in national disputes.
Strict obedience to the government of one's country.

'But do we really need a religion to formulate these kind of goals?' I thought as I sat down on a bench for my first moment of nonsleeping stillness in about thirty-six hours. Then I started thinking about lunch. I made a, 'So, shall we be making a move?' face, and Lissen rolled her eyes and sighed.

As we left the temple gates I looked around for Emil, who had slipped from my hand. He had scampered about fifty metres away where he was now crouching in front of a man sitting cross-legged on the pavement. In front of the man was a basket, its lid askew. The man was holding some kind of crude wind instrument

44

made from a varnished gourd. It couldn't be, could it? It was. A snake charmer. I began to hasten over to grab Emil but it was too late, the black cobra, its scales shiny like worn leather, had raised its head and turned towards my young son. It flared its hood like a vampire's cloak. Encouraged by its handler, Emil stretched out to stroke the snake. I stopped dead in my tracks.

I hissed, 'Emil! No!'

I had visions of his arm blackening rapidly as the venom coursed towards his heart, a mad rush through Delhi's treacly traffic, desperate explanations at some grotty local hospital and, well, I didn't allow myself to go any further.

'Okay, okay, sir. Is okay,' said the snake charmer, who lifted the basket with one hand and moved the snake towards his own cheek, allowing it to caress his face. The snake seemed drugged; either that or improbably affectionate.

'Don't worry,' said Rashed. 'They keep them in the baskets to weaken them, and they remove their fangs. There is no danger.'

Emil spent some time stroking the snake, increasingly emboldened, while Asger held back, wisely in my view using his younger brother as a test case and brandishing his wand just in case.

I had taken Rashed aside to consult on the matter while we were in the temple. We had agreed on one of the most famous restaurants in Old Delhi, Karim's, supposedly run by descendants of the chefs who had cooked for the Mughal kings in the Red Fort until the mid-eighteenth century.

'It's near the Jama Masjid,' I told Lissen. 'So we can go and see that at the same time, if you like.'

'But you can only get properly into Old Delhi by cycle rickshaw, is that okay?' added Rashed.

So into two frail and spindly cycle rickshaws powered by two frail and spindly cyclists we climbed. The men, who looked like contemporaries of the Tollund Man, began to move, their heads down, standing up, grinding down on the pedals. Soon we were speeding along quite alarmingly, dodging traffic, pedestrians, the odd cow, and men carrying improbable loads. My usual fanatical insistence on child seats, seat belts and airbags seemed hopelessly fey in such circumstances. It was my first lesson that, when confronted with Indian traffic, you really have to disconnect your imagination or nervous breakdown will ensue. Our rickshaw pedallers hardly raised their heads from navigating the colossal potholes yet somehow avoided the myriad opportunities for collision, before finally depositing us at the entrance to a dark and narrow passageway between two crumbling shops. Here, I took a moment to unclench.

Emerging from the alley we came to Karim's Restaurant. Its kitchen was perhaps ten square metres in all, with a charcoal kebab grill, iron tureens of curry sitting over small charcoal braziers and a group of men making breads on the floor behind. It was separated from the dining room by a narrow open-air alleyway through which motorbikes occasionally passed while, above, pigeons loitered on a cat's cradle of

46

electrical cables. Food seemed to arrive from all around us: from rooms above and to the side, as young men in grubby Karim's uniforms emerged from doorways and stairs carrying trays of terracotta cooking pots. Every surface was thick with the grime of a million meals; the place looked like it hadn't been cleaned since it opened in 1913, but the food was terrific — heavily spiced, heavily charred, but juicy and flavourful, the world's greatest barbecue food.

We stuffed ourselves on mutton burra (tandoor-cooked mutton), dal makhani (a classic Delhi lentil dish), sheermal naan (kneaded in milk) and lazeez murgh saag (spicy chicken and spinach) — most dishes costing around three or four pounds, expensive by Indian standards. A korma I ordered for the boys turned out to be too spicy for them, so I ate that too, along with a whole Amritsari fish, char-grilled and salty. I couldn't resist a helping of butter chicken, rich with its thick, sweet gravy and soft, tender chicken chunks. This wasn't pretty or refined food, but there was a divine marriage between the tanginess of the yoghurt and limes and the sweet, succulent meat.

That was lunch. Oh yes, and we also saw the largest mosque in India, the Jama Masjid; the Jain Bird Hospital nearby (not so much a 'hospital' as a place sick birds are taken to die); the Red Fort; and Indira Gandhi's cremation site. Stuff like that. But, to be honest, I was feeling a bit slothful that afternoon for some reason, and mostly thinking about dinner.

4

Chat, Thalis and Red Light Kebabs

I was probably about six years old when I ate my first Indian meal, in a low-lit, chintzy cave of a restaurant with thick, patterned carpets and high-backed, burgundy velvet chairs. I can still hear the quavery sitar music and remember the efficient, disinterested bustle of its black-clad staff as they pulled out chairs and handed out laminated, folded menus. Someone would have ordered for me: sugary onion bhajis and flying saucer poppadums, with four dips (only one of which I dared taste) offered in a pressed steel stand, followed by an equally sweet korma with king prawns and, if I am not mistaken, featuring both lychees *and* pineapple chunks, along with multicoloured rice which reminded me of the hundreds-and-thousands which festooned a Fab ice lolly. I ate all this viewing the adults through a golden prism of bollard-sized beers.

For a child who had until that point mostly eaten brown things with brown sauces, it was revelatory, the culinary equivalent of the transition from black and white to colour in *The Wizard of Oz*. The sense of wonder continued into dessert: a whole orange, frozen, and filled with permafrost sorbet which I chipped diligently away at like an Arctic archaeologist.

That whole, frozen orange has been about my

only experience of the world of Indian desserts ever since, aside from the odd, tentative foray into Indian sweet shops on Brick Lane, with their gaudy array of alien cubes and spheres.

'We can't have that!' said Sourish, when I told him all this. 'I have to take you to my favourite chat shop. How about tomorrow night?' And so I found myself squeezed in alongside Sourish in his titchy Maruti Suzuki whizzing through the New Delhi night to the snack shops of Bangla Sahid Road.

Sourish talked me through the array of syrupy sweets and snacks — many of them Punjabi — laid out in neat rows behind his favourite store's glass cabinets, and ordered a plate of chat — sometimes spelled 'chaat', as it is pronounced — for himself and one for me, bringing the two perilously floppy paper plates over from the counter to where I sat waiting on a high stool by a table in the corner of the shop.

Chat was quite unlike any foodstuff I had ever seen: a plate of ectoplasm covered in an eclectic landscape of vermicelli, yoghurt, coriander, chutney, lentils, wheat flour poppadums, bhalla (one of Indian cuisine's numerous variations on the spongy doughnut), nuts and pastry. With its barrage of savoury, sweet and sour flavours and crunchy-slippery textures I am afraid I found it pretty disgusting, but ate as much as I could out of politeness.

Perhaps sensing my doubts, Sourish insisted we hop back in his car for a ride across town to his favourite Gujurati-Rajasthani restaurant, Suruchi, on Ajmal Khan Road. We left the car in

49

a side street and wandered down dark, shabby, deserted streets. Sodium lights cast an eerie glow in the fog and groups of men huddled around shuttered shopfronts; the only other light came from the occasional fluorescent tube strung above a street cart. Despite the unpromising build-up, Suruchi was wonderful. We each had a thali: multiple small dishes served on one large circular tray, with breads and rice, pickles, onion and sauces and slices of lime on the side. Suruchi is famous for its hospitality, which meant that no sooner had I emptied one of the small bowls than a waiter would come and refill it, offering more bread and rice. The food was spicy, but tolerably so and included foraged seeds, tart desert berries and dried leaves, marinated in a thick, brown pulp. There were baja roti, made with something called foxtail millet, and gut-busting gatta, a heavy, dense chickpea dumpling that is a classic of the region. And, of course, more bottles of that excellent Sula wine.

I spent the next couple of days continuing my whirlwind introduction to Delhi food. Looking back, I had fallen into a familiar pattern, the same old distractions, and I was using the excuse of researching a magazine feature to renege on the agreement I had made with Lissen. Naturally, she was not best pleased about this.

That night, after I got home from my evening with Sourish and explained my plans for the following day (a posh lunch and a tour of Old Delhi's street food with another journalist), Lissen and I had a bit of a talk, or a hissed

50

whisper, as the kids were asleep on their camp beds.

'I knew this would happen. Tomorrow is my turn for the itinerary, remember?' said Lissen, seething because I was already undermining her plans.

'Yes, I know but, really, this is the last of my food stuff, I promise. I've got to do this for the article.'

Of course, had I known the nature of the payback I would endure later on in our trip for this gluttony, I would have thought twice and perhaps gone to bed early with a water biscuit. But it was at least true that I was researching a piece on the Delhi food 'scene' (there is no such thing, of course, but editors like a 'scene') and used this as an excuse to turn the rest of my stay in Delhi into one great meal after another.

At one restaurant, Fire at the Park Hotel, I got chatting with its chef Backshish Dean, a Punjabi Christian (hence the unusual name). Backshish, a bulky jovial man in his late forties, invited me to join him on a trip to some of his suppliers at Azadpur market (I told Lissen that my lunch at Fire had overrun) — a place where few if any tourists go. It is reputedly the largest market in Asia — the fruit and veg section covers ten square kilometres alone — but there is a good reason tourists don't venture here: this is not a picturesque market; not one for skipping through loading up your wicker basket with nice bits for a picnic. Azadpur is in the business of feeding half a billion people every day, and that is never going to look pretty. Rotting produce carpeted the

51

streets. See the butchers here, in particular, and, if you are even just marginally more intelligent than me, you will never eat meat in India again.

At the end of our trip we visited a cold-storage building over eleven storeys high, where all the stevedores were Nepalis: 'They are used to the low oxygen and they can take the cold and the steep stairs,' explained the owner, Anish, as we stepped aside to let a couple of men pass. They were bent double, bearing gigantic loads on their backs up the narrow wooden stairs.

When you see people whose working lives are this arduous, it does make you think twice about getting angry over the cost of printer ink cartridges, or fretting about grumpy editors. How, I thought, could I possibly complain about my Amazon rankings or poor word rates when there are people in this world who work ten hours a day carrying loads of twenty or thirty kilos up narrow, steep staircases in temperatures of four degrees? Perhaps, I thought, I might try to remember these men the next time I felt cross about my broadband connection, while sitting in my cosy office looking out at the fields.

★ ★ ★

Later that afternoon, still on a quest for stories for my food book, I found myself bouncing through the streets of Old Delhi, squashed into the back of a cycle rickshaw side by side with a character plucked straight from a Salman Rushdie novel. 'I've caught jaundice twice,' Rahul Veerma told me cheerfully as our elderly

52

rickshaw wallah stopped beside a hole-in-the-wall selling kakori kebabs. 'It's an occupational hazard, you might say.'

Veerma, a gourmet communist with a penchant for fine single malts, had agreed to show me around his favourite feeding posts. He is another of India's leading food writers and Delhi street food is his specialist subject, at least when he is writing for the *Hindu Delhi* newspaper. When he writes for the *Hindu Kolkata* it is on that city's fine dining scene. 'The food is generally more refined in Calcutta. They serve it in individual courses and they have proper beef instead of the buffalo you get in Delhi,' he says. 'But I love the vibrancy of Delhi.' Veerma breezily dismissed the paradox of a staunch communist (he was a former trade union leader) writing about posh restaurants: 'Well, I have to make a living, you know' — and accepted a bottle of Talisker as his fee for my tour. It was a price I was happy to pay to delve deep into an urban food scene which many might avoid like, well, jaundice — that being merely one of many ailments you might acquire by eating on India's 'vibrant' streets.

Pier Paolo Pasolini, who travelled extensively in India, wrote of 'that smell of poor food and of corpses which in India is like a continuous powerful air current that gives one a kind of fever. And that odour which, little by little, becomes an almost living physical entity . . . ' I have no idea if what I smelled on the streets of Old Delhi was corpses, but I would not have been at all surprised. Brown dust coated every surface and the gutters ran rust-red with paan spit, yet for all this, the place was utterly compelling. The congestion — vehicular, bovine and pedestrian — is impossible. Stick to the pavements and you'll be there all day. I stuck instead to Veerma as he darted with surprising spryness for a man of his self-professed decrepitude — 'It's my knees, I'm afraid' — around handcarts, cows and piles of fearful, unidentifiable detritus. We stopped only to sniff the air. 'Ah, ghee, can you smell it?' he smiled.

Though it appears the very apogee of chaos, Old Delhi, formerly Shajahanabad, is self-ordering, with traders of one type tending to congregate in parades of similarly themed open-fronted shops, be they electrical suppliers, spice merchants or whores (there is even an abattoir district somewhere in the midst of it all). 'Cities and palaces have risen and fallen on the plains of Delhi, but Chandni Chowk [the avenue which runs through the centre of the old town] is indestructible, the heart of both old and new,' wrote Ruskin Bond. Actually, I am not sure 'indestructible' is the right word. The place looks more as if it has been destroyed numerous times, and not so much rebuilt as propped up, patched over, and re-inhabited regardless.

We had begun by emerging from Delhi's metro into the cacophonous chaos of Chawri Bazar where Veerma persuaded me to try daulat ki chaat, a unique Delhi street food only served in winter between Divali and Holi and sold from handcarts. It's made from frothed-up milk foam, sugar and saffron and had an ethereal, sweet-dairy flavour. As we stood chatting, the vendor swiped a couple of flies from his precious white dome of froth. 'That's why it's only served in winter,' said Veerma. 'It'd be covered with flies any later in the year.' I thought of something Sourish had said to me the day before: 'Anyone who grows up in Delhi can eat anywhere in the world.' I had grown up in mid-Sussex, mostly on things wrapped in clingfilm. But this was no time for squeamishness.

As we walked, Veerma greeted friends and acquaintances, including Sudhir Mishra, the esteemed Bollywood director, tall, elegantly tailored and with a mane of grey hair; and a Hindu spice seller, the only Hindu trader in the heart of the Muslim quarter. We tried aloo tikki — potato patties stuffed with lentils and chutney; cholle bhaturey — spicy chickpeas eaten with a special fried bread; and kulle — hollowed out potatoes stuffed with chickpea, chutney and various fruits; but I baulked at gol gappa — also known as panipuri. It can sometimes seem as if every street corner on India has a man with a trolley selling these bite-sized, hollow puffs of crispy-fried dough used to scoop a highly spiced water. It's not that I didn't want to taste one, but, well, that open barrel of water . . .

I recoiled too at a dish literally an inch deep in oil. 'In Delhi they say, if you can't fit four fingers in the oil, it's not good. The oil is good, you see, it calms the spices. It's all safe to eat, I assure you. In the summer I wouldn't let you try the chutneys, for example, and you shouldn't eat raw, cut vegetables, but anything hot and fried is safe.'

Deep in the red-light district, a warren of alleys where daylight rarely reached, we tried the most sublime kebabs I have ever eaten — made from mutton, tenderised with papaya and mixed with a secret spice blend, before being moulded around sticks and grilled over charcoal. 'He has been making these for twenty-five years,' said Veerma. 'No one knows the exact ingredients, but there will be chilli, coriander, ginger, garlic and onion. What else? Who knows?'

In the Muslim quarter, close to the Jama Masjid, we passed a crowd of men, shabbily dressed even by Delhi standards, crouching on the pavement outside a takeaway restaurant. 'That's faqiri. After visiting the mosque, someone makes a donation to the restaurant so that they can feed the destitute,' Veerma explained.

After an enjoyably whisky-soaked lunch, we ended the day at what he said was the best sweet shop in Delhi, Chaina Rami, at one end of Chandni Chowk. Chaina Rami is another venture which was born out of Partition. The owners fled here from Karachi in 1947. 'You must try their speciality, karadi halwa. It's expensive — 600 rupees per kilo — but you are paying for the ghee.'

I bought a box of the Turkish-Delight-style jellies and commenced stuffing them in my face on the ride back to the hotel on the metro.

I had an odd encounter during that journey home. At one stop, a man draped in orange cotton robes with a wild beard and a turban got on the train and sat opposite me. He had strange white smears on his face. I guess he was some

56

kind of sadhu, although I thought they didn't take transport. Weren't they supposed to walk everywhere? He stared intently at me as I ate my sweets and I began to feel a little self-conscious, so offered him one. His eyes widened and he held up a hand to say no, then moved across so that he was sitting next to me.

Then he spoke softly:

'You know, Gandhiji once said: 'Man is not born to eat, and he should not live to eat. Those who spend their days worshipping the belly are like the beasts.''

By rights, following such an encounter, I should have renounced my life of gluttony for ever, returned to my family purged of my appetites reinvigorated to face the challenges of the second era of my life. But there was no awakening, no Damascene moment; at least not yet. So when I got back to the hotel, we all went out to eat again.

5

Emil Desecrates the Indian Flag

Up, through and above the hazy bruise of Delhi's atmosphere our Kingfisher Air[1] jet climbed, in the direction of the Punjab.

I don't want to begin here on a repetitive note, but I am afraid to say my first impression on arriving in Amritsar was that it really is the most fearful shithole. If it is true, as diplomat Pavan K. Varma has written, that Indians 'have a remarkable tolerance for inequity, filth and human suffering', then Amritsar is a shining beacon of tolerance: rubble- and rubbish-strewn, with roads like Emmental, mildewed buildings, and litter, God, the litter. Even the trees were littered, in their case with kites following the recent Lohri festival. The sky was still full of them, being flown by children from balconies and rooftops. Thanks to *The Kite Runner* I now always associate kites with anal rape, prison brutality and the Taleban, so it was a shame that they were about the only semblance of joy in this chilly, mouldy, foggy city.

---

[1] Kingfisher — a brand of not very good beer — also operates an airline. How is this allowed? It's as if Bacardi won the contract to run Sellafield. You have no idea how much thought I gave to this during our time in India.

At lunch in a restaurant in town, a white woman in a turban was sitting at the next table with her Sikh husband. We all did a double take, and I wondered about her story. Did she wear it freely, or under pressure from her husband? I suppose I made a spurious, hasty judgement, feeling pity for her that she had lost something of her own identity to her husband's culture, that she had perhaps been wholly subsumed by it.

Turbans would, it turned out, come to be the dominant totem of our time in the Sikh capital. 'My turban is ten metres long and my hair is one metre long,' said our taxi driver that afternoon by way of introduction, perhaps pre-empting his most frequently asked tourist question. 'We do not cut our hair,' he added, 'because the hair is part of us, and this for a Sikh is our symbol.'

At the mist-shrouded Golden Temple we met an elderly man wearing a blue turban the size of an immersion heater. He was ex-military, the Sikh equivalent of a marine, he told us. 'How long is your hat?' asked Emil. It was 400 metres long, he told us. Emil and Asger gazed at him, slack-jawed. In their wildest fantasies they had never imagined such a magnificent vision of a man could exist, and they insisted on being photographed with him. Asger was drawn to his ornamental dagger, but Emil was gripped by the turban. A seed had been planted . . .

The Golden Temple offered a rare opportunity to combine our food and spiritual itineraries as it has what is claimed to be the largest kitchen in the world, capable of feeding up to forty thousand people on Divali (the autumnal festival

59

is as important to Sikhs as it is to Hindus, albeit for different reasons). Here volunteers cook for pilgrims using donated food — the living embodiment of the Sikh principle of *kar seva*, or voluntary manual labour. The temple itself is the most sacred site in Sikhism.

Sikhism has always seemed to me one of the least worst religions: its basic teachings include gender equality, honesty and temperance. Sikhs have famously good manners and are the most generous hosts. Unlike Buddhists or Hindus, they are encouraged to engage with the world, to live 'normal' lives as decently as possible, based on the principle of karma. They are also supposed to reject the caste system, though, as I read in Sathnam Sanghera's remarkable memoir of his Sikh childhood in Wolverhampton, *The Boy with the Topknot*, caste still plays a central role in Sikh arranged marriages. Regrettably, they do, of course, believe in God and reincarnation, but they do not hold with idolatry (martyrs are a different matter, they love a good martyr), and have no time for talk of miracles or the supernatural. I've also always admired the fact that, historically, Sikhs have never allowed their quest for achieving oneness with God to let people push them around. Since the Mughal war of 1699, they have been a warrior race, 16 million strong in India, 25 million worldwide. And let's not forget that when, in 1984, militant Sikhs occupied the Golden Temple to draw attention to their demands for an independent Sikh homeland and Indira Gandhi ordered the army to take it back by force, one of her own

Sikh guards responded by assassinating her.

It was another freezing cold, foggy morning, which made walking barefoot on the white marble and soggy red carpet in the temple complex especially toe-numbing. There was a dense mass of several hundred people waiting to enter the temple — or gurdwara — itself, which shimmered enigmatically through the mist from its island in the middle of a shallow ornamental lake.

'No, no sir, not there, this way,' said one of the temple staff, pointing us to the right, exit side of the 60-metre-long causeway, where there were no people.

'Oh, no, we couldn't,' said Lissen. 'It's not right for us to jump the queue just because we are foreigners. These people are here on pilgrimage, it's us who should wait.'

I personally had no problem jumping the queue. If an Indian in a position of authority was inviting us, it seemed rude not to. The only strategy I could think of was to appeal to Lissen's maternal instincts. 'But look at poor Emil's feet, they're almost turning blue,' I said. She relented, and we walked briskly past the crowd who seemed resigned to being overtaken by foreigners. Inside the temple there was barely breathing room with pilgrims squeezed up against the walls. The atmosphere was ripe with the sickly sweet smell of ghee — burned as an offering — fermented with sweat. One could not help but be moved by the quiet reverence of the crowd, many of whom were here on a once-in-a-lifetime pilgrimage to the most impor-tant place in their world, but after we had squeezed our way around and stolen a glance at the Granth Sahib, the Sikh holy book kept beneath a jewelled canopy in the temple during the day, we headed towards that all too rare entity, the free lunch.

With its open sides and lack of lighting, the kitchen, known as the Guru-ka-Langar, was more like a cattle market. Cauldrons the size of upturned Volkswagen Beetles were bubbling with dal over wood fires. While Lissen and I stuck our noses in one, Asger was lured away by a friendly woman who was making chapattis with a small group of her friends. When we caught up with him they all greeted us warmly, hands together, 'namaste', smiling. An elderly woman showed Asger how to shape the dough, and roll it on a board with a small, wooden rolling pin.

A TV crew was at the temple that day to film a government minister who was visiting, but they soon abandoned the minister when they heard that there were two foreign boys making bread nearby, and suddenly we were the focus of an impromptu media circus, smiling for the cameras as the minister shook our hand.

This lasted for a good ten minutes until the TV people felt they had what they wanted, and we moved off in the other direction. In the next-door hall we marvelled at a room filled with a gigantic, chapatti-making machine which looked like a life-sized version of the board game Mousetrap. From there we took our places on the floor of one of the dining halls, which was as packed as the temple. The noise from the clatter of pressed steel TV-dinner-style serving trays from the rinsing troughs was phenomenal, but our meal was more delicious than such mass catering has any right to be.

All the while, unbeknownst to us, inside Emil's head were brewing visions of turbans. Later, as we walked around the Jallianwala Bagh, the park where the Amritsar massacre took place — inspecting the bullet holes in the wall, evidence of the slaughter of over two thousand Indians by the British army under General Dyer in 1919 — Emil sidled up to me and tugged my sleeve.

'Can anyone have a turban?'

'Well, yes, lots of Indians wear them, not just Sikhs. Why?'

'I think they are really cool. I'd really, really, really like a green one.'

A little later we passed an open-fronted shop — as most were in Amritsar — stacked from floor to ceiling on three sides with turban fabric. Lissen pointed it out and Emil grew strangely agitated, insisting we go in. He is usually shy with strangers, in shops and so on, but he walked straight in and asked if he could buy a turban. The three shop attendants, stationed on each side of the room, looked at each other, hoping the other would take charge of the situation, and were still silently passing the buck when the rest of us caught up.

In the end it was agreed that Emil was perfectly entitled to have his own turban, and they even offered to tie it for him. He spent a while deciding on the exact shade of green he wanted, ending with a vibrant Kermit, which was brought down from the shelf and cut to a length of around four metres. The assistant sat Emil in a chair in the middle of the shop and began preparing the material, unravelling it — which took him out onto the street — then soaking it in a little water and scrunching it up to soften it.

By now a small crowd had gathered on the pavement outside, silent but more puzzled than offended. The colours and methods of tying turbans are a religious and social minefield as far as I can make out. Hindus, Muslims and Sikhs all wear them but in various colours and forms, depending on caste and other factors: Rajasthanis wear saffron-coloured turbans to signify their chivalry; Brahmins wear pink; Dalits brown; and nomads black. Hindus wear various shades of green, blue and white to indicate mourning, while wives and single women wear pinks and reds and yellow. Yellow and red together might indicate that a woman has given birth to a son.

Two men emerged from the crowd and, with perfect Geordie accents, asked me how I was liking Amritsar. 'It's a bit different, isn't it?' laughed the elder of the two. They were pharmacists from Newcastle, here for the marriage of the younger man to the elder's sister. I asked how many people had been invited to the wedding. 'Oh, it's going to be quite a small one, just four hundred.' This is far from exceptional in India, he told me, and though they are notably wedding-crazy, neither are large marital bashes an exclusively Sikh phenomenon. The average Indian wedding has around five hundred guests, although, with the frenzy for them further stoked over the years by Bollywood, often thousands are invited.

As we were talking, I noticed Asger, standing alone in a corner of the shop, on the verge of tears. What was the matter? He began to sob.

'I don't want to lose my little brother.'

'Why do you think you are going to lose him?'

'He's changing into an Indian! He's going to stay here! I won't leave him!'

We explained that wearing a turban didn't necessarily incur a change of nationality. 'Why don't we all get one?' said Lissen, more to reassure him than as a serious suggestion. I looked at her. This was a dangerous bluff.

Asger's face brightened.

'Oh, can we?' The idea sank in a little. 'Yes, yes, please. Can I? You too, Daddy!'

'Me? No, ha ha, why would I . . . '

'Yes, why don't we all get them,' said Lissen, smiling slyly.

So over the next hour or so we all took turns in the turban chair as the shop assistant slowly, methodically, wrapped our heads tightly in colourful bandages before an ever-swelling audience of bemused locals. When he had finished, our turban consultant refused to accept a tip for his trouble. 'It is a very great honour to tie a person's first turban,' he said, bowing.

First impressions of life with a turban? You lose about 30 per cent of your hearing, for a start. Has any research been done into hearing disabilities in Sikhs? I wonder. It is awfully tight, too. 'An instant facelift,' said Lissen, looking pleased, but also a little troutlike. The revelation

65

of the day, though, came from Asger. 'We're still the same people, even though we've got these on,' he said, clearly relieved, as we drove out of Amritsar on the way to see the famous border ceremony at Wagah.

Wearing a turban for a couple of days was an education for us all. As Asger pointed out, I was still the same person even though in its improbably youthful tautness my face now had shades of Joan Rivers, I was partially deaf, and had five metres of cloth wrapped around my head. Therefore — and I realise this sounds epically trite, but it's true — presumably, other people who dress differently from me, whether in burkas or turbans, jeans which hang halfway down their arses, or pink cords with wax jackets, or whatever, are just people. Of course, intellectually I knew this perfectly well, and if you had presented me with this knowledge as a great leap forward in human relations (in, say, a copy of *Sikhs are from Mars and the Rest of Us Are from Venus*), I would have reacted with some disdain, but the actual wearing of an actual turban had that little bit more impact. It was a minuscule step in my development as a human being but, I suspect, quite a deeply felt one for Asger and Emil.

I might also add that the Indian and Pakistani participants in the highly charged border ceremony we witnessed that afternoon might also do well to walk a mile in the shoes, or headgear, of their neighbours. We reached Wagah after half an hour by Toyota minivan along what used to be the Grand Trunk Road — the Sher

Suri way — an old Mughal route stretching two thousand kilometres from Calcutta to Peshawar.

It was a lively journey, as the driver appeared to be insane. At one point he hit one of the thousands of feral dogs which live in Amritsar and can seem to outnumber humans. There was the sickening, dull crack of bone and flesh on metal, and a slight jolt as we rode over the carcass, but not a flicker of reaction from the driver, a Hindu, judging by the plastic idols hanging from his rear-view mirror.

There was a carnival atmosphere as the Wagah crowd waited behind a barrier to be allowed to walk the short distance to the border proper. Again, as the only foreigners, we were encouraged by officials to jump the queue, and were allowed to begin the walk ahead of the crowd, which can number as many as ten thousand. They soon caught up with us though, engulfing us in chants, in Hindi, of 'India Victory' and 'Long live India', and we all arrived together at a complex of large, concrete, open-air grandstands.

The crowd, in high, flag-waving spirits, was whipped into a further fervour by execrable pop music blaring from the tannoy and a man with a microphone leading synchronised chanting bigging up India at Pakistan's expense. He segued into a bizarre note-holding contest with his opposite number in Pakistan, whose own caterwauling wafted eerily through the mist along with the chants from the Pakistani crowd, like a strange, aural tennis. As we climbed the steps to our seats at the top of the grandstand nearest the border, we could finally see the smaller but still vociferous crowd on the other side of the high fence that partitions the two countries.

'Look!' said Asger, pointing to the Pakistan side. 'Daleks!'

'No, they're not Daleks, they are women,' I corrected him. 'That's how women dress in Muslim countries.'

'Why are they sitting on their own?'

Experience has taught me that once these kind of questions start, they tend to continue until the child has successfully tied you in knots. There'd be 'What's a Muslim?' next, and before we knew it, we'd be deep into theological semantics. So I left Lissen to it and moved away to ask a flag-waving Indian if I might borrow his flag for a photograph.

He was happy to lend it to me, but one of the guards charged with keeping order among the crowd snatched it from me and ordered me to sit down. He had a large red cockerel's fan atop his head; ill-fitting trousers which terminated at mid-shin; and big, Elton-John-singing-Pinball-Wizard-style boots on. With spats. He looked as if he could — and would very much enjoy to — crush me beneath them but at that moment Emil announced that he needed to pee, urgently. Lissen said she would take him, but the guard told her that boys were not allowed in the Ladies' loo. She told him this was ridiculous and, as they discussed this heatedly, behind them, Emil sighed, pulled down his trousers exposing his bright, white bottom to the world as was his habit in such emergencies, and urinated over the side of the grandstand. This would have been awkward enough, but the urine's trajectory terminated on a small pile of Indian flags which someone had left on the ground below. All parties had, by now, frozen in horror. The guard glared at the paper flags for some time as if struggling to comprehend the enormity of the crime. I was already bracing myself for either the imprisonment of my son and the lengthy ensuing diplomatic negotiations, or the imprisonment of us all, and weighing up whether the fact that we were wearing turbans would work in our favour or against, when, to our great relief, the border ceremony began and the guard was forced to leave the scene of the crime to clear away a group of teenagers who were entertaining their friends in the stands with a Bollywood-style dance routine from the parade ground.

The main event consisted — after a good deal of warming up and agitated pacing by both parties of soldiers — of what is customarily referred to by sniggering Westerners (like me) as a re-enactment of Monty Python's Ministry of Silly Walks sketch. The soldiers on both sides marched with a spastic aggression, like a park keeper who has just spotted some boys tramping on his saplings, thrusting their feet up as high as they could go and moving with a clockworky petulance. Finally, after ten minutes or so of this, they shut the damn gates and everyone breathed a sigh of relief that, at least for today, the Pakistani hordes had been kept at bay.

As we walked back to our car, I reflected that,

for all its absurdity it is also rather glorious that a terrifying nuclear rivalry which threatens to destroy the fragile stability of the region at any moment can be reduced to a meeting of the John Cleese Appreciation Society, Punjabi Branch.

6

The Curse of the Ritzy-Turbaned
Fortune Teller

The fog bound us to Amritsar longer than we would have wanted. No flights were leaving the city, although, having read a news story in *The Times of India* about a crackdown on drunk pilots — apparently a common feature of Indian airspace — I was almost relieved, and at least grateful for another crack at the stunning murgh lababdar, another of those outstanding butter-rich, tomato gravy Punjabi dishes, which I had tried at the Crystal Restaurant in the centre of town the previous day.

When we finally did get airborne and make a nervy, shudder-wobble landing an hour or so later, it was too late to take the train from Delhi to Agra, as Lissen had planned. We ended up staying the night in a posh hotel, courtesy of our travel insurance.

I hadn't realised how Asger and Emil had felt about our slightly shabby accommodation so far on the trip until, in the great, towering gold and marble lobby of the Lalit Hotel Delhi, Asger launched into a long, heartfelt speech about how grateful he was to be staying there, and how fantastic he thought we were as a result. It became known as the 'Five Star Love' speech but it caused Lissen and me concern about how he might react to some of the other hotels we had lined up. We have raised both our sons on the principle of what they don't know about they can't want (they are still blissfully unaware of the existence of Eurodisney, for example, which was some achievement given that we lived in Paris for years), but now they had had their heads turned by chocolate on the pillows, complimentary toothbrushes and fifty TV channels, their hotel horizons had been dangerously broadened.

Our train plans having been dashed, in the morning loomed the first of what would be many day-long car rides to come over the next couple of weeks, as we made our way, first, east into Uttar Pradesh to Agra, then west across Rajasthan to Udaipur. The first chunk of that first drive was spent simply trying to break free from the gravitational pull of Delhi. As we sat at traffic lights, Emil's attention was drawn by a boy beggar who had a monkey. Emil, seeing only the monkey, envied the boy. He already had a name planned if he were ever to get his own monkey, he said. He would call it Ape Booth.

'I wish I was him, look, the monkey is his friend,' he said.

'Well, I don't think the monkey has much choice in the matter,' I said, pointing out that it was tethered by a piece of string, and adding that the boy had no shoes.

Asger and Emil wanted to give the child some money. We had already tried the 'We can't give to everyone, then we wouldn't have any money,' approach to beggars, and argued that giving money to them only perpetuated the problem,

72

but both approaches had rung hollow. This time I went with, 'You know, some of the richest people in the world are Indians and, really, it is their responsibility first and foremost to give to the poor in their country, not ours. The man who owns the company that built that lorry' — I pointed to a Tata truck which was at that moment barrelling towards us on our side of the road — 'and that one, and that one, for instance. Think how rich he must be.'

Imagining that one man could have built all of those lorries kept them occupied for a while, and soon Asger and Emil were distracted again by a group of Jains walking past with white cards suspended in front of their mouths, like home-made surgical masks, to prevent accidental ingestion of insects. This prompted another flurry of questions. But the issue of giving money to the needy on a one-to-one basis continued to trouble me. Really, what excuse did we have for not giving money? It is true we weren't wealthy by Western standards, and we were on a tight budget for the trip; also, I'd seen *Slumdog Millionaire*, so had to assume that many of the child beggars we saw were part of organised gangs. But did any of that change the blatant fact of their abject circumstance?

After seven hours we approached Agra. Around an hour outside the city we glimpsed our first, proper Indian sunlight, just in time to warm us for our visit to the tomb of Akbar the Great, at Sikandra. This was the most perfectly proportioned jewel box of a building, made from white marble and red sandstone. Actually, it literally was once a jewel box: the jewel box to end all jewel boxes, having been home to the Koh-i-noor diamond. The tomb stood in a well-tended park with antelope, baobab trees, egrets and squirrels, which Asger and Emil immediately identified as the ones from *Ice Age*.

'You see the four stripes down their tails?' A tall, elderly man in a white kurta and taqiyah, the brimless cotton hat worn by Muslims, approached us as we stood looking at the squirrels. Asger and Emil nodded. 'They say that they were made by Krishna stroking them with his black fingers. Do you know who Krishna is?' Asger and Emil knew about Krishna — who can be depicted as both blue and dark-skinned — from an animated series they had been watching on Indian television. 'But do you know who Akbar was?' They shook their heads, which the man took as his cue to embark on a potted history of Mughal India.

Akbar, the third Mughal king (grandson of Babur, the first Muslim king to have ruled large parts of India), was a benevolent ruler, the man told us, cultured, enlightened and tolerant of Hinduism.

'But didn't his armies massacre tens of thousands of people?' Lissen asked.

'Don't encourage him,' I hissed. 'He's only doing this to get money.'

The man waved a dismissive arm. 'He was enlightening them.'

I pointedly turned my back on the man, and tried to get the others to do so as well, but he continued. 'The Mughal kings started like giants, and finished like jewellers,' he said, gesturing to

74

the onyx and lapis lazuli inlay which were added by Akbar's son. 'Akbar built in sandstone, but that wasn't good enough for his sons. They had to have marble and jewels.'

The man still seemed aggrieved by this. He went on to explain how Akbar's rule began in Delhi when this descendant of Tamburlaine and Genghis Khan was just thirteen, and commenced the golden age of the Mughal kings (there was a short pause here while we clarified for Emil an ongoing Mughals/Muggles confusion). This lasted for around a hundred and fifty years. Akbar even founded his own religion, Din-e-Ilahi, cherrypicking the elements he liked from Sufism, Hinduism and Islam. 'He was a very tolerant, very reasonable man. But then his sons . . . ' the man shook his head, as if recalling some wayward local boys of his acquaintance. 'Drink, women. They availed themselves of them all, sir, madam. And then they let the Britisher in.'

He glared at me. To change the subject, I asked him what caste he was, realising as I did that I had no idea of the etiquette of such a question. Thankfully, he didn't seem upset, and told us he was a Brahmin, the highest 'teacher' caste, which, until the last decade or so and the rise of powerful lower-caste political movements, was the unassailable ruling class of India. I ventured that, to the outside world, the caste system seemed as iniquitous as, say, apartheid in South Africa.

'Oh, no, sir, you are very wrong. The caste system functioned very well, very well indeed

75

until recently. The caste system is a kind of selective breeding, based on the fact that, according to your particular genetic inclination you will specialise in that area. Each is different but not higher than the others, but historically the Brahmins have been venerated above the others, because they teach. These days Brahmins have no rights, no vested interests. It is the lower castes who have all the power, who are taking advantage of the system. If you like, it is an experiment gone wrong. Originally caste was only a way of sorting out the capabilities of a society. You are in the highest group, for instance,' he pointed at Lissen, 'so you can marry within that group to create a select genetic line, but not beneath you.' Was it me or did he bat his hand in my direction as he said this? 'In those days genetics were considered to be the primary factor. Besides, there was just such a caste system in Christianity, you know. Discrimination happens everywhere.'

'But the caste system is such an awful system of oppression and discrimination, it's caused such misery and suffering, how can you defend it?' asked Lissen.

'Defend it!' he, turned to her, surprised and, I think, a little upset to be confronted by a woman in this way. 'I shall defend it until I die!'

And with that he bade us good day, and turned briskly away without, as Lissen would point out several times to me during the course of the trip, any hint of a request for money.

★ ★ ★

76

The cursed fog descended on Agra again that night so that, when we drew back our hotel room curtains the next morning expecting finally to see the shimmering marble dome of the Taj Mahal, there was instead an impenetrable, vaporous cliff face. Downstairs, there was literally fog in the entrance lobby of our hotel. At this rate we would bump into the Taj Mahal before we saw it. As always in life, I was readying myself for colossal disappointment.

'Don't worry, Michael,' said Lissen, whose burden of being the family's eternal optimist she bears with tireless resolve. 'It'll be clear by two o'clock. At your age you'd think you'd have learned not to worry about things you can't do anything about.'

'But that would account for pretty much everything in my life,' I said. 'Then what would I have to worry about?'

'But don't you get it, you don't *have* to worry. Have you any idea what it is like living with someone who is in a constant state of anxiety? How much effort it takes to balance that so that our children don't grow up like you, or worse? Yesterday Asger cleaned his hands with bacterial gel after holding my hand! Can't you see the effect it has on them? And I never get a chance to worry about anything, because I am always the one who has to pull us through, sort things out, calm everything down. When do I get a chance to worry?'

★   ★   ★

77

We decided to visit Agra fort in the morning, in the — probably forlorn — hope that the fog might lift after lunch so that we would be able to see the Taj. Leaving the fort we saw our very first real elephant, just a glimpse of a swinging shoestring tie tail. I had to lift Emil up on to my shoulders as the beast lumbered off in to the traffic and I felt a jolt of excitement shoot through him as he finally spotted it. That was his Taj Mahal, enough for his day in Agra to have been deemed a success, but all I could think of was that I had the one chance to see the actual, real Taj Mahal in my life, and the fog was going to ruin it.

Of course, by two o'clock the fog had cleared, revealing a perfect deep blue sky against which to view the most perfect building in the world, preferably, as I did, with my arms held in apologetic embrace around the woman I loved.

I had feared the Taj itself would be a cliché, but when you first catch sight of it (as you adjust from the darkness of the Great Gate — itself the most perfect building I had ever seen up until the point we passed through it), shimmering through the heat haze, it is as if all previous images are erased and you are seeing it for the first time. The challenge then is to overcome the sense that you are seeing yet another image of the Taj Mahal, to go beyond the soothing symmetry and comprehend fully that you actually are there.

For the first ten minutes or so, as our guide reeled off his various facts — Shah Jahan's wife, Mumtaz, died giving birth to their fourteenth child, was buried here in 1631, blah, blah — I was not really listening. Some things did make it through: the Taj is built on an earthquake-proof foundation of wood and rubble with its four towers built leaning outwards so that their collapse wouldn't damage the main building; its façade is studded with three million semiprecious stones; it cost 14 million rupees to build at a time when ten grams of gold was worth fifteen rupees; and its architecture appears to have been a collective effort. It is, then, the world's first, and perhaps only, example of a successful design by committee.

Of the four of us, only Emil had a critical view of the Taj Mahal: 'I think it's dumb to build something that big and then only bury one person in it,' he said, shaking his head at the wastefulness.

★ ★ ★

There was a palm reader at work in the hotel lobby that evening. I would no more pay money to someone who claimed to be able to predict my future from the creases in the skin on a particular part of my anatomy than I would to someone who said they could give me the tooth fairy's telephone number, but Lissen would. Along with the career of Sandra Bullock, my alcohol consumption and how to load the dishwasher, fortune tellers had long been a source of discord in our marriage. To my horror and very much against my strict orders (which, oddly, seemed almost not to bother her), she

79

happily gave this man — who, I might add, was wearing a ritzy, multicoloured turban with gold accents — 500 rupees to shower her with bullshit.

'You really should go down and try him,' she said, excitedly, when she returned to the room. 'He was spot on. Absolutely amazing.'

'So tell me exactly, just one thing that he told you that he couldn't possibly have known — a fact, I mean — which was accurate.'

'Well . . . he said I liked to travel.'

'You're in bloody India!'

'He said I was worried about my weight.'

'What woman isn't? A fact . . . ?'

'Right, okay. How about this: he said that I was going to live to eighty-five and be incredibly rich!'

'Well, why didn't you say?'

Ignoring my sarcasm, Lissen insisted that I go down and try him. I refused. She persisted. I have been married to her long enough to recognise those occasions on which she is more likely to win these small but keenly fought wars of attrition. Tired and perhaps slightly softened by the day's magical experiences, I am ashamed to say I caved in.

'Here's the deal,' I said. 'I'll go down and talk to him and offer him a proposal. I'll tell him that if he can tell me one single true fact, give me one piece of evidence that he can read my palm, then I will go ahead with a full reading. If he can't, I'll leave. Okay?'

She agreed, so I took the lift down to the lobby and waited with a glass of red wine from

80

the bar for the palmist to finish spinning his absurd tales to an enraptured Australian couple.

At last the space beside him became free and I sidled over, trying to indicate that it had just at that moment occurred to me to have a reading, for lack of anything else to occupy my time.

I made my proposal, and to his credit the man didn't take offence, and agreed to the challenge. He took my left palm in his hand and studied it with arched eyebrows.

'From an early age you always respected your mother and father,' he said in a sing-song voice. 'You never answered back or questioned them.'

'I am afraid you couldn't be further from the truth,' I said.

'But wait!' he said, as I stood up to leave, his words echoing through the lobby and reaching me just as the lift doors closed. 'You also have an interest in travel . . . '

Of course, for all my proud rationalism, despite my mockery of him, and even though I reminded myself several times of that ridiculous costume turban, I still spent the night tossing and turning, worrying that the palm reader might put a curse on me. Such are the burdens of the feeble-minded rationalist.

7

The Motorway Mariner

Vinod Kumar was a tall, thin, shy Brahmin with a Clark Gable moustache, a shirt that had clearly been laundered more times than a 1,000-rupee note, and immaculately oiled hair sculpted into a simple side parting from which it did not budge. He had better English than his modesty allowed and a tender dignity which instantly put us at ease. His brow was permanently furrowed with concern for our well-being, and we, in turn, trusted him from the moment we met him. The trust was well placed. Vinod could read a road like an old sea dog senses the moods of the ocean, anticipating, it seemed, all eventualities a heartbeat or two before they materialised. This was fortunate, as most Indians seem to have learned how to drive by taking notes from the chase scene in *The French Connection*, as V.S. Naipaul put it in *A Million Mutinies Now*, 'as if anything could be asked of an engine and a steering wheel and brakes'. But, whether it was a herd of camels like a bunch of used teabags on stilts which appeared suddenly around a bend; a suicidal cow who decided the plastic bags were greener on the other side of the road a femtosecond before we passed by; or the various Tata trucks driven by men, presumably whacked on amphetamines, which came blasting towards us at full speed in the fast lane on our side of the highway, Vinod responded with swift, smooth evasive action. In another world he would have made a great stock-car racer, or was at the very least the one person I have ever met who I would trust to drive me across Belgium.

Just how lucky we were to have Vinod was brought home to us a couple of hours outside Agra as we entered Rajasthan, en route to the Ranthambore National Park where we were going to try and spot a tiger. We crested a hill and found ourselves in the midst of a serious car accident which, judging by the still-spinning wheels of the overturned auto-rickshaw and Tata truck involved, we had been moments away — less than one of Emil's lavatory breaks, for example — from being protagonists in ourselves. As Vinod edged us through the carnage I glimpsed the faces of a woman, pale and unconscious, and of a man with blood gushing from his hairline as he sat, slumped, with his legs stretched out before him like a marionette with its strings cut. I sank down into my seat.

'Should we stop to help?' Lissen asked Vinod.

'No, ma'am.' He shook his head, his eyes flicking nervously to the rear-view mirrors and the crowd which had already gathered. 'Local people can riot after an accident like this. They could be violent towards you.'

Away from the accident, now deep into the arid, biblical landscape of rural Rajasthan, the people actually seemed more friendly than ever. Many waved at us as we passed, recognising Vinod's white Toyota Innova as tourist transport.

Rajasthan, the 'Land of Kings' as the tourist brochures have it, was once made up of twenty royal states, each with a maharaja or, in the case of Udaipur, a maharana, and, perhaps because it was not part of the British Raj's domain, it seems to have opted out of the twentieth century entirely. Occasionally, the roads disappeared altogether to be replaced with dirt tracks. The villages consisted mainly of mud huts with straw roofs and perhaps a parade of shabby shops with a workshop at one end for car repairs and a couple of open-air barbers. For several miles we passed vast fields full of kilns and stacks of red bricks; then miles of aircraft-hangar-sized chicken farms; then fields of wheat.

My nerves could no longer stand the constant drama of a front row seat, so Lissen rode up front with Vinod now, and managed within minutes to extract a good deal of his biography, including the fact that he had recently got married and the first time he saw his bride was on his wedding day. The car was a joint investment with his brother, he said, and the sole means of earning money for three families, a total of twenty people.

The idea had been for us to catch a train for part of this journey and for Vinod to meet us at Ranthambore, but fog again wrecked those plans — the train people were measuring delays in calendar terms — and so we settled in for a day watching rural India fly by from the Innova. This journey at last brought the classic images of India: a woman in a red sari in a green field; buses with their roofs packed with passengers;

buffaloes pulling carts; gaudy temples.

At one point, slowed by cattle in a small village, I looked to my left to see a small puppy, perhaps a couple of weeks old and by Indian mongrel standards relatively presentable, cute even. A man dressed in a drab polyester shirt and trousers was standing nearby waiting for a bus. He saw the puppy too and, as it ambled blithely towards him, he picked up a large rock, the size of an aubergine, and threw it at the dog. I didn't see the stone make contact as we had driven by, but I did hear the puppy yelp.

The puppy stoning stayed in my mind for some time afterwards, weeks in fact. I toyed with the incident, drawn to it as I am to testing the sharpness of a kitchen knife's blade with my thumb, returning to the blank look on the man's face, and the dog's penetrating yowl. 'That's what cute gets you in this place,' the man seemed to be saying, and the terrible thing is, I understood him perfectly. I doubt I'd survive much beyond teatime on my first day in rural India before I started stoning puppies to displace the injustice of it all.

If you are wondering about the tigers, by the way, we spent three, four-hour-long game drives in the freezing morning and chilly evening, rammed in alongside a group of boorish Dutch tourists whose gargantuan buttocks hogged most of the bench seats in the back of our open jeep, without spying so much as a whisker (although Emil swears blind he saw the top of a tiger's hat peeping above the tall grass).

We were told by our hotel manager that there

was an 80 per cent chance of seeing a tiger, but no one we met during our three days in Ranthambore had seen one either. Coincidentally, the newspapers were that week reporting that the official figures for tigers in India had been grossly exaggerated. There were supposed to be over forty in Ranthambore, but if you told me there were four, I wouldn't have been surprised.

We did see sloth bears (Baloo, in other words), which have been poached to the brink of extinction because they are apparently great dancers; as well as crocodiles; an owl; and an excessive number of deer-type things which, to tell the truth, became a bit of a bore after a while. Shortly after seeing the bear, still in the middle of the park and theoretically at least surrounded by various toothed beasts, Asger announced that he needed the lavatory.

'We'll have to stop,' Lissen said.

'We can't stop,' I said. 'What, are you suggesting he just gets out of the jeep and walks off into the bushes? There are tigers about! We just saw a bear only — what? — a mile away!'

But the park ranger, who looked about fourteen years old, assured us there was no risk, that there were no dangerous animals in this part of the park and that, if there were, they would be put off by the jeep's smell, so that's precisely what Asger did. This presented me with a dilemma. Should I go with him, and be ready to lay down my life should he be attacked? In theory, yes, but would that really be best for the family in the long run? So I decided on a compromise: I would stand up in the jeep and keep watch.

During our final drive our guide claimed to hear bird warning signals, suggesting that a tiger or tigers were nearby, and he got very excited over what he claimed was a paw print. In my, by now, cynical frame of mind I could quite easily have imagined that one of his colleagues had been out at dawn on his bicycle with a plaster-cast stamp. We ended up spending an hour waiting in silence along with about thirty other vehicles parked in a wide circle around a patch of marshy grass, like paparazzi outside the Ivy, but, again, no Shere Khan.

The park itself was at least a sumptuous visual feast, with beautiful grasses, gargantuan, tasselled banyan trees and the evocative ruins of the Maharaja of Jaipur's hides and temples dotting the landscape. The hotel we stayed at was also ripe with colonial atmosphere, right down to the snooker table and a photograph of that noted animal rights campaigner, Prince Philip, and his wife, Queen Elizabeth II, standing proudly over the last tiger shot (by Her Maj) here, a fourteen-footer which met its end in January 1961. But the best thing to come out of our stay at Ranthambore was that we got to know a family from Mumbai, the Guptas, who were stopping by at the hotel on their way back home after a family wedding in Jaipur. Their sons, Kamil and Balbir, were the same ages as Asger and Emil, who, in their playmate-starved state, ambushed them on sight. The boys got on well, and played together late into the night. Kamil and Balbir spoke four languages, English included, but the boys chose instead to communicate via the universal language of the under-tens (Power Ranger fighting), running around as the dog-sized bats — which during the day we had mistaken for large black fruit hanging in the trees — swooped and twittered above their heads, and God knows what else lurked in the undergrowth.

Their parents, Badri and Nita, invited Lissen and I up to their suite (considerably larger than ours, and with a balcony) where we shared a bottle or two of Sula wine. Badri offered me my first Indian whisky, which tasted uncannily like toilet cleaner.

Badri and Nita were part of India's new rich, the emerging middle class which has grown wealthy from India's derestricted market economy. Badri ran his family's cleaning products company, which had outsourced much of its production to China. 'But you can't trust the Chinese,' he told me, as he and I engaged in 'men talk' on the balcony while the women were indoors. Nita occupied herself with her children and Bolly-wood gossip, which, frankly, I was much more interested in. When they heard we would be coming to Mumbai later on in our trip, they insisted we come for dinner, and we promised we would get in touch once we arrived.

Lissen, it turned out, meant it.

8

Red Teeth, Pink City

The jealous are troublesome to others, but a
torment to themselves.
William Penn, *Some Fruits of Solitude*

The French anthropologist Claude Lévi-Strauss
described India as a 'very old tapestry . . . worn
threadbare by long use and tirelessly darned'. It
perfectly describes Jaipur. It looked to me as if
an entire sixteenth-century city had been
excavated, a dab of cement applied here and
there, a million shards of gaudy Perspex signage
flung up about the place, and a carpet of plastic
bags and rubble strewn around to lend an air of
ongoing commerce, then put back to use.

Aside from the main tourist sights — the
Palace of Winds; the palace where the current
maharaja still lives; and the Dali-esque Jantar
Mantar observatory — all was crumbling
masonry, dust, dirt and litter. Since 1876 Jaipur
has, famously, been painted pink (it is the Pink
City, to Jodhpur's Blue and Jaisalmer's Golden).
Originally this was done as a gesture of welcome
to the visiting Prince of Wales, although now the
city is more a faded shade of salmon, like a
German game show host's blazer.

Like all good tourists, we felt obliged to pay
to ride on the back of two elephants up to the

sixteenth-century Amber Fort just outside the city as part of a nose-to-tail convoy that waded through a continuous torrent of amber elephant piss and boulders of dung. Asger declared it the best day of his life. 'My greatest ever wish has come true,' he sighed as we climbed aboard the elephants. I was delirious with flu that day and mashed off my face on the Indian equivalent of Day Nurse. As a state in which to parade up a hill on the back of an elephant, I can actually quite recommend this: the mental fog induced by the alcoholic cough mixture allowed me to maintain a serene, catatonic distance from what would otherwise have been an intolerable assault by the dozens of hawkers who line the path that zigzags beneath the ramparts. Even by the standards of other major Indian tourist sights, the Amber Fort's salesmen were tenacious: having somehow missed us when we left in the Toyota, one of the photographers chased and caught up with us on a motorbike a few miles away to try and sell us the photos he had just had developed. We couldn't not buy them after that.

It was my day to control the itinerary and so I had arranged for a lunchtime cooking demonstration at the Sankotra Haveli, an historic house which has been home to the Chandrawad family for over two centuries. We were welcomed by three of the women of the three-family household who lived there: Ritu and Padmini, who were sisters-in-law, and one of the daughters, Namita, all hugely fun company, and deeply passionate about food. They showed us

90

how to make a goat curry and I learned more about Indian food in that hour than I had from most of the books I had ever read on the subject — tempering spices in oil, for instance, and how they used some chillis for colour, and others for heat.

A leading Jaipur family, the Chandrawads have had close connections with the maharaja for centuries, formerly working as his tax collectors and still employed as go-betweens in his dealings with the Indian state in the various legal wranglings which continue to rumble on as a result of Indira Gandhi's abolishment of royal titles in 1971.

India has over 30 million court cases outstanding, the ladies told us. Cases can take decades to conclude and it is estimated that it would take three hundred years to deal with the backlog, to the extent that, it is said, around 10 per cent of India's GDP is tied up in legal disputes. Combine that judicial constipation with the fact that the Jaipur royal family is the richest in India, and it makes for a reliably sized income for the Chandrawads, I suppose. The current maharaja, the eighty-year-old Brigadier (retired) Sawai Bhawani Singh II, had recently taken the government to the Delhi High Court to win back 800 kilos of gold seized in 1975. He had fallen foul of a law — since repealed — which stated that possessing raw gold was illegal and that any found should be turned over to the authorities. The maharaja claimed not to have realised he had the gold, and defended himself by citing his military action: 'A person of such high devotion to the country's cause would not go and break the laws of the country knowingly,' he said. Well, what more evidence do they need?

As tends to happen when food fanatics get together, we soon got down to swapping extreme dining stories. Ritu trumped us all with a dish she had tried in Assam in which they feed a dog with rice then kill it, open its stomach and eat the rice. One for *Ready, Steady, Cook* . . . Her sister-in-law explained how twenty-six people from the three branches of the Chandrawad family lived together in the house which was arranged, Persian style, around a quiet, lawned courtyard; sharing a kitchen, they took it in turns to organise the day's menu. I wondered how these committed foodies avoided conflict in the kitchen. 'Well, it's been drilled into us that we all have to get on,' said Padmini. 'Of course we do disagree on some things, but we manage to hold our tongues when we see something wrong.'

On the way back to the hotel I asked to be dropped off at the Jaipur Literary Festival which happened to be taking place in the city at the Diggi Palace that week. I had seen from a festival programme I'd picked up at the hotel that one of my favourite authors, Geoff Dyer, had been due to appear. I'd missed his talk, which he had given a couple of day's earlier, but I had some vague hope, a weird intuition that I might bump into him (it only now strikes me that this is, effectively, stalker-speak).

Alexander McCall Smith was on the outdoor stage when I arrived, discussing crime fiction. I sat behind the film director Stephen Frears, and listened for a while as McCall Smith chatted amiably, in a panama hat, with William Dalrymple — who helps organise the festival — sitting front and centre in the audience, every inch the literary maharaja.

Being surrounded by famous writers, writers far more successful, talented and award winning than I'll ever be, put me in a foul mood. I am hardly ever invited to literary festivals, and on the very rare occasion on which I have been nominated for a prize it has been with a wearying sense of inevitability that I have turned up, dressed like a penguin, to hear the other person's name being read out (once, it was Jeremy Clarkson's, so you can imagine how that felt). On such occasions I have tried my best to do that 'I'm so happy for them' smile while applauding vigorously, and then had to get very drunk very quickly.

I got up and headed for the bar, spotting as I did a tall, skinny man with sunglasses and a satchel heading away to one side of the crowd. It was Dyer. I hovered, watching where he went, and followed. Halfway across the lawn, I paused to ask myself what I was doing. What did I possibly have to gain from this? Was I hoping he would ask who I was, and then profess his admiration for my work and invite me for a drinking session which would last until the small hours and feature outlandish parties with important literary figures and lots of drugs?

Yes. Yes, actually, I was.

'Excuse me, are you Geoff Dyer?' I asked, craning round in front of him as he walked. He replied that he was. I gushed something about how I loved his writing, was so pleased to see him, having sadly missed his talk, and that I just wanted to say 'Hi' and thanks for all the pleasure his books had given me, which he accepted neither particularly graciously nor ungraciously, keeping his sunglasses on all the while.

We chatted a little about what he was working on: a book analysing some or other Tarkovsky movie frame by frame, and another about tennis, he said.

'Tennis,' I said, trying desperately to keep the conversation going. 'Hasn't David Foster Wallace pretty much done that?'

This was not the right thing to have said at all.

'Uh, can't stand him. One of my allergy writers,' said Dyer. 'Completely allergic to him.'

'Oh, um right, sorry. Like me with Rose Tremain,' I said. Dyer chuckled. 'You know, the best thing any reviewer ever said about my first book was that it resembled Geoff Dyer in the clever bits,' I continued, trying to change the subject.

'Oh, ha! Right. Glad they didn't say you were like me in the rubbish bits!' he laughed. At that moment a beautiful young woman with lustrous black hair passed by. She was an acquaintance of Dyer's, so he excused himself and headed off to the bar with her, leaving me standing there like some kind of putz.

I left the festival in a somewhat bitter frame of mind, and wandered through the centre of Jaipur along a street lined with kitchenware stores. This cheered me up. I love a good kitchenware store and was curious to see the, to me, alien equipment on sale. I was very taken by the mini grinding machines — replete with small millstones — used to make the masalas and ginger-garlic pastes which form the basis of many Indian dishes. If I'd had the counter space back home, and the luggage space, I'd have bought one.

I turned off the main street and straight into the twelfth century. Here men toiled (no one just *worked* in the Middle Ages) with hammers on metal, or over charcoal fires. I spent some time watching one man making a dessert by pouring batter into hot oil through a slotted spoon so that, as it fell, it coagulated instantly into small spheres; molecular gastronomy, Indian style.

The traders of this dark, fetid alley offered a wide range of services, from shaving to shoe repairs, fortune telling to dentistry. I stopped at a barber's to ask, out of curiosity, how much a haircut would cost. 'Twenty rupees if you sit still, sir. But only ten if you move and I stand still.' I don't think he was joking either. I spent a while looking at the spices. 'Very good for diabetes,' said one stallholder, letting some fenugreek cascade from his hand.

I watched a paan seller making his fat chewable spliffs which he packed tightly with pastes and herbs, jams and, I think, some kind of tobacco, rolled up in a betel leaf and sold for 10 rupees. His small work surface was crammed with over twenty different pots and tubs of ingredients, all ranged around a half-dozen, ace-of-spades-shaped leaves. He spread and sprinkled,

95

scattered and rolled with a swiftness clearly born of years, perhaps decades, of practice. Seeing me looking at him, the man smiled a gappy, red-toothed smile and beckoned me over.

'Good for digest,' he said, patting his stomach. Then patted his throat: 'Good for neck.' And before I could protest he had stuffed a fat pouch of rolled-up leaf into my mouth and indicated that I should let it sit in one of my cheeks. A jamboree of flavours began to spread through my mouth — sweet, rose, fennel seed, menthol. I could see the appeal, although the way it stained my tongue, teeth, lips and mouth bright red was less attractive.

'Ha!' I thought. 'I bet Geoff Dyer isn't having an authentic Indian experience like this, lounging in a bar with the literati.'

Then the man asked me for 200 rupees.

9

A Freebie Too Far

For freelance journalists — at least, the burnt-out crack-ups working at the frivolous, first person, off-the-top-of-your-head-with-a-little-help-from-Wikipedia end of the spectrum — the only real perks of the job are the blags, the freebies; you could call them the bribes, though, please, not to our faces, we do have some feelings you know. But don't judge us harshly: the free stuff is the career wreckage we cling to through the otherwise mostly enervating vicissitudes of freelance life.

For travel writers, the holy grail of freebies is the business class upgrade, but for others the motive force driving their careers could just as easily be how many electronic gadgets, clothes, make-up, CDs, DVDs, dinners or canapés they can stuff in their swag bag each week. Legends in the trade of how far journalists have taken this are legion. There is one travel writer, for instance, who while staying for free at a five star hotel in London, took her curtains along to be cleaned by room service; the well-known car journalist who was in the pay of a famously third-rate Asian car manufacturer for years and plugged their rubbish hatchbacks at every opportunity; or the commissioning editor on an interior-style section of a national broadsheet who wangled an entire fitted kitchen. Those happy few who edit the gadget pages for men's magazines literally drown in iPads and electric shavers.

It is a mutually beneficial relationship: the companies get their products plugged; the PRs can demonstrate the coverage they have secured for their clients; while the journalists fill their boots, and of course get paid for their work. And if the advertising department of the publication is able to ring the manufacturer with news of positive coverage, the latter will be more likely to buy advertising space. It is true that the journalists are, in most instances, free to write what they want about the product and thus maintain at least the façade of integrity but, equally, they will be aware that if they write anything negative, further freebies might not be forthcoming from the same source. Sometimes — especially with online content — they simply cut and paste the press release. Knowledge of all this brings a whole new subtext to one's reading of consumer magazines: if you want to know where a magazine's loyalty lies, read the adverts, not the articles.

My moral glasshouse is a shattered shell, of course, as I have been a modest achiever in this field for many years, seeing freebies as compensation for the paltry remuneration, zero job security, nonexistent social status and general, all-round shitty treatment which are a freelance journalist's lot. I have had the upgrades, the cars on loan, the holidays and hotels, but feel no great remorse about it because

I can genuinely say that I have never let a freebie influence what I write. Looking back, this was an extremely foolish strategy which I greatly regret but my writer's vanity always just bested my venality and, as a consequence, I have burned so many bridges among London's PR community that it is only the fact that they have a burnout rate comparable to journalists' and are constantly renewing their staff, that any of them still answer my calls.

One who did was the PR for a travel company which works with the Umaid Bhawan hotel in Jodhpur. I had asked for three nights at what I had heard was one of the grandest hotels in India in return for a mention in a national newspaper article. They agreed, but the extent and nature of their hospitality only began to become apparent as Vinod drove us up the broad, circular driveway of the 347-roomed, art deco palace belonging to the maharaja of Jodhpur and deposited us at the foot of the steps to its front entrance.

We had been driving for seven or eight hours and emerged from the Innova bleary, shoeless, with boiled sweets matted into our clothes, and bed hair. We tumbled out on to the red carpet where several liveried servants waited to greet us, one bearing a silver tray of drinks. As we ascended the stairs, from the balcony up above, two other members of the hotel's staff rained down red rose petals upon us.

We had spent a day looking out of our car window at some of the most gruelling poverty in India. People in rags scratching an existence from refuse and cow dung, yet now here we were checking in beneath a vast sandstone dome, surrounded by the stuffed heads of leopards and tigers, then being led to our antique-filled suite, with its living room the size of a football pitch. The bathroom was the size of our living room at home, and in each room there was a television screen the size of our bath. Asger and Emil seemed remarkably unfazed by the transition and, once again, I marvelled at their equanimity towards their ever-changing circumstances. As Lissen later said, we could have told them that the next day we were going to be taking a rocket to Jupiter and they would have started calmly packing their rucksacks.

The man with the twirly moustache who had shown us to our room introduced himself as our personal butler, Piyush. 'I will be on service for you at all time. Simply ring,' he told us, handing me his card.

'Could I perhaps arrange some yoga, or some tennis for you?' he added, as he walked around briskly turning on lights. Lissen and I looked at each other.

'Hey, how about we try yoga?' said Lissen, turning to me. 'You know I've wanted you to try that for ages. I know it'd be great for you.'

'Do you have a tennis partner I could play with?' I asked, swerving the question.

'Yes sir, that can be arranged,' he said.

And that's how I found myself playing tennis the next morning against the all-India squash champion of 1996, in borrowed trainers with my own butler standing beside the court holding a box of tissues (he'd noticed that I had a runny nose), on a silver tray alongside a glass of perfectly chilled orange juice. Despite his best efforts to throw the match, the squash champion won. I blamed the borrowed shoes.

Lissen and the children preferred to remain in the hotel for the first day in Jodhpur — the kids playing in the pool while Lissen was slowly driven insane by Piyush shadowing her everywhere ('Would madam allow me to escort her to the lavatory?'). I had yet another masterpiece of Indo-Islamic architecture to inspect: the Mehrangarh Fort, a building of such gravity-defying majesty that, for me, it rivals the Taj Mahal as the greatest of India's Mughal-era buildings. Yet there were virtually no foreign tourists at the fort; India as a whole receives fewer visitors per year than Madame Tussauds in London (around 4.5 million, and that includes visitors from Pakistan and Bangladesh). Thrillingly, they were filming a Bollywood movie in the fort the same day and my growing obsession with Indian movie gossip meant that I was able to recognise one of the stars, the politician-actor Vinod Khanna, co-starring with actress Esha Deoll.

Afterwards, suddenly feeling guilty that I had done no research for my food book for days, I jumped in a taxi and asked to go to Jodhpur market, where I had heard there was a shop selling the best lassi in India. It took some time to locate it, but along the way I found a stall selling the greatest samosas I have ever eaten, for around 20 pence — crispy, fiery hot, with a swirling cavalcade of aromatic flavours. When I finally found the lassi shop in the corner of the market their makhania saffron lassis were indeed heavenly: thick, sweet, fragrant and creamy. After downing two of them, I asked the man behind the counter what the ingredients were.

'No, no sir, sorry sir. Secret!' he said. Saffron, green cardamom and sugar, for sure, perhaps some vanilla, but in truth the secret of this sublime drink was almost certainly the yoghurt they used, a yoghurt which came from milk produced by cows whose diet one could only shudder at but which, nevertheless, was clearly, tragically, unrepeatable anywhere other than Jodhpur.

Back at the Umaid Bhawan, my family had been feasting on unicorn steaks and enjoying ambergris body scrubs and the like. I left Lissen perusing the hotel's 'pillow menu' (I am not making that up, you could choose from five different types) to take a tour of the kitchen with the hotel's chef — again in the hope of finding material for my book. The chef had inherited the maharaja's recipes, he told me, and has used these as the basis for the food he serves guests (who had recently included Prince Charles). The chef was trying to promote classic Rajasthani cooking, predominantly the Khad cuisine of the Thar Desert, which uses milk and whey to cook with instead of water, which is scarce. There are few vegetables in Rajasthani cooking; instead they use grains and pulses along with wild berries, long thin beans called sangri and lots of pickles — also dictated by the climate and mean-spirited landscape. This is one of the hottest and driest parts of India; if they are lucky it rains three months of the year, and in recent years it has hardly rained at all. Many of the ingredients in classic Rajasthani dishes only grow wild, so this is to a great extent foraged food, and extremely nutritious, although the international clientele at the Umaid Bhawan also demanded their Caesar salads and burgers, so the chef gave them those too, he told me with a shrug.

At the end of our time together, sitting in his office, the chef mentioned that he was having trouble sourcing a few of these more Western-oriented items, including organic meats, European cheeses and good couverture chocolate. I told him about some of my favourite producers and helped him find them online, for which he seemed very grateful. Just how grateful would soon become apparent.

A while after I had returned to our room, our butler rang to ask at what time we wanted to dine that evening. I told him that we were planning on going into Jodhpur to eat.

'Oh dear sir, chef had arranged something special for you,' he said. 'He will be disappointed.'

'He didn't mention anything to me,' I said. Besides, as much as I would have liked to, we couldn't afford to dine at the hotel. Dinner for four could easily have set us back over £100 — the equivalent of four days' food budget. I knew a meal in town, even at a decent restaurant, would cost a fraction of that. We would never ordinarily have been able to afford to stay at the Umaid Bhawan in the first place — room rates start from many hundreds of pounds a night rising to £20,000 for the royal suite. Our fellow guests looked as if they shopped exclusively on New Bond Street, and were doubtless packing Louis Vuitton trunks; we were in high-street backpacker mode, and had the opposite of matching luggage. (Piyosh had managed to suppress his horror upon seeing the numerous odd socks and knackered pants hung out to dry in our bathroom, restricting himself to a single raised eyebrow, before taking them away to dry.)

But if the chef had arranged something, there was a good chance that would also be free. He wouldn't arrange something special, and then ask us to pay for it, surely? The trouble was, I couldn't come right out and ask. That would be crass. Journalists usually prefer to couch their naked grasping in terms of 'would you be interested in supporting this press trip?' or, ' . . . participating in this feature', or 'facilitating a consumer review of your product,' or at least use 'complimentary' instead of the more brazen 'free'. But nor could I risk a bill which — considering the 'special' factor — might run into considerably more than a hundred pounds. Somehow, I had to find out without asking directly. I rang the butler back.

'I've been thinking,' I said. 'Can you tell me more about the 'special things' the chef has prepared?'

'Oh don't worry, sir, I've told the chef that you have made other plans. It's no problem.'

'Ah, yes, right, I see. But I was just wondering about the nature of the things he had planned.'

'No, no problem, sir, I have told the chef you are dining out.'

'Ah, right, okay, thanks.'

I hung up.

I told Lissen about my conversation. 'Oh for goodness' sake,' she said, picking up the phone. 'Hello, is that Piyush? This dinner tonight. Is it free? It is, good, thanks. What time should we be ready? Fine. We'll be there. Bye.'

At seven o'clock Piyush knocked on our door. We had mustered our best outfits: shirts instead of T-shirts, proper trousers instead of shorts, but our footwear options were limited to either flip-flops or hefty walking shoes, which rather undermined the whole ensemble. He led us to the central dome of the palace, were we were presented with multicoloured ceremonial turbans which he helped us tie, along with drinks. We then followed him in single file out to the rear terrace where dinner was usually served. But he didn't stop at a table among the other guests; he continued down the steps, which were lined with torches, towards the marble pavilion in the centre of the lawn.

Piyosh paused halfway down the steps. In the distance we could see the floodlit Mehrangarh Fort. Perhaps he wanted us to enjoy the view for a little, I thought. But at that moment the night sky erupted in a plume of fireworks detonated a kilometre or so away at the bottom of the hill: fireworks which had been laid on especially for us. Once the fireworks subsided, we continued to the pavilion where a local Manganiyar musician sat playing a kind of sitar with a bow. He continued as we ate a sumptuous eight-course meal, the highlight of which was a saddle of

105

rabbit so tender and punchily spiced that it haunts me to this day.

It was one of the most extraordinary evenings we will ever experience together as a family, but while Lissen and the children had the good grace to accept a generous gift and show how much they appreciated and enjoyed it, I felt intensely awkward about the whole thing: the butler, the musician, the fireworks, the food, and the onlooking terrace diners who, I imagined, probably assumed we were competition winners.

'Come on Michael, lighten up,' said Lissen, noticing my clenched jaw and restless eyes. 'Just enjoy it, will you.'

But I couldn't. I simply could not appreciate the moment for what it was. I don't really know why I had decided at that point to come over all coy about such a lavish gift — Lord knows these kind of things had never troubled me before. Perhaps it was the the fact that my children were there that made it all seem more tawdry than usual, I don't know — but so consumed with guilt was I, so great was my sense of fraudulence, that instead of savouring what anyone else would have seen as a transcendent, magical experience, I felt utterly wretched throughout. As so often happens in my life, I was regarding proceedings from a distance, one step removed; observing the evening when what I should have been doing, as all those god-awful self-help books would have it, was 'living the moment'.

10

Face Time with the Thunder Bucket

Of other holidays one might perhaps choose to recall the beaches or the shopping, the wonderful weather, or that gorgeous little bistro you found which no one else knows about just a spit from the Eiffel Tower, but in the run-up to our trip, all we ever heard about from India veterans were harrowing tales of the catastrophic bowel movements which had afflicted them there. Everyone, it seemed, had either been to India and experienced awful toilet trouble, or knew someone who had, and for some reason they particularly relished the retelling — almost always unbidden, sometimes despite me explicitly pleading with them to stop — of the sundry hospitalisations and emergency repatriations which ensued, detailing every enforced lavatory visit with the survivor's pride of the war veteran in his most traumatic battles, painting vivid word pictures of gushing torrents, great Niagaras of vomit and diarrhoea.

It was made very clear to us that if we went to India it would not be a case of 'if', but 'when' we would find ourselves up to our ankles in our own bodily waste, enjoying 'face time with the thunder bucket', 'riding the porcelain pony', and so on.

'The world is divided between those cultures

which touch their own feces and those which don't,' wrote the Australian travel writer Robyn Davidson in a description of a trip to India. After I read that, just before we left, I began to wonder if we shouldn't just pack four space suits and be done with it. Should we even be taking children to India? What kind of irresponsible parenting decision was this? Didn't I have enough parental guilt already, what with already having passed on my flawed genes, and the countless goodnight stories told through a fug of Pinot Noir? The most extreme thing my parents ever put me through was a slightly rainy camping trip to Tenby.

In the end I compromised with copious supplies of Imodium, Cipro and amoxicillin, plus two odd socks to slip over hotel bathroom taps. I also vowed that, whatever scatological calamities we did experience on our trip, any account of the journey would be a 100 per cent excreta-free zone. There would be no war stories, no splash by splash reruns.

In fact, we all had our comparatively gentle introductions to Indian bacteria at around the one-week mark (as the India veterans had predicted), and the truth is that by far the majority of incidents of digestive discomfort during my time in India were caused by overeating, but shortly after leaving the most expensive and exclusive hotel any of us had ever — or probably will ever — stay in, we were struck by the big one. A rampant and malicious bacterium did enter our systems and, one by one, like an assassin picking off an improbable posse of fugitives as they rode through the night, it felled us.

Asger toppled first, complaining of stomach cramps as we drove from Jodhpur to our next stop, out in the desert. By the time we checked in to our next, somewhat less salubrious, hotel we had all started to look a bit Gothic and ended up taking it in turns to keep the toilet seat warm throughout the following night and day.

'I want to die,' Asger whispered to me during one toilet visit in the middle of the night, as the cockroaches scurried underfoot and goodness knows what else shuffled around outside our door. 'I can't go on. It's not nice being sick in another country.'

What he really wanted to say was, 'Please, please can we go home now?', but he was trying to be brave, as he sat, quivering, sweating and bent double on the lavatory. Which, of course, was even more heartbreaking. That night, with his temperature way above forty, I feared much worse was to come, not least because we were still in the middle of the Thar desert, many hours from a hospital.

One's children are a great open wound into which fate can prod its finger at any time, and for someone almost permanently crippled by guilt about one thing or another, it was almost too much to bear that my decision had led to my son suffering in this way.

I was brought up a Catholic, and though I had rejected all that decades ago, the guilt filter through which all good Catholic boys' actions must pass remained. I am not claiming that guilt is the exclusive preserve of the Papists, just as a work ethic is not the preserve of the Protestants (Inquisitions don't happen all by themselves, you know), but as a Catholic it is drilled into you that you should feel remorse for pretty much everything that might bring well balanced people joy.

I can remember being led from my Catholic school, St Wilfrid's of Burgess Hill (sadly, this wasn't even one of those aristocratic, sexy Brideshead-style Catholic upbringings: more *Father Ted*), across the street to the church for my first confession at the age of five, being sent to sit in a dark room with a priest, and desperately racking my brains for something, anything, to confess (picking my nose in class? picking my nose in bed? Was nose-picking an actual sin?). These days, of course, one is all too aware of just how badly the 'young boy alone with a Catholic priest' scenario could have turned out, so I realise I got off lightly with merely having the holy fear of God put up me and to say a dozen Hail Marys sitting in shorts on a cold wooden pew, but the programming had begun. Henceforth, everything I did had to be considered confession fodder to appease the whisky-breathed priest.

Though I have been tempted for old times' sake, not to mention a childish urge to admit to something truly unspeakable just to see the look on the priest's face, I haven't been to confession for around thirty years. I used to joke that I was so lapsed a Catholic that I didn't feel guilty about it any longer but, if anything, my guilt receptors are more highly tuned than ever, probably because I have more to feel guilty about these days. Alcohol is one of the best methods I know for quietening that guilt although, admittedly, it does tend to exacerbate problems in the long term.

Watching Asger and Emil suffer through sweats and cramps compounded the guilt I was already feeling about the India trip. What had possessed me to bring them all this way and expose them to such poverty, illness and danger? Why should they suffer for my midlife crisis? Even before the dysentery, the children had started to show signs that they weren't quite as resilient as I had expected. There had been the odd teary interlude as the tedium of the long drives began to take its toll; random, squabbly tension between the two of them at bedtime; and explosive tantrums when homework time loomed.

Attempting to school Asger and Emil on the road had given me a fresh appreciation for parents who educate their children at home. I can only assume the people who do this have a whole different arsenal of threats and bribes that we don't know about. The more time we were spending together, the more hotel rooms and decisions we were sharing or delegating entirely to them, the less our children were viewing us as parents and more as equals. That was positive in some ways, but trying to impose authority when it came to the school books — or anything else for that matter — was becoming increasingly futile.

The stomach upset gave them a good excuse

for a longer hiatus from the school books. It was two days before we felt brave enough even to clamber aboard the Innova again, during which time Vinod had waited with patient concern, sleeping in even less salubrious digs in a nearby village, fetching us medicine and bottled water, which he would thoughtfully leave outside our room when he sensed we were sleeping, his worried frown growing deeper by the day.

He seemed almost as relieved as we were to leave for the final leg of the drive to Udaipur. Lissen, Emil and I had recovered somewhat by then but Asger was still suffering, stretched out in the front passenger seat. Vinod drove as if he were carrying a goldfish in a very full bowl.

★ ★ ★

The parched landscape of the Thar looked a fairly lawless kind of a place, with little sign of involvement of the Indian state — there were few road signs, no public buildings, just endless, dusty scrub, punctuated by the odd sackcloth settlement or random smallholding. Wood was scarce and so the corrals for livestock had been made from tombstone-like blocks of red sandstone.

It was a surreal day's drive. At one point I was convinced that I had seen Baz Luhrmann, the Australian film director, standing beside the road with a large motorbike. At the time I did wonder if this was a vision caused by the self-prescribed cocktail of drugs and bottles of Kingfisher I was taking to combat the sickness, but we later read

112

in a local newspaper that, improbable as it sounds, Baz Luhrmann actually was travelling through Rajasthan taking photographs for an exhibition in Mumbai.

As well as camp Antipodean movie directors, there were more camels and wild dogs, fields of wild chillis, cumin and mustard, and vast tracts of sand dunes shimmering in the distance to look at. Once in a while, we would pass a sorry row of small, open-fronted huts selling plastic sachets of paan mix and washing powder, but even in these remote settlements, the schoolchildren would always be dressed in proper school uniforms and have perfectly combed hair, and they would wave and smile when they saw us, running to keep up as Vinod weaved to avoid them.

I was feeling guilty, too, that we were passing through so much of India without ever properly engaging with it, so at one village I asked Vinod to stop. As he did, I had second thoughts, fearing it might take on the air of a royal walkabout. This proved founded as we were engulfed by children asking us where we were from, where we were going, and whether we knew Ryan Giggs. The adults kept a distance to begin with until one of the barbers came out of his shop to ask if I wanted a shave. I actually needed one, but instantly regretted saying yes when I saw his elderly equipment, and sat rigid in my chair as he lathered me up and scraped a rusty blade over my face.

Since Delhi, almost subconsciously, I had been collecting what I had come to think of as 'lives of quiet desperation'; without really

113

realising it picking out people — the destitute, the sick, the injured and impossibly burdened — as we passed by in our car, and imagining a life for them: where they had come from, where they hoped to go, and where they in all probability would end up. It was an unforgiveably condescending thing to do, but, as I say, it was subconscious, more a case of catching glimpses of lives which I then found impossible to shake off. Much later I read something that Peter Matthiessen, founder of the *Paris Review*, had written which chimed with this:

'In India, human misery seems so pervasive that one takes in only stray details: a warped leg, or a dead eye, a sick pariah dog eating withered grass, an ancient woman lifting her sari to move her shrunken bowels by the road.' This is what I was experiencing, a random accumulation of stray details.

There had, for instance, been the children I had seen wrapped in rags, crouched by the roadside, employed, presumably for money, in banging bits of rock together to no apparent end other than the endless churning of grit. There was the mother with a child in a sling on her back, bent over, alone, in a vast field, picking a crop by hand; and another woman sweeping the endless, swirling red dust on a petrol station forecourt, each new truck which arrived kicking it all up once again. And the cripple who had tied sections of bicycle tyre around his knees to protect them, as he dragged himself along the road.

At one road toll, instead of an automatic

barrier, there was a man whose job it was to wheel a segment of fencing back and forth to allow vehicles to pass, all day long, back and forth, wreathed in fumes. Occasionally we would pass small groups of women randomly stationed by the side of the road tending to the kerbstones. And, most hauntingly of all, there was the beautiful young woman we nearly ran over in the middle of nowhere — at least ten kilometres from the nearest settlement — walking down the middle of the road with an utterly blank expression on her face. Vinod made the universal twirly-fingered sign for psychological illness. What would happen to her? Where would she go? How could she survive here?

These desperate lives were not restricted to Indians. In Jaipur one evening I had come across two Western women in thin cotton dresses with an excess of cheap jewellery dragging two unfortunate little girls in their wake, both barefoot and looking thoroughly dejected. Esther Freud has a great deal to answer for, I thought to myself as I passed them, trying to avoid eye contact (and any potentially awkward self-reflection).

And then there were the animals, like the puppy I'd seen stoned; or scrawny goats, not much more than fur-covered ribcages, grazing on dust; and the countless buffalo, standing morosely in the middle of frenetic highways (Vinod told me that they have sussed out that the exhaust fumes help keep insects at bay), chewing plastic bags at one end, and defecating them out of the other.

So, despite the nervy barber visit — which,

incidentally, resulted in the best shave I have ever had — I was glad we had stopped off in this little village and made some, albeit fleeting, human contact with people whose lives I might otherwise have condemned from a speeding Toyota.

In his exquisitely sad story of dead end lives in a small town in northern India, *Delhi Is Not Far*, Ruskin Bond describes the village of Pipalnagar where 'there is not exactly despair, but resignation, and indifference to both living and dying'. Later on he writes, 'There are days and there are nights, and then there are other days and other nights, and all the days and nights in Pipalnagar are the same.' But there was also great warmth, at least towards us, in this particular Pipalnagar.

11
Mafia Monkeys and the Altruistic Imperative

A few hours later we bade an emotional goodbye to Vinod before catching our flight to Udaipur. Emil jumped up and hugged him tightly around the neck and the two had to be prised apart. Vinod was as bashful as ever, but I could see he was moved. We made all the usual noises about how, if he were ever in our neck of the woods, he would be very welcome to visit us, but we all knew we would be unlikely to meet again. I hope India treats him as honourably as he treated us.

At the airport we played our now customary game of 'What can we get past Indian airport security?' which this time included two large bottles of water, a small sword and a toy gun, but not for some reason a wooden model of a tiger which Emil had snuck into his rucksack, and which was confiscated without explanation. 'Emil, cry! Start crying now!' I hissed, but Emil is not the type to weep to order and the wooden tiger was lost for ever.

With Lissen and the boys still feeling a little delicate, I went out alone that evening to a lakeside restaurant, the Ambras, in the centre of Udaipur. Couples sat at candlelit tables waiting hours for their food but not much caring, gazing

117

either into each other's eyes or at the impossibly enchanting Lake Palace hotel, floodlit by a full moon in the middle of Lake Pichola. Although I am used to eating alone — indeed, if the food's good, I quite like dining solo — I did feel as if I was playing gooseberry to pretty much the entire restaurant. Happily, the food, when it came, was sumptuous: a dhungar maans, a Rajasthani-style smoked mutton dish, with aloo chatni wala — potatoes in tangy mint and coriander. I managed to find room for yet another lababdar, but this one was scorchingly hot. Within seconds of my first, incautious mouthful my forehead was running with sweat. Soon my shirt was soaking, but I continued eating despite my flaming tongue and drenched clothing. From time to time the waiters would approach the table, then, on seeing my condition, back away slowly. Word spread quickly among the staff, so this happened at regular intervals. Roll, up, roll up, and see the sweaty weirdo on table nine!

I managed to persuade one of the staff to come closer and, wiping a shower of sweat from my forehead with my sleeve, asked for a large whisky. They brought me an Indian 'single malt'. I sipped, tentatively. Again, it tasted of toilet cleaner but I managed to knock it back, which relaxed me enough to continue as, for all its nuclear heat, there were still nuanced flavours in the lababdar and, besides, I now needed something to eradicate the flavour of the whisky.

★   ★   ★

118

The rest of the family still felt fragile from the stomach bug the next morning but Lissen had long ago arranged for a trip to the famous Jain temple at Ranakpur, and insisted I go alone. I had been reading about Jainism as we'd travelled and had used their bizarre practices to score cheap anti-religion points in our ongoing discussions about faith and belief.

Jainism is an easy target. Its followers are devoutly non-violent and hold all life to be sacred, a belief they call ahimsa — which even extends to micro-bacterial life. In theory, Jains must not eat root vegetables because of the disturbance their harvesting causes to the things which live in soil, and they aren't supposed to walk outside during monsoon season in case they step on bacteria in a puddle. Ball sports are a no-no too, as the mere act of hitting a ball on a bat is considered violent.

Jains believe all attachment brings suffering, and the truly devoted ascetics among the four million of them worldwide — by far the majority of whom live in India — give away their wealth amid great ceremony and leave their families to roam India on foot, sweeping away insects in front of them with a brush made from peacock feathers as they walk (clearly, they can't drive or fly anywhere, for fear of injuring bugs — think of the accumulated karma). They are not allowed to beg for food but must wait for it to be offered; are not allowed to bathe; and have their hair pulled out, follicle by follicle, every six months. One strain of these Jain sadhus, the Sthanak-vasis, commit public suicide by starvation in a

119

rite known as sallekhana. Oh yes, and when the Sthanakvasis defecate, they must spread their faeces out to dry within forty-eight minutes so that it will not become home to bacteria. I don't imagine they are terribly popular house guests.

Reading about all this reminded me of a fascinating theory by the cognitive scientist Steven Pinker. He has suggested that extreme religious observance — outré clothing, funny hats, self-harm, rituals, processions, all the silly show of faith — has an evolutionary purpose directly linked to the human race's strange and unique altruistic imperative. It is, he says, a way of showing that you are part of a tightly knit group, and of reassuring others in that group that you are the same as them, that you have the same values and beliefs, and thus deserve to be treated well. People tend to behave in an altruistic way towards people who are demonstrably more like themselves than unlike. 'One way to test who's genuinely committed is to see who is willing to undertake costly sacrifice,' he writes. Here, I think, must lie much of the explanation for the behaviour of Jains.

Theoretically, Jains shouldn't use soap, take Western medicines (because of animal testing), or handle money, but the reality is that many are prosperous business people. In particular, I very much enjoyed pointing out the hypocrisy inherent in the fact that a number of Jains have grown wealthy through the diamond trade. 'So they can't pull up a parsnip, but they can dig for diamonds, or at least let others dig for them?' I said to Lissen. Jains are, I should also add,

120

responsible for a greater number of terminations of female pregnancies (and quite probably female babies) than any other group in India — according to one study, Jain boys outnumber girls 1,000 to 848.

But I was still intrigued by the Jains, and had heard that Ranakpur was a 'must-see', so I agreed to take the day trip alone. I left my family taking tentative nibbles of dry toast in our hotel room, and headed up through the Aravalli hills to the north of Udaipur with my driver for the day, Amin. We soon found ourselves among rocky, red, parched mountains dotted with cacti. I asked him to stop in one of the small villages we passed through so that I could get out and explore and, seeing my interest in how the people lived in this part of the state, Amin gave me a brief lecture:

'Rajasthan lady is very very hard work. In field, pump water, teach school, collect cow manure. Sometimes they have to pump the water for ten minutes before it comes. Men sleep.' Do these people have any idea that there are men in the West who think it natural to help with the shopping, the cooking, the childcare and the household chores? I wondered. And, if they do, are such things dismissed as myths, or considered a symptom of the crazy dysfunction of Western society?

Halfway up the mountain range a little south of Ranakpur we passed through a cordon of monkeys, standing guard on either side of the rocky mountain bend like the mafiosi in *The Italian Job*. 'They are waiting for the bus,' said

121

Amin. Apparently the monkeys are familiar with the bus timetable on this road because the buses slow down to let passengers make offerings to these sons of Hanuman, so they all gather at specific times in anticipation.

The temple was squat and frilly and really rather magnificent. As I passed the female guard on the door, having followed her command to remove my leather belt and shoes, she belched a loud, garlic-chutney burp in my face. Surely that, I thought, could be classified as an act of violence.

The early-fifteenth-century temple is famous for its 1,444 columns, each of them intricately carved and densely packed within the building so that it resembles a stone forest. Legend has it that the stonemasons who built it were paid not by the hour but according to the amount of shavings they ended up with at the end of each day, hence the astonishing ornateness of the carvings. As an exercise in getting people to take Jainism more seriously, it works, at least it did as far as I was concerned. It was one of the more transcendent religious buildings I have visited. In a book I bought outside the temple I read that Jains do not actually believe in God and happily accept the idea that the universe simply came into existence. I was beginning to warm to them, although certain of their habits would still probably put me off trying to get to know any personally.

As Amin drove me back to Udaipur, I began to reflect on why Lissen was so adamant that I should have visited Ranakpur, and why she'd wanted to go to the Golden Temple and the Bahá'í temple in Delhi, come to that. There was more to it than just sightseeing or ticking tourist attractions off a list. She must have known I would find more to ridicule than respect in the rituals they hosted, but she kept drawing my attention to what she perceived as the benefits for their followers — their sense of community; the inner ease which comes from a belief in a higher power; their values, which bring order and balance to their lives, and which even I had to agree were generally, at root, admirable.

It was as if she were softening me up for something, though surely not a leap into any kind of spiritual direction? She knew me well enough never to attempt that.

12

Dharavi Days, Bandra Nights

As our plane eased its way down through the brown toxic haze, Mumbai's mildewed tower blocks emerged through their dense smog-cosy. We caught sight of its slums too: corrugated hutments hugger-muggering their way up to the airport's perimeter fence like some abstract collage. I watched Asger staring fixedly through the porthole, as if trying to make sense of it all by the sheer force of his gaze.

'People live in those sheds, whole families,' I said. 'Often for their entire lives. There are more than nineteen million people in Mumbai, and more than half of them live like that.'

Asger looked at me sceptically, and pressed his nose back against the plane's plastic inner-window.

I had probably read more about Mumbai than any other part of India, in books like Suketu Mehta's magisterial *Maximum City* and Gregory David Roberts' *Shantaram*. Frankly, their tales of 500-rupee hit men and carnivorous rat swarms had left me terrified. The picture which emerges from these books is of a venal, stupid, corrupt, suppurating wound of a city. It was hard to imagine a more hostile environment for a flabby, neurotic food tourist and his unworldly brood. I've travelled in some fairly inhospitable places — the Gobi, the townships of Johannesburg, Crawley on a Saturday night — but none had anything like the form of Mumbai, and I had worked myself up into quite a lather about this part of our trip. Right up until the moment our plane had taken off from Udaipur I had questioned Lissen's decision to come there at all, wondering if we couldn't just hop over it and head straight for the south.

'Michael, what exactly is it that are you so frightened of?' she said.

'Filthy hotels, disease, robbery, murder, trauma, gangsters, abduction, terrorists . . . '

'You are getting worse about this kind of thing, you know. When I met you, you were forever off on trips to dodgy places. You seemed to find it exciting. What happened to you?'

'Events.'

'Well, we're going. You can't go to India and not visit Mumbai. And, you know, Mumbai is supposedly far safer for visitors than Delhi, especially for women. You spend so much of your life worrying. Why not just decide not to?'

She was right, of course — not about the worrying, which I preferred to look upon as 'preparedness' — but about Mumbai. Even after just a short time there, a different sense of this 'large and unbeautiful metropolis', as Paul Bowles called it, began to emerge: of its exuberance, its ceaseless pace, and the ambition and audacity of its residents. Mumbai made Delhi seem suffocating and stuffy, and Rajasthan look like a medieval backwater.

Taking advantage of my relief that Mumbai

125

was not as awful as I'd feared, Lissen even persuaded me to visit a slum. Organised tours to Mumbai's slums do exist, but none fitted in with our schedule so, after an intense period of negotiation in which I finally agreed terms — a fifteen-minute visit, no longer; that we would only wear our shabbiest clothes, and carry no handbags, cameras, toys or watches — we piled into a battered Fiat taxi and asked to be taken to Dharavi, which will probably forever now be known as 'the *Slumdog Millionaire* slum'.

At first, the taxi driver simply couldn't understand our request. He spoke English, so it wasn't a language issue: it was simply unthinkable to him that we would want to go there. Then, once we had convinced him, he point blank refused. The next taxi driver responded to an extra couple of hundred rupees and, an hour or so later, deposited us on a rubble-strewn roadside beside a busy alleyway.

Lissen and I looked at each other, took a deep breath, and, holding the children's hands firmly, entered the slum . . . which turned out to be not at all as bad as we had expected, barely distinguishable from the rest of Mumbai, in fact. Most of the buildings were concrete, some of them two or even three storeys high, although virtually all had roofs made from that now familiar collage of tarpaulin, plastic and corrugated iron. The place was buzzing with industry too: there were mountainous stacks of plastic barrels; bulging white sacks; piles of old bicycle wheels, and so on, all supplying the small factories and workshops which lined the narrow

126

streets. There were proper shopfronts with fantastic hand-painted signs as well as dark, smoky caves where men in grimy vests operated Victorian-era machinery. We saw people making everything from handbags to cooking equipment, more often than not out of recycled materials. Ladders lined the alleyways, giving access to the first floors; clothes hung all around, soaking up the smoke from grills and braziers; and the noise was astonishing — from the machinery, radios, bicycle bells, mopeds and people.

The Mumbai government is trying to rehouse many of the 600,000 or so inhabitants of Dharavi (some say as many as a million live there) in high-rise suburbs; not for humanitarian reasons, but to free up valuable inner-Mumbai real estate. If they genuinely wanted to improve people's lives, there are, apparently, far worse slums than Dharavi on the outskirts of the city whose inhabitants would benefit more from relocation. Most of the people who live in Dharavi have jobs of one kind or another, or at least participate in Dharavi's economy. According to many who know the area and its people, there is a strong sense of civic society among the slum dwellers, all of which means they are understandably reluctant to leave.

After a while though, we took a turn into an obviously poorer part of the slum. Here the children were virtually naked and the stench from the wet litter which lay everywhere nauseating. The huts were layered with crusty scabs of plastic, wood and cloth sheeting and

127

had the look of something almost geological which had emerged organically from the mire over decades. Now we were tiptoeing through sludgy litter, leaping warily over open sewers filled with an impenetrable black ooze, its surface slick with rainbows of oil. Some of these alleys were covered, had neither natural nor electrical light, and were so narrow we had to walk in single file, although that didn't stop a moped squeezing past us in one.

When I was a child I seem to recall there must have been an unspoken rule of fatherhood which stated that a dad should never betray his ignorance on any matter to his children, nor his fear, nor any shred of inadequacy, no matter what the circumstances. Children must not be allowed the slightest glimpse of fatherly frailty, or all would be lost, Gibraltar would crumble, the Empire would tumble. I was well into my teens when it dawned on me that there might be some things that my father didn't know, that he might have been bluffing in certain areas (his fluency in Swahili, for example). In contrast, I fear that my own children sussed me out fairly early on: with Asger, it was probably the first time I changed his nappy, in a windowless room just off the delivery ward where he screamed until his little face turned radish red, and my blood pressure scaled new heights. With Emil, the let-down came a little later I think, when, after an afternoon's cussing, I assembled his IKEA bunk bed, essentially, upside down.

I gave up bluffing entirely after that, and vowed to try my best to admit to my faults and

128

inadequacies, so it will have come as little surprise to either of them that, deep in darkest Dharavi, I began to panic. I had lost sight of the tower blocks in Bandra which I had been using to keep my bearings until then, and now had no idea which direction we were going or how to get back to the main street. I gripped Emil's wrist so tightly he pulled it from my grasp. Asger had begun singing softly to himself, something I have noticed he does in times of stress. Even Lissen looked concerned. People were no longer smiling at us, or coming up to talk but staring from the eyeless sockets of their huts.

As we stood at a cramped, airless crossroads, a young woman emerged from a low door and asked, in English, if she could help. 'Please, yes, just please tell us how to get out,' I gasped. She told us to follow her and, within a few turns, we were back at a main road where we flagged down a taxi. I gave her a few hundred rupees, possibly as much as five and, quite rightly, she accepted it as a reasonable fee for services rendered.

★   ★   ★

From our hotel room we had a perfect view of the beach north of central Mumbai, and when we returned I spent some time staring out at the Arabian Sea as it lashed the rocky coast. To the east were more slums, an ocean of brown and, in between the two, a slender slice of some of the world's most expensive real estate, including what our bellboy assured us was Shah Rukh Khan's house, Mannat (meaning 'blessings'), a graceless glass block. I spent the rest of the afternoon staring into his living room with Emil's toy binoculars trying to catch a glimpse of the world's most famous movie star, later learning to my considerable chagrin that he was actually in London receiving an award.

I spent the evening alone in the hotel bar while Lissen and the kids watched TV and got ready for bed. I was hoping to catch sight of the Bollywood stars who supposedly frequented our hotel but, though I saw plenty of people who looked as if they ought to have been famous — women dressed up like MTV dancers tossing glossy hair to draw attention to themselves in a way which contrived also to say, 'Please, I am just trying to have a quiet night off, don't pester me'; and frowning men with stubble and dark glasses — I saw none whom I recognised. Instead, I fell into conversation with a business-man from Norwich who was in Mumbai to set up a manufacturing deal with a local textile fac-tory. He treated me to his insights into India and its people: how 'the worst thing that had ever happened to this country was the British leav-ing'; about the appalling safety standards at the factory ('I have seen them put hydrochloric acid in Coke bottles and then leave it standing around — and this was after someone had drunk it by mistake and died!'); and how everyone he dealt with was, essentially, a lazy, barefaced liar.

'Just look at these people,' he slurred into his gin. 'What's wrong with them? I'll tell you what: democracy. Look at China. Look how well they are doing. Why do you think that is?'

'Slavery?'

'Democracy. They know what's important. They know how to get things done. Don't talk to me about democracy. What this country needs is a good old-fashioned dictator.'

If he hadn't been paying for the drinks, I would have left.

13

The Greatest Chef in India

I had an appointment for an interview in connection with a magazine article — and, in theory, my book on Indian food — with a chef many consider to be India's finest, Hemant Oberoi, of the Taj Hotel Group. Mr Oberoi spends his life shuttling between the many Taj hotels around the world but, fortunately, our few days in Mumbai coincided with his. I was to meet him at the iconic Taj Mahal Palace Hotel, opposite the Gateway of India, in the south of the city.

It looked just a brief taxi ride away on the map, say, twenty minutes. In reality it took us an hour and a half. Despite an impressive new bridge which sweeps out beyond the city across the water, semi-circumventing the worst of the congestion, the traffic in Mumbai is unlike anything I have ever seen. We need a new word for what it is that the cars and trucks actually do here, because they can no longer really be deemed transport in the conventional sense.

Along the way, then, we had plenty of chances to observe the people of Mumbai going about their daily lives. In Worli we sat for about fifteen minutes, covering barely 30 metres, but spent the time watching (it was unavoidable) a man giving himself a full body wash on a pavement no more than a metre from the traffic. First, he stripped to his underpants, packing his clothes into an old Taj Hotel laundry bag, then he washed himself from a barrel of rainwater. He wrapped a cloth around his waist and whipped his underpants off, giving them a soaped scrub on the pavement before wringing them out and putting them back on, along with the rest of his clothes. All the while a baby screamed from inside his hut, yet he moved at his own pace and, all things considered, with quite some dignity.

The Taj was built by a Parsi, Jamsetji Tata (he of the trucks, the telecommunications, the mineral water and just about every other product or service on offer in modern India), who, legend has it, created the hotel out of spite when he was refused entry by the British to what, at the time, was the city's leading hotel. As with other top tourist hotels in India, today there is airport-level security at the front entrance of the Taj, with X-rays for people and their bags. This was a consequence of the terrorist attack which had taken place there just over a year earlier, in November 2008. As well as the 164 people massacred in Mumbai station, at a nearby Jewish centre and other points across the city, thirty-one people died during a four-day siege of the hotel, as its attackers roamed the building casually terminating guests and staff while the Indian police tinkered with their WWII-era rifles outside. Towards the end of the siege, prompted by their masters in Pakistan via mobile phone, the terrorists set fire to the hotel. Its façade was still shrouded in scaffolding but most of the

133

repairs to the interior were now complete.

We explained all this to Asger and Emil who — unsurprisingly — could not really follow the rationale behind the attack. Together they and Lissen headed for the café for lunch and later went over to look at the Gateway of India before heading back to the hotel. Meanwhile, I was led away backstage to the kitchens in the bowels of the hotel, where I was left to wait in Hemant Oberoi's office.

As I sat, I took in the small, windowless room. 'Never, but never, question the chef's judgement' read a sign on the wall, behind the desk, alongside various Indian Chef of the Year awards and pictures of Oberoi smiling beside the likes of George W. Bush, Manmohan Singh, and Bill and Hillary Clinton.

Sitting there, sweating from the alcohol I had consumed with the textile boss in the hotel bar the night before, my fingers trembling, I was feeling decidedly unwell. I had recognised the symptoms of alcohol poisoning as soon as I had woken up that morning: cold sweats; crushing depression; searing self-hatred; a desire only for a cool bed and a darkened room. But I had an interview to conduct. About food. With a lunch to follow.

The chef himself arrived, reassuringly chef-shaped with a belly stretching the buttons on his chef's jacket and a neatly trimmed moustache. 'Maharastran food is very simple,' he said, in answer to my opening question about the local cuisine. 'You have bel puri and vada pao, khali kababs, pao bhaji, all street food really, but I have been trying to refine it slightly and bring it

134

on to my restaurant menus. Masala Kraft is the only restaurant that serves these things in a five-star environment.'

He was less enthusiastic about British Indian restaurants. 'It's food made by people who haven't even been to India, that's the problem,' he sighed. 'They use tomato purées or canned tomatoes rather than fresh, so the food is less acidic. But it should be acidic. They don't use, or can't get the right kind of, red onions. Or, they use packet masalas. Masalas should be made fresh. All these short cuts, because manpower is so much more expensive in Britain.'

It was time for lunch, though food was the last thing I desired. I followed Oberoi out of his office. One of the kitchen staff approached him as we entered the corridor with some question, and I stood quietly, trying to gather myself, wiping the sweat from my forehead with my sleeve.

'You know, of course, this is where it happened,' Oberoi said, turning to me, having answered the young man's question. 'What?' I asked, unthinking. 'This is where the gunman came. He shot seven of my staff.' Oberoi held my gaze as he said this, still smiling. I hadn't planned to raise the events of November 2008. I'd assumed he would want to move on, but he seemed keen to talk about the attacks.

'I saw them shot dead in front of me. The gunman just walked through, very casually, he might just as easily have shot me, but he didn't,' he continued. 'When I am in Mumbai I stay at an apartment just a short walk away, but right next door is the Jewish centre which they also attacked, so I was literally caught between them.'

I asked how on earth he was able to return to work after having witnessed something like that. 'I was here the next morning, after the siege had ended. I was the first in. That was the most important thing for me, to get the restaurants up and running again as soon as possible. If you don't, then they have won, haven't they?'

In the restaurant, Oberoi and I sat across from each other at a corner table. He watched, not eating himself, as I forced down course after course of staggeringly good food which I was in no fit state to enjoy. At one point I had to make an unedifying dash for the lavatory, where I vomited in one of the stalls. If Oberoi saw the stains on my shirt on my return, he was good enough not to mention it.

It was a wretched experience not, I hasten to add, on account of the food or the company but for the unpalatable self-reflection it forced upon me. The night before I had poured down my throat alcohol of a value equal to, or quite probably in excess of, the amount a Dharavi dweller could live on for a month. That, in turn, had rendered me barely fit to carry out a job I was extremely privileged to be doing; unable to appreciate exquisite food, also of a value equal to or in excess of that required to keep a family alive for some weeks in this city; and had, finally, placed me in a position of stark contrast to a man with more dignity, courage and integrity than I could ever hope to muster.

You could call it a low point. Although lower ones were to come.

14

Party Pooper

I am not a people person, it won't surprise you to hear. I tend not to like gatherings of more than me. From what I understand, quite a few men of my age are like this. I think it might have something to do with the diminished self-esteem that comes with the arrival of the paunch and the bald patch, the inexorable decline in virility, energy and dress sense; all of which is relentlessly reinforced by the media's customary depictions of middle-aged men — in adverts, soaps, dramas and sitcoms — as feckless, henpecked fools. It all combines to make you feel that, past your mid-thirties, you have become not merely redundant, but a bit of a joke. It is so much easier to stay at home with *Newsnight* and a bottle of Merlot.

My avoidance strategy usually starts with feigned illness in the morning (ostentatious coughing fits; taking to my bed; lengthy periods in the toilet, reading), and, when that fails, there'll be protestations of deadlines to meet come the afternoon. Both have worked well enough in the past, but over-use has diminished their efficacy so, these days, when I know I am going to be taken somewhere I might not want to go and I sense all is lost, the best I can manage is a torrid blend of pleading and foot stomping just prior to departure. Then, when that fails, I usually drink myself through it.

As with many of my other handicaps, Lissen has learned to work around this one, usually choosing to simply ignore me during the day prior to an evening engagement, and then employing her extensive portfolio of threats and emotional blackmail come departure time.

Nevertheless, the jockeying regarding our invitation to visit Badri and Nita, whose sons Asger and Emil had got to know at the Ranthambore phantom tiger reserve, began early that day. Badri and Nita had insisted we get in touch in Mumbai, and Lissen had texted them on our arrival. An invitation to dinner pinged back almost instantly and, equally fast, I leapt into action. 'We hardly even know them. What on earth will we talk about? What if the food's terrible?'

Unfortunately my scope for weaselling out of this one was compromised, and I knew it. Asger and Emil had been re-enacting the climactic scenes of Cain and Abel for the last few days and were desperate for new playmates. Alternately cooped up either in a car or a hotel room, or under a tight leash out and about in crowded, traffic-filled cities for five weeks now, they were suffering from late-stage cabin fever, at each other's throats pretty much from the moment they woke up. When they played, it was always with a hint of genuine danger, like lion cubs, or drunken rugby players. Lissen and I were on permanent alert, watching for claws, never quite knowing whether there would be blood. They seemed able to pick a fight over the slightest matter, like Woody Allen's parents in *Radio Days* ('Wait a minute: are you telling me the Atlantic is a greater ocean than the *Pacific?*')

It was yet another aspect of the trip which Lissen and I had failed properly to anticipate, but it was understandable. Asger and Emil had been reliant on each other's company for too long. Though there had been occasional encounters with other children in hotel lobbies, Rajasthan had been light on playgrounds and they desperately needed fresh blood. For once, I couldn't let my social autism stand in their way.

Badri had kindly offered to send his car and driver to pick us up from our hotel at five o'clock, but had warned that they didn't live in Mumbai itself, but in Navi Mumbai. 'You do realise we are about an hour or maybe more away from your hotel?' he told me over the phone.

I have to admit that I was intrigued by this car and driver business, conjuring as it did visions of great wealth and opulence. What kind of a home were we going to visit? Would there be marble courtyards with tinkling fountains, swimming pools and tennis courts? Would there be liveried staff and gold leaf desserts?

I looked Navi Mumbai up on the internet. It was a planned city — the largest in the world — built in the 1970s as an escape route for the heaving population of Mumbai proper. It was inland, to the east, on the other side of the harmless-sounding Thane Creek. Surely, even given Mumbai's traffic, it could be no more than

139

an hour's drive, tops.

Their driver, a surly fellow, arrived an hour late, blaming the traffic which, to be fair to him, was even worse than the day before. I tried to engage him in chit-chat about cricket (a sport which I know little), but he was having none of it, staring ahead at the snarled traffic and responding to my salvos about Ian Botham with grunts.

We crawled through the city along vast, eight-lane highways choked with trucks and buses. Every hundred metres or so the central reservation would be punctured by a poster on a pole of the Hindu extremist leader, Bal Thackeray — 'A cross between Pat Buchanan and Saddam Hussein,' according to Suketu Mehta — looking every inch the Mafia don with large, square sunglasses, his gormless son beside him. We drove past hideously stained tower blocks, Soviet in their scale and porridgy decrepitude; through endless roadside rubble and rubbish; past crumbling temples and, once more, alongside the low-rise hell of Dharavi.

After an hour and a half we came to the Thane Creek, which was to creeks as Australia is to islands — a vast estuary at least a couple of kilometres wide. Crossing it we came to Navi Mumbai, endless rows of monumental, pastel-coloured residential blocks, with many dozens more under construction. If you saw it in a film, you'd assume it was CGI, such was its monotonous scale. This was, essentially, battery accommodation for humans, albeit relatively luxurious with each unit boasting a balcony facing the sun like some kind of Ballardian dystopia. Welcome to the heartland of the Indian middle class.

Finally we arrived, now after dark, morose and anxious (although that may just have been me), at the Meridien Apartments in the charmingly named 'Sector 4' — fifty-nine apartment blocks, each twenty or maybe twenty-five storeys high, and one of them home to Badri, Nita and their sons.

Nita greeted us with her boys, and the four new friends disappeared off into the night to play in the communal park in the centre of the complex. We watched our sons get swamped by a gaggle of curious local children, and then consumed into the pack for a couple of semi-feral hours' play, as fruit bats swooped through the night sky above.

I was, naturally, nervous about this. Ought we to let our children disappear into the Mumbai night, to who knows where, with who knows who? I couldn't read the signs, I couldn't figure out whether this was a benign neighbourhood or the kind of place where kids go missing never to be seen again, spending the rest of their lives toiling in a shoe factory in Bangladesh (I tried to imagine some hard-bitten factory owner trying to oppress Emil, and actually felt a twinge of pity for them). Nita tried to reassure me. 'Don't worry, my boys won't let anything happen,' she soothed. 'They know this park very well.'

She distracted me with alcohol and snacks back up on their second-floor terrace as we waited for Badri to come home from his cleaning

141

products factory. Nita was a keen cook, it turned out, and we spent some time talking about India's regional foods. I was interested in the techniques for thickening sauces in Indian cookery. At French cooking school I'd been taught to use flour, butter and cream, or reduction. Nita explained that Indians use a range of techniques, from fried, blended onions to ground almonds, yoghurt or a variety of pastes, often based on garlic and ginger.

This isn't at all awkward, I thought as we chatted, somewhat relieved. And then I asked if I could see the kitchen.

'Oh, you want to see the kitchen?' Nita said, suddenly flustered. 'Well, it's not really . . . '

'Don't worry if it's any bother . . . '

'No, no, of course not, come with me.'

I had misjudged the etiquette of visiting Indians at home. The kitchen, it turned out, was a place for servants. We interrupted two young serving women at work. They too looked disconcerted and confused to see a guest, and a male guest at that, sticking his nose in the cooking pots. Also — and this is a delicate matter as I realise I had been invited as a guest into a private home — the kitchen was filthy, as if we had stepped into an entirely different home. I beat a hasty, fixed-smile retreat.

'Why can't we move here?' said Emil, when he finally emerged, dusty, sweaty and exhausted, having run rampant in the darkness for over two hours. 'To start with they all wanted to touch me,' said Asger. 'They said they thought I was an alien. But after a while, we just played.'

142

Badri arrived at the same time, warm and welcoming, apologising for his lateness, and immediately fixing himself and me a drink. We sat down to eat on their large terrace, with views over the communal park. Nita, originally from the Punjab, brought out endless plates of food — tandoori chicken, dips, breads, fried prawns, all fabulously spicy — but she refrained from eating herself, while Badri only nibbled.

More awkward.

Lissen and I looked at each other wondering whether we should eat or not. We stopped, but Nita encouraged us to continue. As we would find out on later visits to other private Indian homes, guests are considered temporary deities, and are customarily served by the hosts, who wait until they are sated before they themselves eat. But we hadn't experienced this before, and were nonplussed, which in turn made us hesitant about eating. There was yet more awkwardness when I had to refuse the drinks offered to Asger and Emil.

'Sorry, but they, erm, the ice, you see,' I said, realising as I spoke that Nita might easily misinterpret this as, 'You might give my children diseases.'

But they both apologised and said they quite understood. 'When my aunt visits from Australia, she is the same,' said Nita. 'We have strong Indian stomachs and we forget sometimes.'

Badri offered me another whisky, while Nita and Lissen drank red wine, Nita shyly admitting it was only the second time she had drunk alcohol, the first being the night we had met at the hotel in Ranthambore.

After we had eaten, they showed us around their two-bedroom apartment which was sparsely furnished with no books or paintings on the wall, although it did have a large flat-screen TV and a mammoth massage chair, imported from China like all their furniture. We were invited to take turns in the chair, which vibrated like a paint shaker making aspects of my anatomy which I had previously considered relatively taut, wobble alarmingly.

It was a strange night. We had little in common with Badri and Nita other than our sons' ages, and, as with Vinod back in Rajasthan, we talked encouragingly about them coming to visit us at home, but we all knew it would never happen and that, again, we would most likely never see each other. This was actually quite liberating as it allowed us to ask more personal questions than we might otherwise have done. Lissen was keen to hear whether Badri and Nita had had an arranged marriage.

'Yes,' said Nita. 'We didn't have a love marriage but my parents were very liberal, they let us meet two times before we married.'

Seeing our shock, she added, 'Often the bride meets her husband for the first time on the wedding day itself, you know.'

'So, you didn't, like, have sex before you were married?' I asked, incredulously, pausing with my drink tilted to my lips. Suddenly the smiles faded. Nita and Badri looked downwards. Nita coughed. Badri laughed nervously.

We left soon after that.

144

'Well, that was a really interesting evening, wasn't it?' I said as we drove back to the hotel that night. 'I'm glad we went.'

Lissen didn't say anything. She just stared out of the car window as the silent slums of Mumbai passed by.

15

Arrival in Kerala

Malaria, or in truth the prophylactics prescribed to ward it off, almost put me off going to India entirely. I once took Lariam, a commonly prescribed anti-malaria drug, for a visit to the first International Zanzibar Film Festival in the late nineties, and soon after arriving descended into a slough of depression and paranoia from which, at the time, I convinced myself I'd never escape.

It didn't help that Stone Town, Zanzibar's capital, is a medieval labyrinth of narrow alleyways which at night, when the power frequently cut out, would leave me literally groping for a way back to the safety of my hotel trying to avoid the frightful portraits of its most famous son, Freddie Mercury, whose face loomed, with its alarming dentistry, at every turn. It was enough to make even the most intrepid of travellers jumpy, let alone a less intrepid one in the throes of a psychotic episode.

I remember sitting for what seemed like hours one afternoon, staring fixedly at the skeleton of a dodo on display in the local natural history museum, imagining my own bones replacing them in the glass case. Of the film festival itself, I remember little.

So, Lariam: no.

The idea of feeding it to my children was abhorrent. Yet, so too was the risk of any of us catching malaria. My father caught it during his time in India in the latter stages of World War II. The youngest of seven brothers, all of whom served in the armed forces (beat that, Ryans), my dad enlisted at the outbreak of war aged eighteen and ended up as an aerial photographer in the RAF. He was chased out of Singapore by the Japanese in early 1942 and told me how he had to leave all his worldly goods on the harbourside before bundling into a boat for Sumatra just hours before the Japanese arrived, and was then chased across Indonesia sitting on top of a truck. My grandmother received a letter pronouncing my father missing in action, and for a few weeks assumed he was dead. He ended up in India, close to the Burmese border, and remembered his time there with great fondness, particularly the luscious mangoes which were, he said, so juicy he had to eat them in the bath. From the photos, which I now have, it seems he and his comrades spent most of their time performing in *It Ain't Half Hot, Mum*-style gang shows, although he also recalled his near death from a mosquito bite and I can still remember the look on his face as he recalled his first cup of tea after regaining consciousness from his malarial coma. It was, he said, the best cup of tea he'd ever had.

The various therapists I have seen in my life have pointed to my father's wartime experiences as a source of my own rich palette of neuroses. The father I knew was an Olympic-class worrier. Whether it was the money concerns which

147

dogged my parents through the seventies; the risk of barbecue fires; or the consequences of not finding a parking space in Brighton's Churchill Square shopping centre on a Saturday morning (something I, frankly, wouldn't take a chance on either), my father was not a man you would ever describe as 'carefree'. Even on holiday. Especially on holiday, where everything that could go wrong at home might still go wrong, but with all those 'worse things happen at sea' connotations.

In his defence, he had watched the orange glow from the fire-bombing of London while standing on the South Downs and, from a first-floor window, looked into the eyes of a Messerschmitt pilot as he flew down East Street, machine-gunning the road. Friends, neighbours and his beloved next-oldest brother, Percy, were all claimed by the war. While still a teenager, my father had left his family, put on a uniform and been shipped off to a distant continent, where he had been trained to kill. Like much of the British population at the time, he must also have spent several years mentally preparing for occupation by the Nazis. So, I think he had reasonable grounds to be 'a bit of a worrier', and he passed those tendencies on to me.

Naturally, then, I gave a great deal of thought to what might possibly go wrong during our trip and how it might be avoided, hence the twelve bottles of antibacterial hand gel and the Timothy-Leary-sized pouch of pharmaceuticals. Back at home, my local health travel advisor had shown me a map of malarial India. It depicted a wide band across the centre of the country, starting just below Udaipur, and stretching south almost to Mumbai in the west and, further south and east to Hyderabad in central India, with an isolated pocket encompassing Goa on the west coast.

'See, look,' I had said, showing Lissen the map months before our departure. 'There's no way we can go to India. Do you realise that malaria stays in your body your entire life?'

Lissen looked carefully at the printout and, pointing to the large regions to the north and south, said, 'It's simple. We can just avoid the central bit, can't we?'

'Ah, yes, but what about Goa?'

'Well, from what you've told me, Goan cuisine is the most westernised in all India. I don't imagine it'd be a priority for someone investigating authentic Indian food. Besides, it's not very big, and it's full of Germans.'

So it seemed we would avoid Goa and central India, where the killer mosquitoes lived. As it turned out, later, whenever we mentioned the malaria risk to Indians themselves, they either scoffed at us for being so feeble (as if malaria was some niggardly inconvenience) or pointed out that you can, in fact, catch malaria pretty much everywhere in India, even in Delhi, but that the risk of catching it as a tourist is, in reality, negligible to the point of non-existent.

(We didn't bother with rabies jabs either, by the way. If faced with any snarling, frothy-mouthed animals I calculated on my ability to outrun at least Lissen.)

149

★　★　★

So, from Mumbai we flew directly to Mangalore in southern Karnataka, taunting the mosquitoes as we flew over Goa. It was a not altogether un-fond farewell to Mumbai. Of all the cities we'd seen in India it was the one I genuinely hoped one day to return to albeit preferably with a helicopter.

The lush green vegetation and rust-red soil of Mangalore were a radical contrast to what we had seen of India so far. This was clearly a permanently verdant, riotously fertile landscape, and notably wealthier than the north too, with ornate pastel-coloured villas lining the main roads, and well-kept villages with shops boasting actual glass windows. It seemed another country from the arid, parched, fogbound, poverty-stricken north, or the borderline intolerable, urban chaos of Delhi and Mumbai.

I had found us a place to stay — one of my few contributions to our itinerary — in northern Kerala, the border of which lay an hour south of Mangalore. This is a predominantly Muslim area and, perhaps for this reason, it has seen little tourist development — visitors to south-western India tend either to take the package trips to Goa where the locals are more tolerant of bikinis and booze or, if they are more adventurous, head to southern Kerala, to Cochin (Kochi) or the party beaches around Kovalam.

It hadn't been easy but I had managed to find a hotel, near a town called Kasaragod. The odd thing was, the hotel's web page only had one fuzzy photograph and very few other details, but the other two guesthouses in the area were already fully booked, so it was that or nothing. I emailed to enquire about making a reservation. No answer came. I phoned the number at the bottom of the website. It turned out to be a central reservations number for an Indian hotel group. I asked the woman who answered if I could make a reservation. The line went silent for quite a while, before she returned to tell me that the hotel was still under construction, but that she would get back to me. Needless to say, she didn't, but I had now reached a sufficient pitch of annoyance not to let it rest at that. I was going to make a reservation at this cockamamie hotel whether they wanted me to or not. I ended up contacting the hotel group's marketing department directly and ranting at them via email about 'not publicising their hotel before it was ready and wasting people's time', to which I received a very polite reply saying that in fact, the hotel was almost ready (this was a few weeks before we left), and, although they were not yet accepting reservations, she was prepared to make an exception and they would be happy to welcome me and my family on the dates requested at an introductory reduced rate.

I could hardly back out now. I had long ago relinquished my desire to actually stay at the hotel. No one intentionally stays at hotels which have only just opened or are in the midst of a soft opening. It's holiday suicide. The service will be terrible. The electricity won't work. There'll be constant drilling and cement dust; the room safe will gobble all your valuables and refuse to open; and the kitchen staff won't have had their hygiene training yet, so you'll end up with some fearful gastrointestinal affliction and never see beyond the bathroom. But my bluff had been called, I now had a reservation.

As it turned out — and Lissen, were she here, would point out that 'it', whether it be a dentist visit, picnic weather, public speaking engagement or any kind of pending event always turns out this way — none of my fears were realised. The hotel was almost completely finished; not only that, but it was a gorgeous, if anonymously styled resort, close to to a vast, empty, sandy beach where Lissen and I sat together each evening watching the super-quick sunsets as Asger and Emil hared about trying to catch tiny, see-through crabs which moved at the speed of light. There were cotton trees, with their large, swollen green pods dangling rudely; coconut palms, of course; orchids and, high above, white-breasted eagles surfed the thermals. What's more, we were literally the only guests, with our own cottage, a pool all to ourselves, and, most exciting of all, free rein with the kitchen and its chefs.

The downside? There were, it has to be said, slight echoes of *The Prisoner*. We were basically interned, miles from anywhere, with staff awaiting our command at every turn and fountains eerily erupting the moment you approached them. Also, initially at least, we were served 'health' portions at mealtimes, as this was supposed to be a 'wellness' resort. But we soon put a stop to that. The main cause for concern, though, was

152

the fact that they did not yet have an alcohol licence.

They were not allowed to sell alcohol.

It was a dry resort.

'Cheer up,' said Lissen when we were told this on arrival. 'There's yoga!'

16

The Magicians of Kerala

There was indeed yoga, at seven the next morning. Wearing my still slightly damp swimming shorts and a T-shirt I followed Lissen (who, with smug prescience, had packed her proper yoga gear) down to the yoga studio, a vaguely spiritual building with tinkly water features, old wooden temple carvings, candles and incense.

I had never done (practised? endured?) yoga before. I had never imagined being so incautious as to allow myself to be manoeuvred into a situation where such an eventuality might arise, but when the hotel manager had approached us over dinner that first night to offer us a complimentary session, Lissen accepted before I had a chance to weasel out.

Our instructor was called Prabakar. He was a tall, slender man in his late twenties with a fixed expression of serenity. I took an immediate dislike to him. I protested that I had never tried yoga before and almost certainly would be rubbish at it, to which he answered, calmly, 'I am sure you will like it, sir. Let's start with something easy, just relax.'

Ah, that whole passive-aggressive routine, I thought, little knowing the heights to which Prabakar would take this over the next few days.

He stood perfectly still, with his eyes closed and his hands clasped together in front of his chest as if in prayer, intimating that we should do likewise.

Relaxation on command is impossible for me and so I stood, rigid as a church pew, trying my best to locate this fugitive state. My mind was repeatedly telling me to 'relax' but my body would not comply. With my eyes closed, every noise within a two-mile radius was intolerably amplified. My hearing became a superpower homing in on every distraction: workmen dragging a bucket of cement through sand; crows cawing in a distinctly vulgar manner; a distant train horn; a flushing toilet. A fly tickled my leg hair and I spasm-twitched it away, St Vitus-like.

'Breathe only through your nose,' said Prabakar. 'Now do what I do.' He bent over and touched his toes.

I was unable to fulfil even the first of these commands as my nose was full of matter, so I had to shuffle off to the toilet for a good rummage and blow. Returning, I discovered that not only could I not reach my toes, but that I could barely make it halfway down my shins.

This was a setback as far the whole yoga thing went. It turned out that Hatha yoga, the branch (strain? subspecies?) that Prabakar taught, seemed to involve little else than touching your toes in a variety of ways, very, very slowly. Slowly, like longshore drift, or an amateur production of *Troilus and Cressida*. It was intensely boring. If there'd been a clock to hand I would have counted

155

the minutes, but there wasn't, so I had to rely on my own, by now severely distorted inner sense of time. Halfway through the session — at about the three-day mark — Prabakar invited us to lie down on our backs on our blue yoga mats and, again, relax.

This time I was better at it. I was asleep within a minute.

'What was wrong? I thought the whole idea was to relax,' I said to Lissen as we were driven back to our chalet in a white golf buggy. She didn't reply.

Back at the room, we discovered that Asger and Emil had somehow managed to phone in a colossal room service order. It was news to me that either of them even knew how to operate a phone, but I did know that the cost would be phenomenal. 'We were hungry!' they wheedled, in between mouthfuls of pancake and iced doughnuts. By that point I was more interested in wolfing down as much of the food as possible before they finished it all, and left it to Lissen to explain the extravagant expense of getting hotels to bring you food in your room, and the questionable nutritional value of banana muffins.

I spent the rest of the day with books from the hotel's reading room. These were almost all self-help and spiritual titles. I suppose there is always the remote chance I might learn something useful from these books, but my chief pleasure is in ticking off a list of their most oft repeated clichés and truisms, and all of them were right there in *The Monk Who Sold His Ferrari*.

This was a modern fable about a high-flying

156

corporate lawyer who quits his job and disappears to India on a quest for the meaning of life. It is written in what is a — presumably deliberate — naïf style. The dialogue creaks like a Spanish galleon:

'Just listening to you makes me feel great. You really have changed, Julian. Gone is your old cynicism. Gone is your former negativity. Gone is your old aggressiveness. You really do seem to be at peace with yourself. You have touched me tonight.'

'Hey, there's more!' shouted Julian with his fist in the air. 'Let's keep going.'

It made Chuck Spezzano look like Confucius. I read the whole thing, in rapture at its awfulness. Its key messages are:

Think positively.
Buying stuff = bad. Inner journeys unburdened by possessions = good.
Sometimes sit and stare at a rose. It's nice. And watch the sun rise. Maybe dance in a rain shower.
Success on the outside begins with success on the inside.
The only limits on your life are the ones you set yourself.

Part of my problem with this kind of thing is that I find the realm of the abstract foggy and befuddling. High concepts like 'happiness' and 'grace' elude me. Like many men, I suspect, I am

157

mired in the prosaic, the details. An example: every morning, I scour my muesli for pieces of dried banana, and remove them. I can't abide dried banana. It has no place in the food chain, nor, for that matter, does any other preparation of banana other than 'peeled'. (Neither do I want to see a banana gussied up in a dessert or, as once happened in the meal I cite as the worst I have ever had, in a chicken curry together with pineapple and parboiled rice, at a provincial German hotel.) If I accidentally overlook a morsel of this dried monkey puke and end up eating it, it casts a pall over my entire morning. Genuinely, it screws up a good portion of my day. When your life is lived at that level of petty irritability, looking at flowers isn't going to help.

I read on. 'What would you do if today was your last?' the ex-Ferrari-owning sage asks. I put the book down to ponder this: (1) Drink half a bottle of gin. (2) Send some of my own faeces to that commissioning editor at the *Independent* who screwed me over that time. (3) And perhaps a small envelope to that silly bitch who reviewed my first book in the *New Statesman*. (4) If I could find some, see what all the fuss is about heroin.

I read on. 'When you live every day as your last, your life will lead to a magical quality,' it said. Hmm, yes. Either that or a custodial sentence.

Next, I turned to a book called *The Tibetan Yogas of Dream and Sleep*, whose author was keen to tell all about a technique in which he meditated while sleeping using a method called

'Dream Yoga'. 'If we cannot remain present during sleep, if we lose ourselves every night, what chance do we have to be aware when death comes,' he reasoned.

Well, (1) If you don't get to lose yourself when you are asleep, then when do you get to? and, (2) Why in the name of Brahma's balls would I want to be *aware* when death comes? If you see mine coming before I do, do me a favour and slip me a handful of Nitrazepam in a half-bottle of Macallan's, would you?

But it was when I reached the following passage that I finally realised Eastern mysticism would likely remain beyond my ken for ever:

In Tibet, new leather skins are put in the sun and rubbed with butter to make them softer. The practitioner is like the new skin, tough and hard with narrow views and conceptual rigidity. The teaching is like the butter, rubbed in through practice, and the sun is like direct experience; when both are applied the practitioner becomes soft and pliable. But butter is also stored in leather bags. When butter is left in a bag for some years, the leather of the bag becomes hard as wood and no amount of new butter can soften it. Someone who spends many years studying the teachings, intellectualizing a great deal with little experience of practise, is like that hardened leather.

So, is butter good for the leather, or what? And doesn't it really smell if you leave it in the sun for

159

so long? What a waste of good butter . . .

In the early evening, while the pool attendant, Dinesh, taught Emil to swim (I had tried, but Emil refused to listen to me) and Asger and Lissen did something holistic in the 'mindfullness centre', I played snooker with the entertainment manager, Joy. Early on in the game it became apparent that Joy was doing everything he could to let me win. He would approach a shot smoothly, his cue action would be Steve Davis perfect, and his head would remain stock still, but still the ball would strike well wide of the pocket and he'd then chide himself unconvincingly. I had a major post-colonial guilt pang about all this: Britain had raped India of its natural resources and systematically ground the self-esteem of its people into the dust, and here I was perpetuating the crime. So, I decided that I was going to lose, and started deliberately missing shots myself. The frame dragged on for over an hour as the only way balls were going to drop was if they accidentally ended up right over pockets and we were unable to avoid potting them. In the end, with dinner imminent, I broke down, and in a sudden rush of blood cleared the table from the brown.

As we reset the table, another member of staff approached to tell me that the owner of the chain of hotels would be arriving for dinner, along with her morbidly obese sister (the latter was here to test some of the resort's health and weight loss cures). More ominously, he told me that there was to be a traditional dance performance that evening, to which we were invited.

160

'Is there a fresher hell than traditional dance performances in a resort hotel?' I moaned to Lissen back in the room. 'We might as well all get tattoos, put on nylon England shirts and start drinking cocktails with umbrellas in them and be done with it.' She replied that it might be interesting, and that I didn't know for sure that it wouldn't be authentic, and that we were going whether I liked it or not.

With their sinister minty-blue faces, broad red slashes for mouths, and skirts made out of peacock feathers, the Kathakali dancers looked like radical extremist morris dancers. We were all quite taken with them, costume-wise. But their retelling of a story from the Ramayana was lacklustre, and the initial excitement of their outfits soon waned. The performance lumbered on and on for over an hour, the dancers spinning and jerking to the accompaniment of highly strung drumming, and gurning like the All Blacks, unburdened by choreography.

Above the din, Emil, with the typical intolerance of boredom and insouciant disregard for social niceties of a six-year-old, shouted out, 'This is really boring!' Unfortunately the drumming stopped at precisely that moment, and all heads turned.

Blessedly, this was indeed the end of the performance. Asger and Emil rushed the stage like Morrissey fans, keen to meet the dancers. At their age, I wouldn't have wanted to go within a mile of them for fear of being hoovered up by their skirts and never seen again, but India had already made my children braver than I ever was.

161

We took photos and I noticed Asger and Emil talking heatedly to each other in low whispers, then glancing at Lissen and me. They then spoke briefly with Joy.

Joy came to the front of the stage holding a microphone, hardly necessary as, aside from the hotel staff, there were only six people in the audience: me; Lissen; the hotel group owner, a small Indian woman in her late fifties in a dazzling sari and with a cast-iron hairdo; a nervous young woman in a suit, presumably some kind of assistant; the American pilot of the owner's private plane; and the owner's sister who sat, engulfing her chair like the butter icing on a cupcake.

'Ladies and gentlemen, I would like to introduce to you a very special magic show!' said Joy. The Kathakali singers stopped on their way down from the stage and turned to watch as Asger, then Emil, took to the front of the stage, amid much theatrical arm-flourishing and bowing, and proceeded to perform two tricks they had brought with them from a magic set they had been given for Christmas. Asger's involved a clear Perspex box, which could only be opened in a specific, hidden way. The demo required two hands, which left holding the microphone awkward, so Emil did that for him.

'Does anyone have any money?' Asger asked the audience.

Having been stung by the trick already, Lissen and I kept quiet but the hotel owner volunteered a 100-rupee note. Asger invited her to push the note through the money slot in the box and then gave her the box for her to try and retrieve it.

'Oh, wait!' he said. 'You aren't allowed to pull the box like this.' He demonstrated the only method of opening the box, just to make sure she didn't spoil the trick. 'But you can try to open it any other way.'

The owner did as she was told, obligingly failing to open the box, and she and her group applauded generously.

'It's like we've somehow turned into a reality show version of Little Miss Sunshine,' reflected Lissen.

Unlike his brother's close-up street conjuring style, Emil's trick was more suited to stage performance, though perhaps not quite so fully realised. It involved him waving around an orange handkerchief. It was, though, equally well received and at the end of the evening as we were leaving, the owner's sister beckoned them over, reached into her handbag, and pulled out an assortment of chocolate bars to give them. The evening was, then, deemed a great success, at least as far as Asger and Emil were concerned.

17

Shrivelled Spleens and Headless Chickens

The next day, we rose early and were driven in the golf cart the three hundred yards to the yoga studio. 'Let us pray for peace to spread around the world,' said Prabakar with his irritating beatific smile. At one point he told us to 'relax our spleens'. I had no idea where my spleen was, but visualised an unpleasant brown, shrivelled organ. Relaxed is the last thing that's likely to be, I thought.

Prabakar requested that I concentrate on my breathing, but the more I did this, the less I was able to breathe properly at all. (It reminded me of the time I was being interviewed for some TV thing and, to get footage to show during a voiceover bit, they asked me to 'walk naturally down the street towards and past the camera'. I grew so fixated on trying to walk naturally that I ended up walking in the least natural manner imaginable, like a jerky stop-motion animation figure from a Ray Harryhausen movie.) In the end I began making an odd rasping noise, my vision went speckly, and I had to sit down.

The next instruction — to clear my mind of all thoughts and distractions — proved equally ambitious. It would be nice to pretend that this is because my mind is ceaselessly probing the

164

mysteries of existence, but, sadly, the truth was more along the lines of:

'Okay, Michael, right. Don't think about anything. Stop thinking, NOW! Don't even think about yoga. What was the name of that Murakami book? *What I Think About When I Talk about Running?* Or was it, *The Things I Talk About When I Think About Running?* When was the last time I ran anywhere? What shall I have for lunch? Just a lassi, perhaps. And a plate of those french fries. I am dying for a piece of cheese. A Kingfisher would be nice. I wonder if all those drunk pilots are drunk on beer. Perhaps they get it free . . . Urgh, God! There's something crawling in my ear!'

★ ★ ★

After the third day, I was beginning to get bored with sunbathing, swimming, eating and reading. The excitement of spotting kingfishers (sadly, in this case, the bird variety) and scampering mongooses had begun to pall. Small things had started to annoy me out of all proportion. I even complained out loud about the noise of the ornamental fountains.

'I mean, if we are the only guests here, don't you think they'd turn them off if I asked?'

'Michael, most people love the sound of falling water. It's supposed to be relaxing. This place is perfect,' said Lissen. 'I don't understand how it is that you can always find something to complain about.'

To break the monotony of paradise, I asked to

go along with the chef, a Bengali, on a trip to the local market in Kasaragod. The hotel insisted that a member of staff, a sweet man called Harish in his first job since graduating from hotel school in Mangalore, accompany us.

Kasaragod was a relatively prosperous small town — little more than a high street behind which lay the fish and produce market. Dried fish play an important part in the food of this region and the market reeked of them.

As the only westerner I was the focus of some bemusement and a little hostility. 'Are you here to buy fish, or what?' one young man barked at me as he shoulder-barged past. The chef distracted me with a pala kathi, a small, low wooden seat with a round, serrated blade fixed to one of its ends. 'You sit on it, like this,' he demonstrated. 'Then rub coconut flesh on the knife to shred it.' I want one of those.

Walking back up the high street from the market, Harish pointed out an alleyway. 'That's my house, do you want to see?' I followed him up a path overhung with pepper trees and flowers to reach an elegant bungalow. Inside, it was a cocoon of cool, dark wood and we were enveloped in the smell of aromatic frying spices. Harish's mother and grandmother were cooking chicken, would I like some? It was fabulous, fiery hot, but gently lifted by sweet, luscious coconut milk.

While we ate, I had a chance to talk to Harish properly for the first time. Our conversation opened with pleasantries, some of which I suspected he had been taught at hotel school,

166

such as, 'German wines are becoming very popular, are they not?' But it soon became more personal. He had an endearing verbal tic of starting any slightly intrusive question with, 'But basically sir', and there were many things he was keen to know about life in the West. 'But basically sir, your house, does it cost very much?' he asked. I replied: by Indian standards, probably. By Western standards, not. 'But basically sir, I am Hindu, what religion are you?' I replied that I had no religion. Harish tried to take this in his stride but I could see it troubled him.

His family were having to sell this beautiful old house, he said. Someone had offered to buy it off them to turn the plot of land into apartments and they needed the money. It was his dream to join the Keralan diaspora to get a job abroad so that he could send money home — the pay at the resort was hardly enough to live on, apparently. I had noticed the gaudy, Spanish-style villas surrounded by large gardens just off the highway. The houses were often empty and shuttered and Harish told me that they were waiting for their owners to return from construction or hospitality industry jobs in Abu Dhabi or Saudi Arabia. These were the houses 'built by nurses, masons, wire benders and bank clerks who worked hard and unhappily in faraway places', as Arundhati Roy writes in *The God of Small Things*, set in Kerala. I asked Harish why people preferred to build their homes by the road instead of by the beach — the premium location for posh houses in the West.

167

'People don't think anything of the beach, or the sea here. There is more prestige to be by the road,' he said.

Driving back to the resort, we passed a rowdy scrum of men outside a shabby-looking shop. 'What's that?' I asked. 'English liquor store,' said Harish (alcohol shops seem to have an English association in India). Booze! At last. I asked the driver to stop, and joined the scrum around an open counter. Behind, arranged like a church fête tombola display, were rows of Indian-labelled beers, whiskies and gins. Harish tried to conceal his disapproval as I returned to the car laden with chinking plastic bags.

★ ★ ★

That night, I left my family asleep in our hotel room and snuck out quietly. I had a date with the hotel owner's morbidly obese sister. We met in reception, and were shown to a Toyota people carrier in which we drove, in silence, through the Keralan night. This was not some improbable romantic tryst: we were on our way to watch a ceremony which had not been performed in one hundred and fifty years, a ceremony in which a half-naked man, painted orange and wearing a skirt, dances manically with a soon-to-be head-less chicken.

We arrived at around eleven o'clock amid a carnival atmosphere. The streets of Manikothe, the village where the ritual was to be held, were crowded with people and mopeds, all streaming in the same direction down a narrow side street decked with coloured lights and bunting. There were stalls selling popcorn and candyfloss and, a little way off, the sound of high-pitched drumming.

The temple was little more than a walled-off yard with a small concrete hut on one side. People milled excitedly outside. There was a headiness in the air, a tangible sense of the proximity of something thrilling. We took off our shoes and entered the compound. Inside were many more people, mostly men and most of them bare-chested and wearing only sarongs, either orange or white. Some carried drums the size of beer kegs slung from their hips on which they beat a machine-gun rhythm.

As a clearing formed briefly through the throng, I glimpsed the focal point of the gathering: another man, his torso was bare but he was wearing a pleated, multi-layered red ra-ra skirt with silver trim; a circular tray trimmed with tassels reminiscent of chintzy lampshades around his waist; red rings around his biceps; and a butterfly-shaped headdress over half a metre high. Around one of his wrists was wrapped what looked like two white, long-haired cats and he had bells on his feet. In one hand he carried an ornamental shield and large, kinked sword and in the other arm he cradled a live chicken. His face was painted orange and gold with thick black kohl around his eyes. Part Carmen Miranda, part carnival float, he shuffled quickly around the compound as if in a trance leaning forward like a drunk. He emitted a strange, strangulated song like an eerie auctioneer's patter. Occasionally he would bend down to kiss a small, petrified child, or someone would stuff money into his hands and he would stop in front of them and berate them at length — or at least that's how it sounded.

This was the Theyyam who, for the duration of the ritual, was considered to be a living god. 'He is answering their questions about good fortune in the future and giving them a blessing,' an elderly man standing beside me whispered. 'This man is asking him about some businessmen who owe him money. The Theyyam is saying that he is cursing them for him.' The supplicant, wearing a white lungi, stood holding his hands together timidly in front of his chest, his head wobbling appeasingly (there are many interpretations of the classic Indian head-wobble — that it indicates agreement, disagreement, embarrassment, reassurance, confusion, or imminent rage: for what my empirical observation is worth, all I think can be true).

The Theyyam was close by me now and about to pass. It was now or never. I stepped into his path, touching the elderly man who had been explaining things to me.

'Could you ask him something from me?' I said. The elderly man nodded, warily. 'You see there's this commissioning editor . . . ' I told him the man's name. The elderly man translated and I am sure I saw a flicker of uncertainty, a very slight pause, deep inside the man within the Theyyam mask, before he launched into his jabbered curse and moved on to the next pilgrim.

After an hour or so of this, even the living god

himself began to stoop and slow and he was ushered into the temple building for a sit-down (or, I suspect, a dose of some or other 'energy booster'). I was feeling rather exhausted myself, so left the temple compound.

I got chatting with some locals who, in broken English but with great earnestness, explained that the Theyyam was actually just a man from the village — a tradesman, I couldn't figure out what sort — who had been chosen by a committee of town elders to be the divine one for a week of ceremonies.

His role was a cross between a witch doctor, a storyteller and a class warrior, retelling ancient fables of vampires and devils, often targeting higher castes. Of all the religious activity I saw in India, this was without question the strangest: an extraordinary communal suspension of belief, like all religious observance, I suppose, and yet the commitment of the Theyyam and the reverent enthusiasm of the temple elders and the crowd was remarkably affecting. The ritual seemed to serve an important social function as a collective safety valve having, as I understand it, much to do with caste or class struggle, the small man fighting back against a social and economic oppressor, and so on.

It would have been easy to laugh at the carnival-absurdity of it all, the delusion and theatricality, the orange stage paint and the, ultimately, headless chicken, but I actually felt privileged to have witnessed this once-in-a-lifetime ritual, this powerful Keralan magic.

18

The Night Train to Ernakulum

It was starting to get hot, a properly suffocating heat which weighed heavily, particularly at night when the humidity clung like a wet flannel to our faces, cruelly robbing us even of the fleeting relief from the cool side of the pillow. Asger and Emil took frequent cold showers and had given up eating almost entirely. This was not, then, the moment to embark on our first lengthy train journey, but as we climbed aboard the longest train I had ever seen at Kasaragod station, a twelve-hour journey to Cochin on the south coast of Kerala lay ahead of us.

We had booked first-class sleeper tickets. The negligible difference in price between the classes meant it wasn't worth economising, and in terms of cosseting forms of transport 'First-Class Sleeper' is right up there with turning left when you board a 747, or those springy Dunlop moving walkways they have at Heathrow, as far as I am concerned. Sadly, though, Kerala Railways' notion of first class did not quite chime with mine. Our compartment was truly decrepit, lacking both air conditioning and inner doors. Indian Railways is said to be the largest employer on earth with over a million and a half workers; but none of them appeared to have been assigned any cleaning duties. And it turned out not even to be our compartment. Soon after we had distributed our luggage and settled the argument about who would be sitting by the window, a short, spherical couple in their Sunday best appeared at the doorway. They looked at their tickets, then at us, then back at their tickets.

'Sorry to be disturbing you, but these are our seats,' the man said, showing us his tickets. You need some kind of Rosetta Stone to decipher Indian train tickets but, following the intervention of a guard only marginally less clueless than us, it turned out that the man was right. Two of us had berths in the cabin, the other two had been allocated bunk beds out in the corridor.

'Not to worry,' I said. 'It's simple. Would you mind awfully taking the beds in the corridor? We are travelling together as a family, you see.'

'No, no, I am sorry, no,' replied the man. 'We are having difficulty, you see.' He gestured to his and his wife's girth. 'We cannot be climbing, so we have booked these lower beds specifically. Sorry. But you can of course stay here together until it is bedtime.'

And so he and his wife and their luggage squeezed in alongside us and immediately proceeded to assemble their dinner on the sticky blue vinyl seats. Dinner included a plastic bowl of curd rice with pomegranate seeds glinting like rubies, some kind of curried okra, chapattis, and a dal, which filled the cabin with aromas of ginger, garlic, lemons and coconut.

Before he started to eat, the man offered us some of their food. I took some of the rice wrapped in a chapatti, and Lissen tried the okra but the children politely declined.

The train trundled on for some time, mostly at milk-float speed, with garishly coloured mosques, pink and orange villas and patches of red earth breaking the monotony of the passing coconut plantations. Once the important business of eating had been taken care of, the man commenced his inquisition.

'So,' he began, getting straight to business. 'Do you earn good money?'

'I, er, well, okay, I suppose,' I replied.

'So you are travelling in India?' he asked. We explained the purpose of our trip, where we had been and where we were going, to which he listened attentively, interjecting the odd encouraging note, 'Ah, yes. Very good. Very good.'

He talked for a while about his children, one of whom was studying in Abu Dhabi, another working as an engineer in Dubai. He was keen to confirm the rumours he had heard about marriage in the West. 'I hear you are not staying married. At ten years . . . puff!' he cast his hands up in the air. He launched into a story about a Turkish woman of his acquaintance who — and this was the central element of the story — divorced and married another man. 'She just fell in love with this man, Stephen Fry,' he said (I am guessing it wasn't *the* Stephen Fry). 'And married him!' I tutted sympathetically, and Lissen added, almost wistfully it seemed to me, that, yes, divorce did seem to be an easy option for many.

During all this, the man's wife had grown

174

increasingly restless. She obviously wanted to take the floor and finally burst out with: 'But who is looking after your mother and father while you travel?'

'Um, my parents have their own house. They look after themselves pretty well,' said Lissen. The woman frowned, but her husband made a placating gesture, patting his palms down as if to say, 'I'll handle this.'

'Do you mean, you have left your parents alone?' We answered that, where we came from, it was normal for one's parents to live separate lives in this way. They looked aghast. To change the conversation, I asked where they had been.

'We have been to the wedding of the son of the state secretary of Kerala,' the man said, puffing up slightly in his seat.

'Are you and he friends?'

'Yes, well, I am a member of the Communist Party Politburo and he is in the party.'

'Was it a big wedding?' asked Lissen.

'About five thousand people,' replied the man. 'It was a secular marriage. We went really just to show face for about ten minutes.'

For this they had travelled about sixteen hours by train from Trivandrum, some distance further south of our stop, Cochin. Apparently, the reason our seats were spread about the place was because the entire train was full of guests from the wedding that weekend, many of them high-ranking members of the Keralan Communist Party (including the enjoyably named Keralan education minister, M.A. Baby — as in 'Yes, ma'am, that's . . . '), and other such VIPs. I

175

later read in a local paper that, though clearly on quite a scale, the wedding of the son of Keralan state secretary Pinarayi Vijayan to a fashion designer had been tempered 'by an austerity drive. Guests were served just lemon juice and payasam! [a kind of rice pudding]'

We continued to chat for a while until, once more, the wife grew agitated. Her husband looked at her, exasperated, as if to say, 'What now?'

'I've just seen a movie star,' she blurted out. 'Suresh Gopi.' I snuck out into the corridor for a look. The man I saw disappearing down the carriage was indeed the famous Keralan action movie star, whom I recognised from DVD covers and posters. He fitted the classic 1990s Indian movie star mould perfectly: short, fat and mustachioed — more like someone who might come to fix your dishwasher than a film actor, and quite unlike the current crop of muscle-bound stars.

Passing him in the corridor was the biryani man, selling hot piles of steaming, spicy rice. We bought some to share with our new friends and the several cockroaches which seemed to have emerged from the very fabric of the train.

Asger and Emil were unusually keen to get to bed that evening, excited by the prospect of sleeping on the large shelf above our heads. Having grown up watching James Bond movies I was also taken by the glamour of the sleeper carriage, even one as dilapidated as this. After a sobering encounter with the train's lavatory (a hole in the floor through which you could see the

176

tracks passing by below), we started getting the boys ready to sleep. Lissen joined Emil in one bunk, Asger took the other, and I retired to the corridor bunk where I lay, hugging our luggage as if it contained the riches of Croesus and the train was crawling with Persians. I was paranoid about thieves who, as Lonely Planet myth has it, crawl along Indian train corridor floors at night slipping off with bags. That wasn't going to happen on my watch.

I was woken gently some hours later by the guard telling me that Cochin was approaching. Rousing the rest of my family took a little more effort but eventually we found ourselves dumped on Cochin station platform at a little after two in the morning surrounded by a bevy of eager porters.

Lissen had the address of a hotel or guesthouse that a travel agent had arranged for us, and which turned out to be another hour and a half's journey. We were all a little frazzled by the time we arrived in the pitch dark outside a large, modern concrete house in a suburb of Ernakulum, the new part of Cochin, and I am afraid I may have behaved slightly disgracefully.

In my defence, I was preoccupied with getting the kids to bed as quickly as possible so, on finding that there were no beds for them in our room, I may have grown just a little cross with the smiling, elderly man we had obviously roused from his own bed to let us in.

He apologised profusely and hurried away to find camp beds for the children as I fumbled for the air conditioning. There was none. The room was like a sauna, crawling with geckos and buzzing with mosquitoes. By now, whipped up into an unedifying pitch of irritability, looking back, I may have snapped a little at the man when he returned, struggling with the first of the camp beds.

He again smiled apologetically and showed me how to turn on the ceiling fan, which began to rotate lazily, generating the merest whisper of a breeze. I tutted loudly and may have mumbled something along the lines of, 'Call this a hotel, I don't know how they think they can get away with this, I'm going to be calling the travel agent in the morning . . . ' and so on, as the man, on returning with the second bed, again apologised, and wished us a good night.

Lissen was the first to wake the next day, returning hurriedly to the room.

'Michael, you do realise this is a private home, don't you?' she whispered.

It turned out the Pakalomattons, the Syrian Christian family who owned the house and whose patriarch had shown us to our room in the middle of the night, were letting us stay as a favour to the travel agent (who hadn't been able to find any other accommodation within our price range), purely out of the goodness of their hearts.

I reflected on the night before: the metaphorical tossing of my hat and cane as we arrived, the throwing of the queeny tantrum. Clearly, I had a good deal of grovelling to do but, as we gathered for a lavish Keralan breakfast laid on by Mrs Pakalomatton — or 'Mariamma', as mothers are called in Syrian Christian tradition and who, to compound my guilt, we later discovered had recently returned from hospital following serious illness — no reference was made to my behaviour, either overtly or in the demeanour of our hosts, which remained the epitome of graciousness and generosity throughout our stay.

The Pakalomatton family were part of a small community supposedly descended from the Indians converted to Christianity by St Thomas the Apostle after he landed on the Malabar coast in AD 52. This part of India was under Syrian rule at the time, hence the name. According to Mr Pakalomatton, church services were still being conducted in Syrian in Cochin as recently as fifty years ago, and some are still conducted in Latin.

The Pakalomattons were relatively wealthy, owning plantations on which they grew cardamom, bananas and coconuts. Cochin is, of course, famous as a centre for the Indian spice trade and many of its residents — the majority of them Jewish, although that community is now virtually extinct — grew fabulously rich during the Middle Ages selling ginger, cardamom, cumin, turmeric, cloves, nutmeg and, above all, pepper (Salman Rushdie has a great line referring to this in The Moor's Last Sigh, which is partially set among the spice traders of Cochin, calling it, 'Not so much subcontinent as sub-condiment.' Well, I laughed.) Our hosts were quite comfortably off, and had now retired to divide their time between the Church, various charitable deeds and the local country club.

The Pakalomatton family were devout Christians. Their house, built in the seventies with its timewarp rooms lined from floor to ceiling, as well as the ceilings and floors, with dark wood tongue-and-groove panelling, was decorated throughout with icons and religious pictures. The bookcase featured titles such as, *God is a Matchmaker*, *Listen to Mother Teresa* and *From Jesus With Love*. All of the family seemed to spend a good chunk of their time helping people less fortunate than themselves, working with charities and as volunteers at local schools. When I explained over breakfast that we were planning to spend the day exploring old Cochin across the river, Joseph, the elderly father, offered to give us a lift to the ferry in his Suzuki. As we edged out of their driveway into the busy traffic, a shabbily dressed man approached the car. Joseph lowered the window and, without a word being said, handed the man a few notes. 'He has cancer. We support his family,' he shrugged.

The ferry terminal was jammed with people. Out of sheer capricious sadism the man in the ticket booth was refusing to serve the people who had gathered at his window, and so the crowd continued to press tighter, finally abandoning the whole pretence of queuing to press themselves as one against the window.

With three minutes to go before the ferry was due to leave, the clerk interrupted an important project involving rummaging for debris in his left ear and grudgingly began issuing tickets. This prompted a sudden chaotic surge which swept Emil away from us. We caught glimpses of him in the mob and, then somehow above them, crowd-surfing like Iggy Pop. I couldn't help but notice that he was making far better progress through the throng than we were and, as he came within a few feet of the ticket toad behind the glass, I saw this as the perfect excuse to ditch any last semblance of civility and hurled myself through the crowd, yelling, 'That's my son!', grabbing one of his ankles and using the momentum to bring my face up against the glass.

'Four tickets please!' I shouted, elbowing an elderly man on the side of the head. I could feel my lungs becoming compressed as the rest of the queue, seeing my success, pushed even tighter, the ticket clerk laboriously counted out my change, licked his index finger and slipped four small, three-rupee tickets from his stack. Meanwhile, Emil was forced safely up on to my shoulders, like a cork from a bottle.

In Fort Cochin we took photos of the famous Chinese fishing nets — large, cantilevered frames which tip up and down into the water and seem to exist solely for tourists to photograph. The locals claim they first arrived here via the court of Kublai Khan. The area was teeming with tourists, mostly late-middle-aged French couples dressed in flowing white cotton, the men carrying those camp little man-bags French men favour, the women effortfully dressed down, but still as rigidly coiffed as Madame Chirac.

We peered over the wall into the Dutch cemetery. I understood why it was there but, still, how thoroughly extraordinary to find such a thing on the coast of India. We walked over to St

Francis' church, built by the Portuguese in 1503 and the oldest church in India (Vasco da Gama was once buried here). Inside, we came upon a timeless tableau: a priest, sitting behind a grand desk to the rear of the church, counting out great wads of notes handed to him by two furtive men in suits.

The heat was pressing in, so we caught the bus back to the Pakalomatton house. Nearby, we passed another church, a more modest, local one and I had a strange, momentary pang, an unsettling mix of homesickness and nostalgia. An unaccountable compulsion was welling, some vestigial need to go back, just one more time, just to make absolutely sure that all that Catholicism business was as irrelevant and absurd as I remembered it to be from my childhood. After Mariamma had fed us with a delicious lamb curry back at their house, I stood up and announced — much to her and Joseph's approval — that, as this was a Sunday evening, I was going to church. Lissen's mouth dropped open but before she had recovered the faculty of speech I was out of the door and heading through the muggy evening along the unlit street to the church, gripped by . . . well what on earth was this? Spiritual homesickness? Some kind of breakdown?

I heard the Bontempi organ music carrying on the muggy breeze before I saw the church. When I got there it was packed, with fifty or so people seated outside watching the service on two TV screens augmented by a large PA system. I slipped into the last outdoor pew beside a freshly scrubbed family. Inside the church there were, oddly, no pews; the congregation sat on the floor beneath tinsel-decked walls and ceiling fans on full speed.

I was surprised by how much of the mass I remembered. I could mumble my way through most of the prayers and responses, while the ghost of muscle memory helped me keep up with the peculiar hand jives just before the Gospels and when to kneel, stand, sit, and so on. I listened to the priest ranting in a strange, robotic voice about the unspeakable misfortunes likely to befall his congregation soon unless they mended their ways. As with his peer, whom we had seen counting money earlier in the day, this priest had a robustly pragmatic, Geckovian relationship to wealth: 'Richness is always good, wealth is always good,' he preached. 'It does not say [in the Bible] 'Fight against rich', it says 'Do not take from the rich by force'.' This, it turned out, was the preamble to a lengthy admonishment to the congregation that they weren't contributing enough during the offertory.

I once tried to explain the concept of the offertory — handing over money to a priest halfway through the service — to Lissen who, as a Dane, was brought up a Lutheran. In Scandinavian countries they automatically deduct money from your income tax to pay for the Church, so there is no need for such naked commerce during the service itself. To this day she thinks my parish priest must have been some kind of felon. I thought it best not to mention that he tended to spend it on Rothmans and Johnnie Walker

The mass and all the memories it evoked — of the hundreds of hours of grinding tedium spent in church; of the pure evil (and I use that word advisedly) of the sadistic nun, Sister Stanislaus, who taught me as a six-year-old, her range of contemporary pedagogical techniques pretty much limited to beating young children with a wooden ruler; my indignant teen anger at the Church's stance on contraception; the grotesque wealth of the Vatican, and its attitudes to homosexuality and women priests — finally and for ever cured me of any lingering attachment I might have been momentarily deluded enough to have believed I had to the Catholic Church.

I walked slowly back to the Pakalomattons' house that evening feeling that the last spiritual tie to my childhood had finally been severed, and that I was more adrift than ever.

Mr Pakalomatton was the only one still up when I got back.

'Did you have a nice time?' he asked me as I came into the living room, where he sat reading.

Just lie, Michael. Don't upset the man.

'Well, to be honest, I stopped being a Catholic about twenty-five years ago and that mass reminded me why.'

'Oh, I see . . . '

'It's just that, it seems to me, we really ought to have grown out of religion by now, don't you think? I mean, as a species. We've been through the Age of Enlightenment, we are all supposedly rational now. Why do we need all the super-stition?'

'But, you know, Michael, you come from a

184

rational point of view so you think the mass is about superstition. You can call it superstition if you like, but I expect you and I are still asking the same questions: 'What am I here for, what is my aim, how should I live?' — is that not so? My religion helps me on an emotional level to try to understand these things.'

'But why not let us all be rational? Why do we need to gussy our questions about existence or our belief in a greater power in all that ritual flimflam?'

'Because there is still room for the emotional. And that, if I may say so, is where you are falling down.'

19

Club 18-80

Our taxi deposited us beside a broad, forest-lined canal where Devassia the Boatman was waiting to punt us across to the other side. Asger and Emil sat beneath pink parasols to shield them from the noon sun, trailing hands in the water as unperturbed by their surroundings as if they were in a boat on the Serpentine. The sharp-sided punt barged through the thick tangle of water hyacinths, describing a struggling arc as the current did its best to nudge us off course.

Our destination for the next few days lay just across the water, on Pathenkayal Island. The Philipkutty Farm homestay was five small cottages with solid teak pillars and narrow, carved wooden doors, ranged around sandy courtyards and centred on the main reception building. This modern villa doubled as the family home of the owners, the Philips, another Syrian Christian family, who farm the surrounding 35-acre plantation on land reclaimed from rice paddies back in the fifties.

Head of the family was Anu, who greeted us as we climbed up out of the boat. She showed us to the front room of the house where we filled in forms while sitting on big squashy, vinyl sofas, sipping lime juice.

Anu's husband, Vinod, died five years ago of a

heart attack, and since then she has run the farm and guesthouse together with her mother-in-law, Aniamma Philip (whose father reclaimed the land on which the island is built). Also a widow, Aniamma is addressed by family and guests alike as 'Mummy'. Together they share the house with Anu and Vinod's two children, a boy, Philip, twelve, her seven-year-old daughter, Anya, and Peanut, the vomiting dachshund.

The island is surrounded by a raised footpath but the plantations lie below water level and flood frequently. A pump runs constantly, yet that can't always cope with the worst of the monsoon and last year they lost several of their nutmeg trees. Anu explained all this as she showed us around, pointing out cardamom plants, cocoa bean trees, tapioca, vanilla, love apples, bananas, mangosteen, hibiscus, cinnamon, breadfruit, passion fruit, fig and mangoes. Their main crop, though, is coconuts; they harvest the nuts, of course, and tap the sap, known as toddy, which ferments rapidly into a potent liquor and is the preferred drink of the dissolute in these parts. Anu called over a farm worker to show us how they did this. He shuffled quickly up the trunk of the nearest palm, a sharp knife and a small cup tied to his belt. Balancing on the branches at the very top of the tree, he bent forward and cut a small groove in the flower to release its sap. After he had filled the cup, he tied a tourniquet around the flower with a strip of palm, and shimmied back down. Anu passed the cup for me to try. I took a sip. The toddy was amazingly sweet, drinkable, but very yeasty.

187

Back at the cottages, Asger and Emil got to know Anu's son, Philip, having temporarily traded their Nintendo for his fishing rod. Mummy was about to start one of her regular cooking classes. I asked if I could join in, and sat beside an elderly Home Counties couple who had also arrived that morning. Mummy quickly rustled up three or four dishes in a fragrant blaze of fenugreek, mustard seeds, garlic, chilli, curry leaves and onion, using a pressure cooker — a very common piece of equipment in Indian kitchens — for one of the dishes. She showed us how to open a coconut without losing any of its juice by tapping around its upper perimeter with the blunt side of a meat cleaver, as you would tap around the top of a hard-boiled egg with a butter knife to remove its shell, then used the sharp side of the cleaver to lever the top off. I noted the way she tasted food from the ball of her hand with one swift, elegant stroke straight from pot to spoon to hand to mouth without it ever touching her fingertips. Masterful.

The plan was that we would enjoy all of this food together with our fellow guests that night. When I heard that at Philipkutty guests dined communally around a Lazy Susan I groaned inwardly.

'If I'd wanted to go on holiday with a bunch of complete strangers I'd have gone on a Club 18–30 package,' I hissed to Lissen as we got ready for dinner in our cottage. 'Well, first of all, you'd need a time machine then, wouldn't you?' she replied waspishly.

In fact, as we approached the dining area, it

became immediately apparent that we were far closer to 18–30 status than our fellow guests, not one of whom was a day under sixty; for several, sixty was a distant memory.

This was both good and bad. On the one hand, the more time I spend with the elderly, the more discomfortingly apparent it becomes that I am creeping closer to pensionable status myself. Observing the decaying process close up, knowing that, once upon a time, these wrinkled, stooped humans with their cataracts and walking sticks could put on their own socks, climb stairs two at a time and sleep through the night without having to visit the lavatory eight times, was unsettling for me, like being last in the dentist's waiting room and hearing the screams from the surgery of the patients who have gone before you.

On the other hand, more often than not, I found myself empathising with their talk of creaking joints and failing eyesight. Recently, when in their company, I have not only begun to make mental notes of the treatments and medicines they recommend but, most worrying of all, I have found myself positively envying their lifestyle.

Retirement does sound lovely. Your time is your own. Your children are old enough to have spent some time in therapy and have maybe come round to liking you again (and research shows that parents actually get happier once their children leave home). Doctors take you more seriously. You can read and watch daytime television without feeling guilty; perhaps do a little light pruning; then have the afternoons free for napping and sundowners. Plus, the older you get, the more toxic habits like drinking and smoking are tolerated as the last, pleasure-seeking gasp of the grave-bound.

Clearly, it was not right for a thirty-nine-year-old to be thinking like this. It was Lissen who had noticed how I had begun to prefer the company of her parents and their friends to that of my own friends. She accused me of having a 'biddy fetish', and, slowly, we had been working together to wean me off the company of wrinklies until I was back to a normal level. But, here, I was facing an overdose. Lissen was concerned.

'Michael, you won't go on about suppositories, will you?'

I promised not to.

'Or colostomy bags . . . '

I made a face.

'I mean it. Not everyone over seventy has one, you know, and some people don't like to talk about that stuff while they're eating. And if you ask any of them if they take Viagra, I *will* leave.'

We sat down to dinner amid ongoing cross-table introductions. There was a gay couple, Dan, sixty-one, and Kenneth, sixty-four, from the east coast of America; two Cambridge dons in their late sixties; a couple in their late seventies from Dorset; a gastro-enterologist and his wife from Sussex, mere striplings at sixty-two and sixty respectively; a Jewish couple from New York, he a retired corporate lawyer turned high school teacher, she a voluntary worker, both of them, I'd guess, well past eighty; and a textbook retired Home Counties colonel in his early seventies, replete with ruddy complexion and *Daily Telegraph* sensibilities, travelling together with his retired 'lady friend'.

It was, then, effectively, the cast of *Midsomer Murders* but, you know what? I don't think I have enjoyed such stimulating company for years. I could have spent hours talking to each of these fascinating, eccentric, curious and intrepid people. And not once did anyone feel the need to discuss medical histories or funeral plans.

The Dorsetshire couple had arrived that morning and looked precisely as if they had teleported directly from their village pub. They were in no way prepared for the realities of twenty-first-century India and had been the victims of a bag theft at Mumbai station the day before; she lost her credit cards and passport and they had spent twelve hours arranging a replacement.

'We met in Mumbai in 1962,' the husband told me, almost personally affronted by the changes to the city since then. 'I couldn't recognise the place.' Nevertheless, they seemed unperturbed by the theft and were looking forward to the rest of their trip. 'To be honest, if I were poor and living in Mumbai, I'd probably try to steal someone's bag, I can't blame them,' said the woman.

For all his knee-jerk opinions on immigration, corporal punishment, the smoking ban and the 'nanny' state, the bright pink *Telegraph* colonel turned out to be riotous company, regaling us

191

with hair-raising stories of tours of duty in Northern Ireland and the Falklands. 'I was also in Hong Kong,' he continued, a faraway look in his eye. 'Protecting it from the Chinese hordes. Wouldn't go back now, of course. I know what they've done to it.' His lady friend, though obviously very fond of the old goat, had evidently learned to switch off during his more extreme soliloquys, and quietly suggested that I do the same. 'I love him deeply,' she told me with a chuckle. 'But sometimes I wonder if he really believes half the things he says.'

With the gastroenterologist I talked about one of my pet subjects: stomach upsets and how to avoid them. He seemed blasé about the risk of infection. I assumed that he, like me, would have insisted on covering the taps with old socks and brushing his teeth with bottled water, and made a point of nudging Lissen just as I asked him about this so that she could hear his answer. He looked at me oddly.

'Good grief, no!' he chortled. 'That's taking things a tad far, don't you think? Actually, I got sick on the very first day in India! Soon got over it.'

With the New Yorkers I talked films and yoga; his passion was the former (he had loved *Inglourious Basterds*), hers the latter. They had also been in Mumbai and had visited the Jewish centre which had been attacked by the terrorists in 2008. 'Do you know,' the woman said, still shaken by the visit. 'The terrorists had actually been for dinner at the centre four days earlier. They'd come, they said, to learn more about

Judaism. They'd eaten dinner with the children there. But they had only been scoping the joint. They came back and massacred them all.'

I chatted for the longest time with the Cambridge professors. She was currently involved with a major project translating pre-seventeenth-century travel literature, while her American husband was writing a history of the Arabian Sea prior to Vasco da Gama. He told fascinating tales of marine archaeologists finding ships filled with silver bullion, each block individually wrapped and stamped with the owner's name, along with porcelain, all from China. 'Lots of it is being sold on the internet,' he said. 'There's a big market for this stuff in China. There are so many legends from that time which are turning out to be true — all the stuff about the Chinese trade with the Middle East and the sea routes around India.' I asked him what had sparked his interest in archaeology as a child. 'I grew up in Yemen,' he replied. 'I can remember finding Roman coins in the sand, just lying there, where two thousand years ago there had been coast and shipwrecks. Before da Gama, Aden was like the Venice of the Arabian Sea, trading with pretty much the rest of the known world.'

Towards the end of the evening I asked the assembled group about their thoughts on ageing and death. How, I wondered out loud — prompting a sharp kick under the table — were they facing up to their imminent demise?

There was a brief pause. 'Well, I've had a heart bypass, two replacement hips, I take about ten different pills morning and night, and almost everything hurts,' said one of the Americans. 'But when I start to feel sorry for myself, I think about all of my friends who are no longer here, and think, well, it's better to be where I am than where they are!'

20

Lissen Springs a Bit of a Surprise

In our beds that night, once the distant chanting from the Hindu temples and the hymns from the Christian churches across the water finally drifted away on the evening air, it became all too apparent that we were surrounded by a well-populated forest. I'm not a forest person. Back in Ranthambore our tiger-hunting guides had taught us how to identify the location of predators by the worried shrieks of birds. The worried shrieks from the mynahs and other birdlife here pretty much lasted all the night, as did the more troubling, non-bird shrieks. Then there was the gentle patter of regurgitated wood which rained down upon us from the rafters as a thousand tiny woodworms chomped themselves full, and, in the early hours of daylight, every once in a while there would come the unmistakeable sound of distant retching from Peanut the dog, chucking up his breakfast.

When the next morning Asger excitedly reported having seen a sea snake, I was close to calling for a taxi to the nearest Holiday Inn (which, thinking about it, was probably in Mumbai). Lissen gently dissuaded me — I think she said something like, 'Oh for fuck's sake, stop being such a pussy for once, will you?'

Instead, we compromised, and agreed to rent

a houseboat for a night. From the terrace outside our room we'd watched several of these jackfruit-wood boats with their coconut fibre roofs putter past over the previous couple of days. I'd photographed the first one, amid great excitement. We'd waved to the next couple or so. After the twentieth passed by, we realised that they were as common as Ford Fiestas.

Our very own two-storey *kettuvallam* was waiting for us, tied to the coconut trees outside our cottage the next morning. It was a shabby old thing, but it had two bedrooms, each with a bathroom, a small kitchen out back and a lovely deck upstairs where we lazed, eating fried bananas, drinking beer and watching the scenery pass by.

It didn't take long, though, for disenchantment to settle in: at the noise and pollution of the engine; at the number of other tourist boats, of which there seemed hundreds; even at the over-sweetness of the bananas.

'You know your problem, don't you?' Lissen said, putting down her book for the tenth time to look at a passing boat I was pointing at.

'Surfeit of talent, wit, intelligence, sex appeal?'

'Boat envy.'

It is true. For the last hour or so I had been complaining that every other boat which passed us was either larger, more luxurious, faster, cosier or in better condition than ours.

'Can't you just enjoy that you are here, with us, on *this* boat?'

I promised to try. We chugged slowly onward, down broad canals through flat, neon-green

196

countryside with only the odd pastel stucco church, seemingly in the middle of nowhere, to break the view.

Occasionally men would row up to us in coracles offering produce. One had some gorgeous blue lobsters. The cook asked if I wanted to buy some to augment the dinner he was preparing. Looking back, I suspect this was a prearranged meet, which is fair enough. I picked a few, and after possibly the worst bargaining encounter of my life, paid 2,200 rupees for them (about £30 — a very great sum of money for food in India). The cook then did his utmost to overcook and over-spice them, which made me even more annoyed.

As the sun set, the captain moored beside a small, scrappy village. He and his crew stripped to their underwear, rolled out some mats in the kitchen, and went to sleep. I retired to the upper deck to finish off the beers until I was chased off by several colossal crows which descended on the fried bananas we'd left behind.

At night, I was woken by something crawling up my leg. I turned on my bedside lamp to see a hundred little shadows scurrying for cover, and spent the rest of the night alternating between lying rigid with fear and doing sudden, spastic, horizontal star jumps.

The morning brought a welcome cool wind up on deck. I picked up the boat's binoculars for a spot of birdwatching. I saw several birds. Some were white, some black. Many had unfeasibly long necks, others, I'd hazard, judging by their proximity to the water, were water birds, although I should add that I'm not an experienced ornithologist.

Then Lissen joined me on the upper deck.

'Michael,' she said. 'So the plan was to head through the Western Ghats and across Tamil Nadu to Madurai, then on to the east coast, right?'

I nodded. That was the plan.

'Well, I wasn't going to tell you about this until tomorrow, but it might be good now, seeing as you are captive.' She stood in front of me, looking me firmly in the eyes. 'We aren't going to the east coast. We aren't going to Pondicherry or Madras.'

'Yes we are, that's the plan.'

'No we're not.'

'Yes, that's the plan.'

'No it isn't.'

From the look on her face, I knew this wasn't just a misunderstanding about the itinerary.

'You remember Dorthe and the yoga teacher?'

I nodded, warily. We had a Danish friend, Dorthe, who in recent years had visited India, initially to practise yoga, then to train as a yoga instructor. I liked Dorthe. She was the most centred, relaxed, self-possessed person I knew. Dorthe brought calm to a room merely by entering it.

'You remember her teacher, in Mysore?'

Another wary nod.

'I've arranged for us to study with him for a month. You are going to do an intensive yoga course. It's a new type of yoga, a little more hardcore than the kind we tried the other week, less spiritual, more physical. Michael, I'm very worried about you. Your health. Worried about your drinking.'

I laughed out loud. 'You are joking, right? Don't be ridiculous. I'm perfectly healthy. Maybe I could lose a kilo or two but, otherwise, I'm fine. If you think I'm going to make a fool of myself doing yoga a second time . . . '

'We've been having this conversation for years. You have a drink problem. Everyone you know would back me up on this. You drink far too much, and it's getting worse. Christ, you even drank a whole glass of that undrinkable coconut toddy Anu gave us yesterday. You're still out of breath after climbing the six steps to get up here. You've told me yourself that you can't focus on anything. I know you're fed up with feeling old, you're fatter than you should be too. I think yoga could help. I've been arranging our schedule since we left Mumbai, while you've been out or sleeping.'

'But what about my food book? I have to go to Pondicherry because there's going to be a chapter on Franco-Indian cuisine. And the Madras spice blenders, I have to see them . . . '

'Well, maybe you can continue on there alone after Mysore. Michael, this isn't a discussion. And I don't like ultimatums, but . . . ' She looked at the beer bottle in my hand.

Rarely a week passed back home when we didn't row about the amount I drank, usually when I went to open a second bottle, or had drunk alcohol on several successive evenings. Just before we left for India there had been much discussion in the media concerning middle-class alcoholism. In one piece, probably in the *Daily Mail*, Lissen had come across the ten questions which they say determine if you are an alcoholic, printed them out, and left them on my keyboard one morning:

1. Do you lose time from work due to drinking?
2. Is drinking making your home life unhappy?
3. Is drinking affecting your reputation?
4. Have you ever felt remorse after drinking?
5. Do you crave a drink at a definite time daily?
6. Do you want a drink the next morning?
7. Do you drink alone?
8. Have you ever had a complete loss of memory as a result of drinking?
9. Is drinking jeopardizing your job or your business?
10. Have you ever been to a hospital or institution on account of drinking?

Apparently, if you answer 'yes' to three or more of these questions, you are one. Without going into specifics (okay, six, maybe seven), I could.

More importantly, I could also answer yes to my own, personal telltales that one has a drinking problem:

1. Do you check the alcoholic percentage of wine when buying it?
2. When drinking socially in a private home,

are you acutely aware of who has drunk what, and how much alcohol is left in the house?
3. Have you ever danced to Boney M while wearing your wife's grandmother's wedding dress?

Part of the problem in admitting I was an all-out alcoholic lay in the fact that, as I was prone to saying when accused of this, 'I don't pour vodka on my cornflakes in the morning.' I was not classic Alcoholics Anonymous material. I had no glorious, gutter-licking war stories of drunken hijinks, car crashes, broken limbs or fights (good grief, I'd run a mile from the merest hint of fisticuffs). There wasn't even much history of staggering. There were a few Ray Milland-style Lost Weekends perhaps, and a couple of *Leaving Las Vegas* binges, but doesn't everyone have one or two of those in their closet?

I was a classic — far less cinegenic — middle-class 'risky drinker', as were several of my friends. When discussing our alcohol intake, we would usually allay our guilt by citing the health benefits of red wine, reminding each other to have at least one dry day a week, cloaking our consumption in the respectability of wine appreciation, the overblown hyperbole of the oenophile: you're 'tasting' the stuff, not drinking it, you see. Besides, I was too frightened, too controlled to step over the line into complete, tramp-style dereliction. I would never have allowed myself to become a daytime drinker, at least not on a workday. But I would think about drinking on and off throughout the day. In the morning, if I knew I would be drinking that evening, it would be a source of pleasurable anticipation. I would look forward to the first glass I would pour — is any sound as laden with promise as the squeal-pop of a cork being pulled? — when I started to make dinner at around 6 p.m., in the same way, I expect, any addict looks forward to those first moments of brief serenity granted by their substance of choice. And then I'd look forward to the second glass after the kids had gone to bed.

Perhaps if I had been able to leave it there, I might reasonably have argued that there was no great problem, but I couldn't. I was pathologically incapable of not finishing an opened bottle of wine. This was a source of constant friction between Lissen and I, she being perfectly able to drink just a glass or two and enjoy the rest of her evening without ending up falling asleep dribbling on the sofa during *Newsnight*; whereas I was compelled to drink myself into oblivion the very minute an opportunity presented itself. Mindful that she was dealing with a husband on a slippery slope, Lissen long ago vetoed spirits in the house, otherwise there would probably have been many days on which dinner would never have been served at all. But she was also mindful that it wasn't her job to police my drinking and so I continued under some measure of control, but still to excess. And the truth was, since we'd moved to the country, I was drinking more and more. Too much.

I did say I that I had no dramatic drinking

stories to tell, but that doesn't mean I didn't have plenty of shameful, alcohol-related memories: of lying about how much I drank; of being incapable of passing through an airport without visiting a bar; of sitting for hours in bathrooms waiting for the effects of alcohol poisoning to pass; of driving drunk along country roads which I told myself would be deserted at that time of night. But again I returned to an often-employed defence: 'I'm not an alcoholic. I'm a drinker, like my father and my grandfather before me, and it didn't seem to do them any harm.' My dad drank every single night that I knew him. He would start with a gin and tonic, move on to a couple of pints, and perhaps finish with a whisky and tonic, filled up to the brim. And his father, too, was a boozer. According to family lore, he once went to the pub in the midst of having a stroke. Now, that's dedication to the grain and the grape.

But Lissen had heard it all before, I was out of fresh excuses, and had no real defence left. On that ruddy boat, while puttering slowly along the Indian Norfolk Broads, I ran the gamut of Dr Elisabeth Kübler-Ross' four initial stages of grief: denial, anger, bargaining and depression, but as we returned to terra firma, I had come around to the fifth and final stage: acceptance.

I agreed I needed to change. I agreed to go through with Lissen's one-month intensive yoga plan. I agreed not to touch alcohol for the entire month. If I did, Lissen made it quite clear, she and the children would go home — the unspoken threat being that I would not necessarily be encouraged to join them. And I agreed, above all, to take the whole endeavour seriously.

21

The Triple-Breasted, Fish-Eyed Goddess of Madurai

I like to think that I live my life like a chess grandmaster, always thinking several steps ahead, obsessing over future events and how I can minimise the negative impact they might have on my life (for, assuredly, events never have a positive effect). This is not an easy personality trait for others to accommodate. In fact, I have been told it can be frustrating/stifling/aggravating/suffocating for those around me and, now I think about it, many great chess players end up living alone in the woods with straggly beards, posting paranoid frothings on right-wing noticeboards with a rifle rigged up to the front door, sometimes forgetting to wipe their bottoms, don't they?

For someone who likes things planned, to know he is in control, Lissen's bombshell was thoroughly discombobulating. It turned out the catalyst had been the Mumbai incident with Chef Oberoi. It was news to me that Lissen had even been aware of it, but apparently the vomit-stained shirt had been a giveaway. Since then she had been quietly rearranging our schedule online from the various hotel rooms we'd been stationed in, coordinating with the yoga teacher — or 'yogacharya' — in Mysore, and finding us accommodation near his 'shala', as I now learned one called yoga schools. The new plan was that, from the Backwaters, we would drive east, inland, stopping off for a couple of nights en route to Madurai airport, from where we would fly to Mysore.

Back on the boat I argued, of course, then got cross, then whined and pleaded, but could tell from the outset that Lissen was resolute. There would be no gentle snuffling out of Franco-Indian cuisine in Pondicherry — a shame, as it was probably the one place in India I could have got hold of a good white Châteauneuf. Instead, we would apparently veer north to Mysore and stay there for at least five weeks, immersing ourselves in the — to me — utterly alien, possibly barmy and almost certainly patchouli oil-scented world of hardcore yoga.

So it was in a state of some unease that I watched the extravagantly verdant scenery of the Western Ghats, the most scenic part of India we had travelled through so far, pass by as we drove 900 metres up into the delicious cool air, along steep hillsides bulging with tea bushes like great green mushrooms and silver birches planted for their shade. No matter how steep the inclines, the tea pickers, all women, managed to scale them, bent permanently double with baskets on their backs. We stopped at one especially dazzling vista to relieve our scrunched-up limbs. Noticing us, the tea pickers on the other side of the valley slowly stretched themselves upright, and waved silently to us as if from a dream.

We spent the night, together with a selection of local wildlife, in a deserted hotel high up amid a cardamom and pepper plantation. With the owners away and only two, slightly intimidating young men in scruffy jeans and T-shirts left behind to run the place, it had something of an Overlook Hotel (from the movie *The Shining*) atmosphere.

Cardamom is India's 'Queen of spices' to pepper's King, and the green cardamom from the Western Ghats is considered to be the best in the world. They export 90 per cent of all they grow, so it is an important cash crop. We followed the forest path outside the hotel on foot for an hour or so until we came to a small processing plant where a couple of old men were drying peppercorns and cardamom pods in large ovens like tumble driers. In a book I picked up in Delhi, Dr H.K. Bakhru's informative and enjoyably sex-obsessed, *Indian Spices and Condiments as Natural Healers*, the good doctor claims that cardamom can 'increase sexual stamina and virility'. He recommends that, should you need a boost in that area, you boil powdered cardamom in milk with some honey and drink it every night. (Then again, he also claims that chilli, mixed with coconut oil and rubbed on the scalp, can cure baldness which, tragically, it cannot.)

The cool air was very welcome; less so were the ants the size of Brazil nuts, the fat rodents, and the other unseen critters we heard scuffling around in the dark outside our room, including, quite possibly one of the young men warned us, king cobras. It didn't help that we had an open-air bathroom — something of a design flaw if you are in the middle of a jungle inhabited by aggressive, venomous creatures, I couldn't help but think. As soon as I saw that bathroom I knew it meant trouble. During the night, after tossing and turning with a full bladder for some hours, my need to pee finally conquered my fear of what I might find there and I tiptoed across the bedroom and turned on the light. There before me, frozen as if caught doing something they shouldn't, was enough wildlife for an entire Attenborough series — moths the size of microlights; hideous wasp-type things; various rodents; caterpillars; bats; and mosquitoes. These assorted beasties, which also included an astonishing, blood-red snail the size of a loaf of bread but — thank you, Jesus — no king cobras, then went berserk trying to flee the light, and I was engulfed by a blizzard of wings and antennae.

Lissen came to my rescue, alerted by what she later described as 'girlish screaming' from the bathroom, to find me doing another of my frantic insect dances, flinging my arms in the air and thrusting my head from side to side while hopping from one foot to the other. Her only regret, she said later, was that she didn't capture it all on video.

The next day we drove through yet more staggering scenery. Cotton trees lined the way, their dangling pods making them look like weird, Gothic Christmas trees, weirder even than the tamarind trees with their elderly pianist's fingers. There were fields of sugar cane, coconut plantations and grapevines. Goat and buffalo herds slowed our progress at times, and Asger and Emil squealed in excitement at spotting a flying squirrel, a creature they had previously assumed existed only in the realm of cartoons. The temples grew more frequent and more colourful, and the weather hotter and drier, the sun somehow sharper on this side of the mountains. There were very few tourists here: the one group we did see had disembarked from their coach and gathered on a bridge to video a group of women washing themselves in the river below, so that's probably a good thing.

Before making our final jump north to Mysore, we stopped for a couple of nights in Madurai, a dusty, low-rise city, over two and a half thousand years old. Lissen wanted to see the city's Sri Meenakshi Temple, one of the greatest examples of Dravidian architecture in India, considered by some the Taj Mahal of the south.

Asger and Emil were also keen to visit the temple, having found out from our driver that it was home to a tame elephant who administered blessings with its trunk. In fact, we met the elephant while out for a walk in the centre of Madurai, on a street carpeted with onion skins. We asked the elephant's keeper if he did out-of-hours blessings and he made the universal gesture of rubbing his middle finger together with his thumb. I held up a 50-rupee note and felt a large, hairy trunk pluck the note from my hand and then plonk down on my head, soft and heavy like a rolled-up carpet. It was stubbly with hairs, and wet from the piss-coloured puddle he'd just been drinking from, but even though I

209

pointed this out to them, Asger and Emil still jostled to take turns to hand the elephant more notes and brace themselves for the wet trunk slap.

The temple was mesmerising. We entered through one of its mammoth ziggurat gates — or gopurams — decorated with a cast of plaster gods, goddesses and mystical creatures, including the triple-breasted, fish-eyed goddess to whom it is dedicated. We visited in the evening, leaving our shoes outside and crossing a courtyard whose stones were still warm from the day's sun. Inside, the temple was smoky and dark and packed with pilgrims. All around were niches filled with small statues stained with ghee. The air was soapy with jasmine and sandalwood.

Gandhi, who took his decision only to wear khadi (homespun cotton cloth) while living in Madurai, once wrote, 'To seek God, one need not go on a pilgrimage or light lamps fed with ghee and burn incense before the image of a deity. For he resides in our hearts.' It seems nobody has told the Madurai pilgrims this, for they still burn ghee as if they have an Indian Ocean of the stuff, although quite how they make butter flammable, I still don't know.

We said hello once more to the elephant, who was busy with his trunk slapping schtick and other pilgrims (and showed no indication that he recognised us, we were all a little disappointed to note), and sat for a while beside the temple's sacred pond where, apparently, writers are supposed to place their new works. The idea is that if a book is any good it will float, and if it's

210

not it will sink — I couldn't help thinking this would be less painful than having the fucking *New Statesman* review it.

Following the tolling of a bell, we assembled with the crowd in the Shiva temple to watch the nightly puja in which, amid great ceremony and solemnity, the effigy of Lord Shiva is carried to the bedchamber of Meenakshi, one of his wives, to whom, legend has it, he was married in Madurai. The air was thick with smoke and noise from clanking finger cymbals, trumpets, the haunting squeak of woodwind nageshwarams and frantic, mad drumming. Emil clung to my legs and watched as Shiva's silver-plated palanquin was carried through the temple to its nightly resting place. People pressed in on all sides to get a glimpse of the god and to touch the various statues around us, performing small, automatic gestures of absolution upon themselves.

When it was all over, we sidestepped the crowds, leaving the Thousand Pillared Hall ('985 actually,' says my Lonely Planet book with its customary, joyless pedantry), and escaped down a dark, empty corridor which eventually led us back to the twenty-first century.

22

Glutton for Punishment

The human body is thought to lose around two litres of water in the form of sweat during the course of a normal twenty-four-hour period. I, rather carelessly, appear to have lost all mine in one go.

Ten minutes into my first session of Prana Vashya yoga, I lie on my spongy green mat surrounded by a salty puddle of my own emission. The doors and windows of the room on the first floor of the shala are all closed — despite the 30-degree heat outside (at just after seven in the morning), and the fearful fumes from the changing-room toilet just behind me. I appear to be melting like a Cornish Mivvi dropped by a careless toddler on a seafront board-walk on a hot August afternoon. Around me, eight horribly fit, whippet-thin yoga warriors, with alarming muscular topography and limbs like magician's balloons, are moving at a fluid, measured pace according to the relentless com-mands of our instructor, my new yoga guru, Vinay. My face cascades with sweat, a pastiche of the real tears of pain I feel like weeping.

I have vicious pins and needles in my lower legs and feet; alarming chest pains; and my penis has shrivelled like a petrified Shar Pei. Before being told by Vinay to lie down on my front and rest, as I am now doing, I have twice been forced to stop due to sheer physical disarray and simply stand there, heaving like a triathlete at the finish line (a Cornish Mivvi, a Shar Pei *and* a triathlete). For, as well as the positions — or 'asanas' as they are known in yoga — one of the unique features of Prana Vashya yoga, the extreme, 'boot camp' form of yoga Lissen has so thoughtfully enrolled me on, is that it requires participants to maintain a constant rhythm of deep breaths throughout the entire two-hour session. This I am supposed to do even while holding the asanas, some of which resemble endgame Twister positions; others of which look like the positions victims of the Spanish Inquisition's more outré torture devices would be left in, once removed, weeping, from said devices; while yet others are ludicrous, freeze-frame disco moves. I must maintain this slow, deep-breathing rhythm even as we move from one position, sorry, *asana*, to another. And we must breathe only through our noses: mouths must remain shut, according to traditional yoga teaching. As a result, every single muscle in my body aches with a tremendous yearning for bed, rest, or death. My pain is beyond naming.

That was the first ten minutes.

Vinay, who created Prana Vashya yoga and is the owner of the shala, is pacing the room. In his kindly, croaky voice, not a little reminiscent of Yoda's, he is gently coaxing an extra stretch here, encouraging slower, more regular breathing there, while I, more thoroughly humiliated than I have ever been in my life, lie face down on the

213

mat, gasping like a beached haddock, afraid to move for the pain that would assuredly result, and sweating like a piece of Cheddar wrapped in plastic left in a car boot on a summer's day. Above, the ceiling fans mock me with their insolent inertia.

After I have spent ten more minutes lying face down, recovering, Vinay gently taps me on the shoulder and indicates that I should start again. I try to get back into the rhythm, breathing deeply and pushing out the air so that every molecule of oxygen is squeezed from my lungs by my stomach, as we have been instructed to do. At one point, I am poised for five breaths with both my palms flat on the floor, my backside in the air and my legs straight, standing on my toes, like a caterpillar in mid-inch. Vinay stands silently behind me and, before I realise it, he places his toes underneath my raised heels, trying to encourage me to stretch them so that they touch the mat. It is an extraordinarily intimate gesture — to have another man's bare feet beneath mine definitely crosses some border or other — and it catches me quite unawares.

But I struggle on, rasping for breath, sweat pouring into my eyes, wishing I was anywhere but here in this fetid, steaming room full of strangers with their bodies like carved clothes pegs. I can feel them all sizing me up out of the corners of their eyes, judging me for the physical and therefore, in their eyes, spiritual wreck of a man I undoubtedly am.

How did I let myself end up here? Heaven knows I'd had a clear enough omen earlier that

214

morning before I'd even left the apartment. The night before I had put my swimming shorts — which, in the absence of anything more appropriate, would now be doubling as my yoga shorts — out on the windowsill to dry after hand washing a couple of weeks' dust from them in the toilet bucket (from which you will gather that the third-floor apartment we had rented was none too ritzy). When I came to look for the shorts at six o'clock the next morning prior to this first class, they were nowhere to be seen, having been carried off by the breeze in the night. I leaned out of the window and spotted them on a balcony roof, one floor below. Which is how the first day of the rest of my life very nearly began as my last.

I tried to reach the shorts with a broom, stretching out of the window as far as I dared, but I couldn't quite hook them over the end of the handle. For the life of me, I don't know why I didn't just go back to bed and forget the whole silly business altogether (actually, I do know why I didn't: Lissen was there and, once the shouting had subsided, she would have rendered me unconscious with whatever blunt instrument lay near to hand, removed my testicles with a pair of rusty nail scissors, and sewn them on to my forehead), but still drowsy and propelled by some deep, testicular-related primal fear (Must. Get. Swimming. Trunks.), I climbed out of the window and shuffled cautiously along the ledge before crawling on my belly along a nearby mezzanine roof from which I was just able to finger one of the draw-strings.

In terms of 'God doesn't want you to do this, it'll all end in tears', it was a powerful message, but one which I chose to ignore.

★   ★   ★

Two nights earlier we had arrived in Mysore, or 'Mysuru' as it was recently renamed, following a fraught drive from Bangalore Airport, five hours north. The city had bewitched us that night as we drove through its half-lit centre, still packed with people at ten o'clock. One street seemed to be lined entirely with gold merchants whose open-fronted shops glowed yellow, like a row of Aladdin's caves. Mysore was frenetic and crumbling like all Indian cities, but built on a more human scale than others we'd stayed in, and tidier than most (apparently it was rated India's second cleanest city in 2010). We instinctively felt that it was a welcoming and approachable place and breathed a collective, almost homecoming sigh, which in a sense was apt, as Mysore would be our home for the next month. The travelling had ended. We had been on the road now for two months. It was time to unpack our bags and, instead of gallivanting through the great canvas of India, get to know a small corner of it more intimately.

Lissen had arranged for us to rent a flat just outside the city centre within walking distance of the shala. The five-storey, concrete building was on a broad, busy, freestyle two-three-four-lane road along which flowed a continuous rabble of auto-rickshaws, trucks, men pushing handcarts

216

laden with fruit and vegetables, flea-bitten ponies pulling colourfully painted wooden rickshaws, and families on mopeds.

Inside, it was sparsely furnished with random bric-a-brac. There was no air conditioning, but there were ceiling fans although, as the landlady warned, the electricity was prone to cut out from time to time. Soon we were unpacking, sweeping up the cockroach poo, and trying to get used to the idea that we didn't have a bus, a train or a car to catch for a day-long drive anywhere.

The next morning was spent trying to figure out the basics of life in Mysore — where to buy food, how to get hold of the large barrels of drinking water we would need, how to keep mosquitoes at bay and best steel ourselves for cockroach combat. The last of these was less straightforward than it might have been now that Asger had become vehemently opposed to violence of any kind (other than that which he directed towards his brother, naturally). The seed had been planted during our visit to Gandhi's grave in Delhi where we had explained the concept of non-violent protest, vegetarianism and so on, and this had grown when he had heard about the concept of reincarnation for the first time, and the extremes the Jains went to. 'Don't kill it. It might be a relative!' he would cry whenever I swatted a mosquito. So, the cockroaches would have to be eliminated without any blood (or the cockroach equivalent) being shed.

Our local supermarket, 'Big Bazar — Simbol of Shoping' (sic) — posed more questions than it

217

answered. It looked very grand from the outside, but its fruit and vegetables were literally rotting on the shelves, there was no meat (understandably, I suppose) or fish, and very little dairy. It was all a bit of a mystery. Instead, it sold shiny nylon tracksuits, violently patterned polyester shirts, sweaters with slogans vaguely alluding to prominent educational institutions ('Varsity Oxford', 'Harvard Cool', and so on), and nylon trousers with creases so sharp they could fell an oak. Where did people do their actual shopping?

Lissen had arranged an appointment with our new yoga instructor, Vinay, later that afternoon, to introduce ourselves and, she hoped, put me at ease about the whole affair. His shala was a ten-minute walk from our apartment, through quiet, dusty-red streets of traditional, single-storey houses, across a makeshift cricket ground, and past a small shanty town. The shala itself was on a quiet crossroads, and was painted reddish-pink with a cluster of auto-rickshaws and their dozing drivers permanently camped outside.

Upstairs on the first floor, Vinay Kumar welcomed us all into his office. There was a desk, his chair, and two other wicker chairs for guests. Behind us was a bookcase with a few trophies and photos of Vinay contorted into all manner of improbable poses, including one in which he lay on his chest, his face smiling from between his feet as his legs arched over his head. Vinay was twenty-six years old, slim, short, wearing jeans, a T-shirt and several gold bracelets. He had unblemished, caramel skin, against which his

218

teeth shone toothpaste-ad white. His eyes twinkled, his hair was lustrous and cut into a boyish bowl. He had an almost shocking radiance. I hesitate to use the word 'aura', but he had about him a vibrancy I have never experienced before, a Ready Brek glow of well-being and serenity.

I think we all fell a little in love with Vinay at that first meeting. Asger and Emil, instead of fidget-fighting, for once simply sat and stared, becalmed by this beatific being. As we sat down, I looked over to Lissen, who was similarly entranced. Looking back, even before I'd sat down in his office, I knew that I was in a safe pair of hands: I knew this man had the skills to change my life. The question was more: would I let him?

I told him that I was old, fat and unfit, that much of me had atrophied, calcified or simply ceased to work, and that I had serious doubts I would be able to do any kind of yoga.

'I can't even touch my toes,' I said.

'Don't worry, Michael,' he smiled. 'It will be hard the first week, ten days, you won't be able to follow all the asanas, but then it will get easier.'

Vinay explained that the class met at six-thirty in the morning every day for the two-hour Prana Vashya session. After a small break, there would then be another two hours or so of pranayama. I shot Lissen a look. She hadn't mentioned anything about prayama . . . praynam . . .

'Pajamarama?' said Emil, wrinkling his nose at Asger.

'You wear your pyjamas,' whispered Asger.

Vinay explained about pranayama: they were some kind of meditative breathing exercises, it seemed, which didn't sound too arduous. I asked if there were any special things I should eat, or avoid eating. 'No, no, you will be doing enough exercise to eat what you want. This isn't a diet,' Vinay said. He then gave me a Prana Vashya T-shirt, and an A3-size laminated printout featuring photographs of him demonstrating eighty different asanas, each an unthinkable contortion of limbs — like traffic accident photographs without the blood.

'Oh, wow, can you do all these?' I marvelled, stupidly, it being patently obvious that he could as it was him, right there, in the photographs.

'Yes,' said Vinay. 'We actually do more than eighty in the session. And so will you.'

I snorted. 'I don't think so. Maybe at the end of the month I will be able to do a few, perhaps.'

'No, no,' he said. 'We do them all. Every day. This is the programme. See you tomorrow!'

And with that we were hustled out of the door to Vinay's uncle, to whom we were to pay a fee of 22,000 rupees — around £300 — for one month's instruction, plus a little less again for the back-stretching classes Lissen was to take in the afternoons (she has back problems which conveniently ruled her out of the hardcore morning class).

That night I began to read a book, *Light on Yoga*, which Lissen had given me while we were on the Backwaters boat. It was a classic yoga text by the world famous yogi B.K.S. Iyengar. 'Never

220

practise without having first evacuated the bowels,' was one of Mr Iyengar's early pieces of advice. On the subject of what would happen if you didn't evacuate your bowels, he was ominously silent. He was not much of an eater either: 'If we eat for flavours of the tongue, we overeat and so suffer from digestive disorders which throw our systems out of gear,' he warned. 'The yogi believes in harmony, so he eats for the sake of sustenance only. He does not eat too much, or too little.' Clearly the yogi has never tasted slow-braised, Chinese spare ribs.

I read this bit aloud to Lissen as we sat, batting off mosquitoes on the sagging sofa in the living room. She took the book from me and read aloud a different passage, which appeared to amuse her:

'He that is born with demonic tendencies is deceitful, insolent and conceited. He is full of wrath, cruelty and ignorance. In such people there is neither purity, nor right conduct, nor truth. They gratify their passions. Bewildered by numerous desires, caught in the web of delusion, these addicts of sensual pleasures fall into hell.'

And with a quiet, almost sadistic chuckle, she got ready for bed.

23

Worzel Gummidge Meets Jane Fonda

That first day of yoga training, I had left my family sleeping in the apartment and, carrying my new yoga mat bought the previous day for 300 rupees at Big Bazar, started out with a hopeful heart and a fluttery stomach for the yoga centre. Along with my baggy swimming shorts I wore a cheap, purple 'Varsity University' T-shirt, also from Big Bazar, and stout, thick-soled, leather walking shoes, the only footwear I had: picture a holidaying actuary, or perhaps a recovering mental patient struggling after his recent reintroduction to society.

Outside the shala a small group of students waited. Most of them had special shoulder bags for their mats made out of brightly patterned material. The fact that I was simply carrying my mat, without any bag, just as it was, already exposed me as the kind of naive, fly-by-night chancer who rolls into town, buys a cheap yoga mat at a supermarket and thinks he's a yogi without so much as a warm-up stretch. Damn.

No one spoke, which allowed me to form convenient prejudicial biographies of them based solely on their appearance. Next to me was a Mossad hitman, glowering beneath his mono-brow; there was an older Chinese man who looked like a character from *Kung Fu Panda*, the mystical trainer, perhaps; a lanky Australian girl, who most likely worked for an environmental charity and almost certainly suffered from veganism; and a square-cut Danish man of around my age, who ran tantric sex courses on windswept beaches in Jutland but probably had all the sense of humour of a hedge. Before I had time to move on to the others, Vinay opened the shala door and we filed in silence up the stairs to the changing room.

Already dressed in my Worzel-Gummidge-meets-Jane-Fonda outfit, I hovered in the main room, which was L-shaped with pink walls and an ox-blood-coloured concrete floor, one of its walls lined with shelves bearing more of Vinay's trophies and Hindu statues. There were signs requesting absolute silence and forbidding drinking, and on one wall an inspirational poster:

If you think you are beaten, you are.
If you think you dare not, you won't.
If you'd like to win, but think you can't, it's
    almost a cinch you won't.
If you think you'll lose, you're lost,
For out in the world we find . . . Success
    begins with a fellow's will:
It's all in a state of mind.
Life's battles don't always go to the stronger
    or faster man:
But sooner or later the man who wins,
Is the one who THINKS HE CAN!

Yeah! That's the spirit! I thought. You can do this, Michael!

There was just enough floor space for ten yoga mats, the places demarcated with yellow tape on the floor. Having instantly forgotten the inspirational message I had just read, I headed over to a dark, distant corner, as far as possible from the sightlines of the other students, like an animal who knows death is approaching, and began unrolling my mat. Seeing me, Vinay beckoned me over to the front of the class.

'Please, here,' he said.

Damn. If the lack of a yoga mat bag hadn't given the game away, now everyone was going to see for themselves just how much of a beginner I was. I could see other members of the class performing warm-up stretches, so I did a half-hearted stretch up, and then down, to try and touch my toes.

Hope no one saw that.

The Danish student knelt on the instructor's mat as, apparently, he was going to be leading the class that day, and we all did likewise. Vinay knelt beside him, they closed their eyes and commenced humming 'om', loudly, and for as long as their breath could carry it. The rest of the group followed and I joined in, self-consciously and thankful that no one of my acquaintance would witness any of this.

Aside from some painful pins and needles in my legs as the blood supply was cut off, I rather enjoyed the 'om' vibrations bouncing around my skull and teeth. I suspected I might be quite good at 'om'-ing. Vinay slid me a prayer book, and I tried to follow the, again, pleasing-sounding but to me meaningless Hari-Krishna-style words.

I could have been pledging allegiance to Satan and his acolytes for all I knew.

We started the exercises with what I now know to be the standard Surya Namaskar, or 'Sun Salutation', stretching up, then down, a straight-backed press-up, alternate leg stretches, the forming of an arch, and so on, except that Vinay's version had an added flourish peculiar to Prana Vashya yoga: halfway through you stick alternate legs up in the air while having both palms on the floor, like an oil derrick in mid-lever. We repeated this an endless number of times, moving at the same, slow, regular pace, without pause. The Danish man counted out breathing instructions as we moved — 'Breathe in: one, two, three; breathe out, one, two, three,' and so on, so that our slow, deep breaths matched our movements.

Just how ill-prepared I was for all this became apparent within minutes. The sun salutations I could just about manage, although after the fifth my thoughts had already drifted to a nice lie-down, but they were immediately followed by other asanas: physical contortions apparently plucked from the Chinese Secret Service manual for especially reticent dissidents. Take the Veerbhadrasanas A, B, and C in which, with our legs planted wide apart, one knee bent at a right angle, we had to hold our arms, first, straight out to the side (the 'A') and then stretched up above our heads clasped together in prayer (B), and finally and most horrendously of all, (C), forming a human 'T' balancing on one foot with the other leg lifted forming a right angle, and your arms stretching out in front of you as if you are about to dive into a swimming pool. I had never imagined my own body could inflict on me such suffering; at least not without recourse to props.

After the initial Veerbhadrasana leg wobbles had made me look like a shivering whippet, my stomach muscles were the next bit of me to announce they were boycotting the session. Even the measured, deep, slow breathing was defeating me — my vision went all blotchy through lack of oxygen. This was exacerbated during the Kumbhakas, or 'breath locks', when we had to take a deep breath and then hold it while performing a particular asana. My thighs started to . . . well, 'vibrate' is really the only word for it, and then all the other frankly embarrassing physical symptoms of someone way beyond the merely 'out of shape' stage began to manifest in mutiny against me. Vinay noticed my distress and told me to lie, face down, and recuperate. Which is where we came in.

'One day this will all be over,' I consoled myself as I lay in my sopping wet clothes on my sweat-logged mat while the rest of the class continued around me.

At our first meeting, Vinay had told me not to eat prior to the session and to drink the minimum amount of water, so, as well as feeling exhausted, I was by now parched and famished. I considered ending it right there and then and walking out after just half an hour in my first session. I imagined making a sheepish apology face, gathering my mat — or maybe just leaving it there on the shala floor, I wouldn't be needing it again after all — and tiptoeing out, trying my best not to drip on the others, never to return.

But as I lay there with my eyes closed, resting my chin on my hands, my fingertips wrinkled like cold cocktail sausages, I realised that two paths lay in front of me. One path involved simply getting up and leaving. I would go back to the apartment and face Lissen's wrath. We would go home soon after, I'd imagine, and things would go back to how they were before we left for India. I'd drink more, work less, get fatter, poorer, more miserable, more negative, more frightened. I'd decline, withdraw, give up, resign myself to an easy, safe, downward spiral towards oblivion. Where would that end? The final, irreparable disintegration of whatever professional competences I had left. Irreversible physical decline. Bankruptcy. Illness. Hospital. Most likely, if Lissen's dark hints were anything to go by, separation from everyone I love, eventually followed by an unedifying death in a pool of vomit and piss in a mixed ward, the smell of disinfectant lingering in my nostrils as my soul shrivelled to a rum-soaked raisin.

But what of the other path? Where might that lead? Short-term humiliation and the relinquishment of any remaining shreds of self-respect, for sure, but I didn't know these people, and would never see them again, so, as long as I could erase the shameful memory (and, Lord knows, there were precedents for that), what did that matter? Pain, prolonged physical distress? Yes, plenty. A world of pain the like of which I could never have conceived possible, assuming I didn't rupture something terminal early on. But Vinay seemed to have an eye on me. Surely he wouldn't let me go too far. Perhaps it was his extraordinarily limpid eyes, the white teeth, or the room-brightening, dimpled smile, but deep down — and I don't know whether this was an informed conclusion or sheer desperation — I was convinced his methods could help turn my life around. I stood back up, took a deep breath, pulled my shoulders back, and began to follow the Danish instructor.

A few minutes later, I was lying on my front gasping like a laboratory beagle, but, at least I had given it a go.

As the two-hour session dragged on, my fellow yogis pulled ever more improbable and extraordinary shapes; shapes which I could never imagine myself capable of: a whole alphabet of contortion. Recovering once more on the mat, I had time to inspect the wall of trophies in front of me. I knew from his website that Vinay had been an All-India champion, but there must have been twenty other cups and awards on display, alongside a statue of Ganesh decked with flowers. Less reassuringly, from my prone position I was also privy to several unedifying glimpses of stretching bottoms, and one particularly upsetting flash of the Chinese man's angry-looking scrotum but at last, some years later, the session ended.

After a ten-minute pause, which I spent sucking in fresh air outside on the balcony, the second part of the session began. This was the pranayama.

Time to relax. Surely a bit of meditation and some breathing exercises couldn't be anything like as tough as the asanas?

The rest of the students sat cross-legged on their mats with the backs of their hands resting on their knees and index fingers and thumbs held together in the universal, 'Look at me, I am meditating!' position. I did likewise, even though it felt like a terrible self-betrayal. ('This is not me. I am not the sort of person who sits cross-legged on floors like some moth-eaten hippie.') Vinay then visited each student one by one, crouching down beside them and quietly outlining the breathing exercises they would do for the next two hours. After a short while, he crouched down in front of me.

'You are to close your eyes, and focus on a place here,' he pointed to the middle of his forehead, a spot known as the trikuti. 'This is your third eye.'

He showed me how to breathe — still through my nose only, of course — counting to four, slowly, on the inward breath, then, equally slowly ('One Mississippi, two Mississippi' wasn't quite enough, it was more 'One Mississippi River, two Mississippi River'), counting to six as I breathed out. Maths has never been my strong point, but even I could figure that this didn't quite add up. The idea seemed to be to push 'old' air from your body using your stomach muscles like bellows: a kind of internal self-cleansing. I was to repeat this high-pressure abdomen breathing exercise thirty times in all, then lie down to recover for an equal number of normal breaths

— still through the nose only.

'When you breathe, think of it as breathing from the bottom of your spine,' were Vinay's final whispered words of instruction as he left to talk to another student. Right. Spine. Okay.

The first time I tried the exercise I stirred up all manner of nasal debris. So that's why everyone had been blowing their noses so ostentatiously during the break, I thought as I scurried into the changing room to find some toilet paper. Worse than this, though, was the searing lower back pain caused by sitting cross-legged on the floor, something I hadn't done since Callaghan was Prime Minister. This set in almost immediately and was followed by knee pain, more pins and needles and, eventually, the loss of all feeling in my feet. Turns out, you need to be fit just to sit and breathe. 'Feel the breathing en masse, together, stronger,' said Vinay, but that didn't help. Again, sensing my distress about halfway through the session, he quietly motioned that I should lie down, this time on my back.

Interestingly, while I was lying down staring at the ceiling fans I noticed that my rampaging hunger had subsided. I was no longer desperately thirsty either, as I had been during the asanas, and, even more inexplicably, I wasn't feeling quite as exhausted as before. In fact, I was feeling quite jolly, almost giggly. How to explain this?

Behind me another of the students began making an alarming noise, like someone trying to inflate a sinking lilo afloat on a sea of sharks using a faulty bicycle pump. I looked around the room. Isn't someone going to help them? It seemed this was merely another stage of pranayama.

When I had finished my first round of exercises Vinay crouched down silently beside me and told me to repeat the four-six exercise, this time using my right thumb to hold my right nostril closed and, alternating, using the index finger of the same hand to keep my left nostril closed. Under any other circumstances if someone asked me to do this, I would back away slowly with a palsied smile, but it helped that the rest of the room was engaged in similarly absurd activities — the rapid bicycle pump breaths and, by now, loud, long 'oms'.

The repeated chanting of 'om', or 'aum', is said to be one of the techniques by which devotees can empty their minds and finally reach enlightenment. I had already sensed a competitive edge in the class during the asanas, with students trying to outstretch each other, but the 'oms' had an even more overt competitive edge as the students competed to see who could hold the note the longest, straining to squeeze the very last, quavering, noise from their lungs. Crushingly, it seemed I wasn't allowed to try the 'om'-ing. At the end of the session Vinay told me to lie down again and simply observe the others.

We ended what had been a morning of considerable physical and emotional attrition with another Hindu prayer song, then bowing while on our knees to Vinay, and quietly, contemplatively, gathering our mats and heading off down the stairs of the shala and back out into the bright, sharp Indian sun.

Even though our apartment was only a ten-minute walk away I fell into an auto-rickshaw, shell-shocked. Once home, though physically a ruin and with my dignity left in a puddle of sweat on the shala floor, the overriding feeling was one of . . . randiness. After emptying the barrel of drinking water in the kitchen and showering, the only thing on my mind was to make love to my wife. I was as horny as a whorehouse window cleaner, gripped by a raging and, given my broken physical state, optimistic carnal urge.

You may have been wondering about our sex life. You haven't? Please yourself. But we had actually managed to keep that plate spinning during the trip, albeit intermittently. This is not the easiest thing to do when sharing hotel rooms with your kids: the act had necessarily been limited to hasty bathroom visits, at which we had become quite adept. The children had started to grow suspicious over the amount of time we were spending 'talking about birthday presents', but it had functioned after a fashion, and did so once more on this occasion you will be pleased/repulsed/entirely ambivalent to hear.

A sudden and — to Lissen especially — alarming increase in my sex drive was just one of a number of puzzling questions to reflect on after my first yoga session. How had pranayama alleviated my hunger and thirst? Was a rampant sex drive a permanent side effect of yoga? What was the Chinese man's scrotum so angry about?

Gandhi would not have approved of the sex

urges, that is for sure. Though by all accounts he had quite the roving eye, in his writings he strongly disapproved of non-reproductive sex: 'Marriage is for progeny, and not just for sexual enjoyment . . . The sex urge is a fine and noble thing . . . but it is meant only for the act of creation. Any other use of it is a sin against God and humanity.'

Perhaps you weren't doing it properly, Mr Gandhi.

24

The Whale and the Trumpet

My body considered that first yoga session to
have been a once-in-a-lifetime aberration and
had no plans to let me repeat it now that it knew
what was really involved. When I woke up the
next morning, everything ached. My muscles
had annealed, and felt ready to snap at the
slightest strain. Merely to have survived the session made me feel like a mountain had been
climbed, never to be revisited.

'I'm not happy,' I said to Lissen, elbowing her
awake the next morning at six. She grunted,
fending off consciousness.

'It's all so competitive. There's no joy, no
laughter. It's all so show-offy, about who can put
their foot in the most ludicrous position and
breathe the loudest. I'm not going.'

Silence.

'I mean it. I'm not. I've had it. I just can't.'

Still silence.

I got up and put on my shorts and walking
shoes and left for the shala.

This time, as I waited with the other students,
I decided to strike up a conversation with one of
them rather than just stereotyping them from
a corner. The Danish man was called Lars, it
turned out. He'd only been doing yoga for four
years, he said and was spending some months

travelling around India, mainly visiting yoga shalas in Goa. He hadn't planned to come to Mysore at all.

'I thought it would be too Madonna-ish,' he said, referring to the singer who had supposedly studied at the shala of the late Ashtanga guru, Pattabhi Jois, in nearby Gokulam. 'But my girlfriend persuaded me and I was so impressed with what Vinay does, it's really serious, very, very tough, you know? So now I am training to be an instructor.'

An American woman arrived, tossing her long red hair. She glared at me, and I shuffled along to make room for her to sit on the bench next to me. She turned to Lars, blocking me from the conversation altogether, and started talking to him about some party she'd been to the night before.

The older Chinese man, who was clutching an exotic flower which he'd brought along as an offering to Vinay's statue of Ganesh, was called Ling and turned out to be from New Zealand, camp, and friendly. I asked if he had done any other yoga.

'Oh yes,' he smiled. 'I have practised Ashtanga yoga for more than thirty years. I used to have a yoga school in Auckland, but this is the toughest type of yoga I have ever experienced. Some days it really kills me. I've never experienced anyone as good as Vinay.'

There were other testimonies to Vinay's almost supernatural powers. One girl said that on one occasion, when she had told him she was struggling, he had remembered that it was her time of the month; another recalled how he had predicted she would be ill.

'I just wasn't performing the asanas as well as I usually did,' she said. 'And I couldn't understand why. But it turned out he was absolutely right. He said I was about to have flu and would need to take a day or two off. I felt pretty good, but the next day when I woke up I felt terrible and couldn't come in.'

These testimonies made me feel slightly better; only slightly. I was, though, beginning to feel less happy about my yoga mat. As I looked around the studio at the start of the session I noticed that everyone else had thicker, better quality mats; some even had colourful woven cotton blankets which they carefully placed over the top of them. My 300-rupee Big Bazar number was clearly inferior. As soon as it became sweat-soaked, it provided virtually no protection from the concrete floor. No wonder I was finding this all so difficult!

I caught myself. Here I was actually coveting other people's yoga mats. How had my life come to this?

This time Vinay led the session himself, performing the asanas along with us, yet also managing to give a continuous stream of instructions on what to do and how to breathe. He never seemed to get out of breath or even exert himself particularly much. Remarkable.

'Breathe towards the source,' he said at one point. 'Focus on your inner light.'

I had no idea what this meant, but I gave it my best shot. If anything, though, I struggled even

236

more during this second session. Again, Vinay gently told me to lie down several times when I had come close to blacking out while trying to maintain the deep, regular breaths and had started swaying.

I might as well cut straight to the main action of the second day: someone — my money is on Ling — farted. Really loudly, like a whale blowing a trumpet. Nobody else reacted but, personally, I couldn't imagine anything more embarrassing than farting unintentionally in a room full of strangers. This buoyed me considerably. I might not be able to lift my foot over my head, I chuckled to myself, but at least I had basic control of my sphincter.

Needless to say, a short while later, following an unfortunate confluence of circumstances involving air trapped in a sweat-sodden T-shirt being forced out by my stomach as I lay down on my front, it would have sounded to others that I, too, had emitted a tremendous flatulent salute. I immediately tried to replicate the noise, as if to say, 'Look, it wasn't me, it was my T-shirt', but try as I might I could not. I, too, was now branded in the minds of my younger fellow yogis as one of the ageing wind-incontinent. Or, worse, they assumed both reports had been of my making.

Pranayama, the breathing meditation session which followed the asanas, brought the now familiar agony of prolonged cross-legged sitting, although at least this time I remembered to clear my nasal passages, and my pain was slightly eased by Vinay showing me how to support my creaking knees with a folded towel and to shore up my ossified spine by rolling up my mat and using it as a cushion. It was all very undignified, or would have been if I'd had any shred of dignity left. I felt like one of those ancient Japanese pines, its collapsing boughs propped up with sturdy posts.

However — and it is a very big however — when I left the shala that second day and stepped out on to the dusty streets of Mysore my physical discomfort was tempered by an alien sense of . . . well, I don't know what it was, really, but the world seemed sharper, brighter, clearer. I was deeply fatigued, yes, in some pain, and limited in my movements, but what was this stirring, somewhere, quite possibly within range of my spleen? A long-dormant spirit, an energy previously believed extinct: positivity.

As I stood, probably with my mouth slightly open, a bit glazed and trying to work out if this was a genuine epiphany or just exhaustion-induced euphoria, the Mossad hitman (who, rather magnificently, did turn out to be ex-Israeli army), passed by.

We acknowledged each other with a wary nod, but something made him hesitate and turn to me.

'How's it going? You look like you're having a tough time.'

'Yes, you could say that, but I think I had a little moment of . . . something just now. Not sure what.'

'Huh,' he made a little puffing noise and nodded knowingly. 'Ananda, maybe?'

'Ananda?'

'If you read the yoga sutras you . . . You have read the yoga sutras, right?'

'I've dipped into them . . . Waiting for the movie.' He didn't acknowledge the joke.

'Upanishads? Patanjali? Bhagavad Gita?'

'Definitely all on my list.'

He rolled his eyes ever so slightly, but my ignorance wasn't enough of a surprise to prompt any great incredulity.

'Yoga is very simply about one thing: ananda. It means lasting, eternal happiness. To reach ananda you must first come to understand, through meditation and asanas, your true nature: that, deep down, you, like everyone else on this planet, are divine. Nirvana, universal conscious-ness, Yahweh, Muhammad, God — whatever you choose to call it, it's all the same thing.'

'Okay, but do I really need to put my feet between my ears or chant 'om' to understand that? I get it. I'm divine.'

'Well, you might get it on an intellectual level but, my friend, you have been programmed and brainwashed, your mind is scratched and scuzzy with emotions, fears, anxieties. Yoga helps you wipe all that away and see yourself and the universe totally clearly.'

I thought for a moment: show him you understand, otherwise he's going to go on for ever.

'Like when you're approaching a tollbooth and you have to turn the stereo down to concentrate?' I said, hopefully.

'When you do yoga you bend, you stretch, you

239

become more flexible, and your mind becomes more flexible along with it. You don't just get fit — if you travel through India you see an awful lot of fat old guys doing yoga. It's not really cardiovascular like the exercise we do in the West — but you get to know your body and what it can do.'

'Okay, I understand that stretching and moving and stuff is good for you, but I still don't really get what's going to happen mentally.'

'Oh, you will, my friend, you will. Harmony. It's all about the harmony.'

'One other thing,' I said. He paused. 'Does yoga also, you know, make you feel a bit . . . randy?'

'Really? You are kidding, right?'

'Well, I am now,' I said. 'Anyway, see you tomorrow!'

He was already walking away, his mat under his arm, a sweat-soaked T-shirt stuck to his back.

⋆   ⋆   ⋆

Back at the apartment that afternoon I read on in Iyengar's book, and in a couple of other books I picked up in a store in Mysore, about the background and history of yoga. My basic understanding (and it is necessarily basic, I'm afraid: early on it appears someone decided that any text written about yoga had to be excruciatingly, life-sappingly dull; put it this way, if you thought Henry James was hard going, good luck reading anything written by a yoga guru), is that the teachings of yoga originated three thousand years ago in the 700-verse

Bhagavad Gita which Lord Krishna took the time to recite on the Kurukshetra battlefield in the Mahabharata. In it he advises the Pandava prince, Arjuna, about the morality of the war he is about to wage with his cousins and, ultimately, how to achieve 'the final liberation', or 'moksha'.

After this divine introduction, yoga seems to branch off into myriad directions and philosophies, but at the core of most contemporary yoga, both in India and the West, is Ashtanga yoga, devised by Mahamuni (Great Sage) Patanjali, a mere two thousand years ago. This is Eight-Limbed Yoga, a practical, precise, direct plan of action aimed at helping practitioners reach enlightenment by working their way through eight limbs — they seem more like steps than limbs to me but, as we have established, I don't know what I am talking about — to reach liberation.

The first two steps are concerned with what we might broadly call one's deportment in life, one's moral code and personal conduct, with a view to maintaining a harmony with others. They are:

Yama — the fundamental moral commandments, or 'outer observances', such as non-violence, truth, generally being good.
Niyama — self-control, or 'inner observance'.

Then come the two limbs on which Iyengar — and Vinay's Prana Vashya yoga — places particular emphasis: asana and pranayama, the former helping practitioners to conquer their bodies, the latter . . . well, what exactly did all

241

that huffing and puffing bring one?

The book explained that prana means 'breath' or 'life force' and yama means 'length', so the whole roughly translates as 'expanding the breath'. According to yogic belief, your lifespan is dictated not by your age or the number of days you live, but by the number of breaths you take, and so if you can learn how to make the most out of those breaths, extend them fully, exploit them to the full, you can extend your life.

'Pranayama cleanses and aerates the lungs,' writes Iyengar. 'It oxygenates the blood and purifies the nerves. But more important than the physical cleansing of the body is the cleansing of the mind of its disturbing emotions like hatred, passion, anger, lust, greed, delusion and pride.'

The lung bit made sense but it was that second, psycho-physiological leap I was struggling with. Was that what I had glimpsed as I had stepped out into the sun after the morning's session, that briefly energised moment? I wondered. Was that a chink of light beckoning from the realm of enlightenment? Or was I just a bit giddy with all the fresh air?

Beyond asanas and pranayama the next two limbs of Ashtanga yoga take things to what was, for me, an even more esoteric and abstract domain, one with which I was not, at this stage, all that concerned:

Pratyahara — withdrawal and emancipation of the mind from the dominance of the senses and exterior objects.
Dharana — concentration.

242

And with the final two limbs we make the great leap to the 'recesses of the soul':

Dhyana — meditation.
Samadhi — super-consciousness, a 'profound absorption' in which you 'become at one with the universal spirit'.

Reading on I was intrigued, and not a little disheartened, to find that Iyengar divided students of yoga into four categories. Unfortunately, the first category of student he describes — 'mrdu' — pretty much reads as it would if I took one of those psychometric personality tests. These losers are, he says: 'Feeble seekers who lack enthusiasm, criticise their teachers, are rapacious, inclined to bad action, eat much, are in the power of women, unstable, cowardly, ill, dependent, speak harshly, have weak characters and lack virility.'

Check, check, check . . .

While I might aspire to be 'madhyama' ('of stable mind . . . virile, independent, noble, merciful, forgiving, truthful, brave, young [come on, that's hardly fair], respectful, worshipping his teacher'), or perhaps even one day 'adhimatra' ('of great virility and enthusiasm, good looking [again, not fair], courageous, learned in scriptures, studious, sane of mind, not melancholy, keeping young, regular in food, with his senses under control, free from fear, clean, skilful, generous, helpful to all, firm, intelligent', and so on), it very much appeared as if I was fundamentally hobbled by my personality right from the start.

Never mind. Dhyana and samadhi might not

243

feature in my immediate destiny but I could already feel that there were meditative qualities about the asanas themselves, particularly with Vinay's system where the regime of regular, automatic, deep breathing lifted one of the burdens of the subconscious — to regulate breathing — externalising it and rendering it, in a sense, beyond one's control. You simply breathed in and out as and when you were told to and, for me, that freed something.

As Iyengar writes, 'A steady and pleasant posture produces mental equilibrium and prevents fickleness of mind.' It hadn't quite done that for me, concentration had been another major failing of my practice so far and would continue to be so, but more importantly, I could definitely see how the asanas might help. For all the agony, indignity and discomfort, the benefits of asanas and pranayama were easy to rationalise, even for a cynic; they were certainly easier for me to accept than talk of universal energy fields, and that was a start of sorts, enough at least to keep me going for the next few days.

The question now was how long would it take for me to start to feel a proper, deep change, and more importantly, could my body, my spirit and my, thus far, four-day-long period of temperance (the longest I had gone without a drink since . . . well, since I started drinking in earnest in my late teens) endure long enough to achieve these changes?

25

Kinder Eggs and Sacred Cows

By the fourth day my body was at least becoming accustomed to the routine of the early start, comforted by the knowledge that I was not alone.

Our apartment block stood on the corner of a narrow lane leading to a busy warren of single-storey houses where children played in the streets and old men sat on doorsteps, chewing. On the corner, a buffalo had stationed herself besides a large pile of garbage, also chewing. Judging by the diligently stacked piles of dry manure discs (for fuel) beside her, she had claimed her pitch long ago. Here, she slowly, methodically, consumed the kitchen waste, paper, plastic and Lord knows what else our neighbours dumped at her feet, sending their children in a near-continuous stream bearing buckets of more of the same.

Of course, we all know that cows are supposedly sacred in India and allowed to roam wherever they want. Well, if that's how the Indians treat the things they hold sacred, I'd hate to see what they do to the things they don't like. It is perhaps more accurate to say the buffalo are 'tolerated' rather than sacred in the sense of being cherished or venerated, as most of India's cows live fairly wretched lives. But, still, nothing prepares you for the sight of cows standing patiently outside ticket kiosks, or at bus stops, or in the middle of a four-lane highway, completely unacknowledged. It is as if they are unseen, ever present, but ignored; a half-ton phantom of meat and skin with great wobbly wattles and dangling undercarriage, somehow rendered invisible. You feel like gently nudging someone and pointing out, 'You do realise there is a dirty great cow in the middle of the street, don't you?' Lissen had a different take on this, saying, only half jokingly, 'We should never live so fast that we can't make room for cows roaming the streets,' one day, as we waited patiently in our taxi for one to move out of the way (although she did say it in a cod-Chinese, 'wise man' voice).

There were rats everywhere and I would watch their acrobatics from the fondly imagined safety of our third-floor living-room window. From there, if I craned my neck to look beyond the palm trees and the hand-painted sign for the piles and fistula clinic next door, I could see the Chamundi hills, Mysore's main landmark, in the distance, fairy-lit at night. Meanwhile, directly across the main road was a tacky yellow and white stucco chapel with a neon crucifix above the door which glowed warning red at night. Next to the church was a boys' boarding school-cum-orphanage, a large, two-storey, red-roofed building with concrete lattice windows with no glass, and a dusty yard to one side. On Sunday mornings the boys would troop, two by two, from the school to the church. Once, as I stood watching, I saw four of them scurry off into the neighbourhood behind our building, and gave a little cheer at their escape, albeit probably temporary, from the misery of mass.

Every morning before my yoga session, as I sat on the toilet following Iyengar's advice, I could hear the light, high chanting of the boys from the school. Their voices haunted those early, creaking, painful mornings. Thoughts of their lives and their futures often shamed me into hauling myself out of the door and to the shala for my daily torture. I felt that, somehow, I owed it to them, as well as to myself, to make the most of the opportunity I had been given — an opportunity thrown into sharp relief, of course, by all of those I had squandered in my life; the risk of the ones that I might yet squander; and of the chances in life those boys would probably never have, and that my sons, I hoped, would.

Outside the shala that morning the usual crew were waiting for Vinay to open up (I later found out that he usually arrives two to three hours before us to go through his own, probably even more rigorous, asana regime). I slumped on the stone bench in the tiny front yard among the pot plants to remove my shoes.

'Ling, what on earth makes you keep coming back for this?' I asked the Chinese New Zealander sitting beside me. 'What about those days when you ache all over and you just can't face it?'

'Honey, I just haul my carcass into an auto-rickshaw,' he said. 'I let it take care of itself from there on, but it's not easy.'

Kim the slightly vacant Australian overheard us and added with what I would come to know, and almost tolerate, as her customary chirpiness, 'Oh come on guys, think how many people would love to be here right now. Think how lucky we are to have this chance to start a new day cherishing our bodies and souls!'

All the time we were talking, Ling had been absentmindedly tapping away on his laptop. I asked what he was doing.

'Day trading,' he said. 'I can just catch the Australian market, then, when we are finishing the session, for those last few minutes I'm, like, going, 'Come on, come on, I wanna get online when Wall Street opens.' You know, I can make enough money in a day to live for a month in Mysore, it's fantastic.

'One day, I'll let you know my secret!' Ling added over his shoulder as Vinay opened the door to the shala and we climbed the stairs.

When we reached the studio Vinay took me aside.

'How are you, Michael?' he said, his brown eyes locked on to mine. Though I never felt with Vinay that he was judging me, his gaze made me feel that he could see things in me that I didn't necessarily want to reveal. He was always so terribly *present*. I mumbled something about it being very tough, and not being sure I was cut out for yoga, or at least this kind of yoga. I complained it was hot, and about how I got dizzy all the time, and felt I was too old, too fat, too out of shape to continue.

'I can see your body shape is already changing, even after just a few days,' he said calmly. 'You hold your shoulders back more,

248

your back is straighter. Well done. Already I can see your positions are better than the first time.' He smiled again, and turned away to accept a flower offering from Ling.

His words were like applause for a needy actor. Vinay wasn't big on encouragement. He neither judged nor criticised. I don't think he saw that as his role, yoga being, essentially, a private, inner practice — nobody's business but the student's. He might occasionally offer gentle, physical support for difficult asanas or jokingly threaten that if we didn't all perform a particular asana properly he would make us do it ten more times (although I don't think any of us bought the tough sergeant-major act), but aside from the odd, Yoda-esque, 'Gooood', or 'You're doing well,' as he circled the class, he offered little else by way of encouragement. It was clear that how we practised was our own responsibility.

You would have thought there was a risk that this laissez-faire approach would mean that the shirkers among us might coast during tough periods, pulling shapes in a vague approximation of each asana, rather than stretching and pushing our bodies to their limits on every half-breath, in accordance with the principles of Prana Vashya. I admit, the thought had occurred to me during my darker moments, but even I could see the futility of that. Why go to all this trouble, cost and pain and not carry it through to the bitter end? That's the annoying aspect of voluntary (or, in my case, even blackmail-induced) self-improvement: ultimately, you really are only cheating yourself.

So, that day, Vinay's words helped buoy my

spirits, carrying me through the first fifteen minutes, despite being distracted by the strange orgasmic noises being made by the stroppy American woman. After that, my own physical parameters came into play and I began once more to buckle in the intolerable heat. The last straw came when trying the Ardha Baddha Padmottanasana, which involved standing on one leg — surely enough of a challenge in itself — with the other leg folded up and the outer edge of the foot resting on your thigh, before bending over with one hand behind your back and the other (and we are very much in the realms of the hypothetical here) palm down on the floor beside your feet. The problem was that my thigh was too sweaty so my foot kept gliding off (I apologise for invoking this unpalatable image). I lost my balance completely, and staggered over on to Ling's mat, creating a domino effect through half of the class. This prompted sharp glances, and I was told to lie down and rest.

At the start of the pranayama session I had felt hungry, yet also nauseous and, as always, parched with thirst. Even the distant and unmistakable sound of an auto-rickshaw driver urinating on the street was unbearable, but, again, by the halfway point the hunger, the sickness and, most miraculously, the thirst had gone. What was this effect of pranayama? How did it work?

A far greater problem was the boredom. God, it was tedious, this slow-breathing business. I longed for the minute hand to sweep around the dial of the shala clock.

'Have curiosity for every single breath,' Vinay said to the group. 'Every breath caresses the nerves.'

I was a little put out that Vinay still wasn't letting me loose on the 'oms', with which everyone else got to round off the pranayama session. I longed so badly to 'om', to join the competition that blossomed then. Why were the other students allowed to compete, and I wasn't? I cornered Vinay after the session for an explanation.

'Ah, it will come,' he said. 'You aren't quite ready for it yet. You must take pranayama slowly, build up gradually. It can be dangerous.'

⋆ ⋆ ⋆

At home that afternoon I read in Iyengar's book about the various obstacles or distractions which might prevent the yogi from realising his full potential. They are:

Vyadhi — physical infirmity.
Styana — languor or a lack of mental disposition to work.
Samsaya — doubt or indecision. 'The faithless and the doubter destroy themselves,' he writes.
Pramada — indifference or insensibility. 'The sufferer is full of self-importance, lacks any humility and believes that he alone is wise.'
Alasya — laziness.
Avirati — sensuality. 'The rousing of desire when sensory objects possess the mind.' Put it another way: mucky thoughts.

251

Bhranti darsana — false or invalid knowledge. 'Lacks humility and makes a show of wisdom.'
Alabdha bhumikatva — failure to attain continuity of thought or concentration.
Anavasthitattva — instability in holding on to concentration which has been attained after long practice.

Check, check, check . . .

Perhaps it was a blessing then that the next day was a Saturday, which meant a day off from asanas and pranayama. That didn't mean the shala was closed, though. Before I'd left the day before Vinay had caught hold of my arm:

'You will be coming to the chanting tomorrow, won't you?' It was not so much a question as a reminder.

'The what? Why?'

'The sun is the energy, but it falls brightly or dim depending on the interruptions from the clouds,' he said. 'So what we try to do is to clear these clouds, these interruptions, to try to experience the rays. Chanting clears your mind, and opens it.'

I made the mistake of mentioning my conversation with Vinay to Lissen who, of course, was then also adamant that we should go along to the chanting. I tried to plead fatigue and, when that failed, pointed out our lack of a babysitter.

'Well, I am sure it won't be a problem if Asger and Emil come along too,' she said, brushing a pile of cockroach carcasses under the sideboard.

So, we all went along to the chanting the next

252

morning. I was starting to have an instinctive, almost physical reaction to Vinay's shala, similar I imagine to how residents of Eastern bloc countries must have felt about the local secret police headquarters, or a horse's reaction to an especially high fence — the clamping around the throat, the plummeting stomach, a general, all-over body clench.

Asger and Emil agreed to wait outside the yoga room — bribed by the promise of chocolate and a game of air hockey at Big Bazar's fourth-floor arcade — as Lissen and I and the rest of the students knelt and sang Hindu prayer songs, led by Vinay, his mother and a young Indian woman. Vinay's mother, swathed in a green sari, was as radiant as he, with clear skin and a shining smile. The young woman turned out to be Vinay's fiancée, a slender, gorgeous girl with a bashful smile.

Lissen used to be a professional singer, so she followed the gentle melodies of the prayers with confidence, throwing in the odd harmonic detour much to Vinay's approval. I did my usual Rex Harrison half-talking, half-singing but I could sense the New York woman — the one who had interrupted my conversation with the Danish man earlier in the week — bristle from across the room. Clearly, she considered herself the diva of the Prana Vashya yoga shala and upped her volume accordingly. The problem was, she couldn't actually hit, let alone hold a note, and her atonal droning cast even more of a pall over proceedings.

Asger and Emil started to play up, opening the

door to peer in, despite strict instructions to stay outside with their comics and Nintendos. I mimed at them to shut the door and go away, but they giggled. Emil made a farting noise with one hand under his arm, a skill he had recently mastered.

Given a choice, I would have been outside making farting noises with them. Chanting was doing nothing for me. As with the prayer at the start of our yoga sessions, without having the first clue to the meaning of what we were singing, I couldn't really see a purpose to it. I know that chanting is an integral feature of the yogic path to enlightenment, but I already knew it wasn't going to be a feature of my own particular path to wherever it was I was heading.

I began counting the pages we had left to go in the songbook, as I used to do with the hymns in church when I was a boy, but it turned out that, cruelly, we had to repeat many of the songs. At one point I heard myself literally chanting 'Hari Krishna', and was struck by a powerful sense of hopeless, almost tragic displacement; it was one of my life's great 'What the fuck am I doing here?' moments. What was I doing chanting these — to me — completely meaningless phrases, sitting in cross-legged agony in a room of strangers while wearing cheap sportswear? This wasn't me. This wasn't the person I ever wanted to be.

At last, with the farting noises from beyond the door becoming more insistent, Asger and Emil gave me the excuse I needed to leave, and I backed out of the room while the others — Lissen, lost in some spiritual, or at least musical reverie, among them — continued chanting.

Asger, Emil and I walked to Big Bazar where we played for a while in the games arcade. We bought some chocolate which, like all the chocolate we had tried so far in India, was semi-melted and horribly mottled. You have to admire the Indians' persistence with chocolate: with its heat and humidity, poor transport and dodgy refrigeration, theirs is not a chocolate-friendly country, despite the stuff being grown here and despite a strong affection for the execrable Cadbury's Dairy Milk, which is sold everywhere. The only manufacturer which appears to have wised up to the Indian climate is Kinder, who long ago gave up selling their Kinder Eggs in egg form, switching instead to a kind of gloop eaten with a tiny plastic spoon.

But even one of these failed to lighten Asger's mood. He hadn't been himself for the last couple of days; something was on his mind. The trouble always in diagnosing Asger's problems is that, unlike his father, he tends to see the positive in every situation and person he encounters. He'd much rather avoid conflict or unnecessary aggravation, and if that means pretending things are fine when they're not, then so be it. After some gentle probing he admitted he was feeling upset, but he didn't know what it was about. He described a 'funny feeling' in the pit of his stomach: I guessed homesickness.

'I don't know what's happening in my head. Sometimes I hate you and Mum and Emil. Some-times I love you,' he said, bottom lip trembling.

This made me reflect again on the wisdom of bringing young children to India in the first place, or even, come to that, taking them anywhere away from their home and friends for more than just a couple of weeks.

The open-minded, liberal, adventurous, middle-class response would be to say that taking children to India gives them a great life experience; they witness a world, a people and a way of life that is starkly different from their own and, somehow, become better informed, more rounded people because of it. But what if experiencing all this misery and suffering, what if having to endure — not exactly against your will but certainly without having made a properly informed decision on whether to or not — the exhausting barrage of the sacred and profane to which India subjects its visitors is more scarring than it is educational? I thought of the Esther Freud wannabes and their children whom I had seen in Udaipur. We had done our best to keep our kids safe and happy during the trip but was taking Asger and Emil to India really not just a form of child abuse gussied up as education? Wouldn't it have been better to wait, as most people do, for our children to become young adults so that they could decide for themselves whether to go back-packing in the subcontinent?

To make matters worse, the Indian media was full of coverage of a recent terrorist attack at the German Bakery in Pune in which seventeen people had died. The bomb had gone off on the night before Valentine's Day, and though it had specifically targeted Western yoga students, most

256

of the fatalities were Indian. The newspapers were saying that Mysore might be among a number of other targets, which also included Rishikesh and Mumbai. What *were* we doing here?

To salve my conscience, after another game of air hockey we jumped in an auto-rickshaw and took off, via the apartment, to the Regalis hotel, which we'd heard had a decent swimming pool. On the way, our driver was stopped by police at a crossroads and arrested. The three of us sat in the back of his auto-rickshaw wondering what to do next and, after watching the poor man empty his pockets for bribes which failed to placate the policemen, we decided to walk the rest of the way.

The Regalis was the main hub for the large Western yoga community in Mysore which has been growing rapidly in recent years thanks, in part, to Madonna and other celebrity yoga fans (and, thus a prime terrorist target, now I come to think of it). As I waited on a sunlounger for Asger and Emil to grow tired of jumping into the pool, clambering back out, then jumping back in (about four hours, this being essentially what they live for), I took in the assembled crowd of yoga students.

They were all, without exception, thin and annoying. Actually, that's unfair. Some were extremely emaciated and irritating, others merely skinny and tooth-itchingly aggravating. You must of course consider my opinion in the context of the bitter fog of self-loathing and body dysmorphia (is it considered dysmorphia if one's revulsion at one's body is justifiable?) through which I

257

observed them, but I have to say, never before has such a bunch of self-regarding, tattooed, Jesus-haired narcissists been gathered together in one place.

Let us list the reasons why I hated them so:

All their sentences end on an upward inflection. (After a while it dawned on me that perhaps everything they said really was a question: perhaps the world perplexes them to such a degree that the only method they have of coping is to machine-gun questions at it in the hope that some might be answered.)

Men with ponytails.

Excessive use of the words 'like' and 'whatever', as in one conversation which I noted down verbatim:

Yoga fool one: Like, whatever . . .

Yoga fool two: Whatever.

Yoga fool one: Yeah, like, whatever, you know, like whatever.

Yoga fool three (arriving with drinks): Whaaa-devva.

Their ramrod back posture. My natural sitting position is essentially like piped mashed potato: a kind of spiralling slump characterised by ever-broadening tyres of flab, but even the men sat with their backs arced and chests thrust forward like aspiring glamour models. I thought the idea of yoga was to loosen up?

Ponytails for men.

Looking at me out of the corner of their eyes

as if I had some freakish disability. I'm just a bit fat and old, for Christ's sake. Give it time . . .
Women with sunglasses bigger than their faces.
Men in Speedos.

After an hour or so spent simmering in my own resentful decrepitude, I picked up a book I had brought with me: it was a copy of Paul Brunton's *A Search in Secret India*, a fascinating description of the author's quest for a guru in 1934 — although it might as well have been 1734, or even 1434, so archaic and backward is the country he describes. He meets a colourful cast of fakirs, mystics, yogis and swamis, some of whom he condemns as frauds, though others do convince him of their powers, not least the fakir who removes his own eye, 'Calmly with the detachment with which one might pull a button from a jacket.'

Brunton was one of the first Western writers to attempt to get to grips with yoga but, initially at least, he seemed baffled by what he witnessed. 'The seventy odd postures which compose the remainder of the system are hardly likely to yield to any except the most enthusiastic,' he writes. 'And that only if they are young enough to have flexible limbs and supple bodies. I certainly do not know how it is possible for any adult European to adventure with the scores of intricate postures which comprise most of their system without breaking a bone or two in the undertaking.'

'What Westerner,' he wonders, 'has the patience to go through all these complicated exercises and master them?'

259

26

All Hindus Now

Humiliation is slowly seeping into my subconscious. Even in dreams there is no refuge from pillory, shame and embarrassment.

That night I dream that I meet Bill Bryson at a book signing. For some reason — which in that annoying way of dreams is never properly explained, and thus all the more unsettling — it's a joint book signing, just him and me. I sit, alone, surrounded by a fortress of my unsold books while Bill is engulfed by fans waving copies of the 'Notes From . . . ' series and his latest book about whatever on earth he feels like writing about. I am dressed as Big Bird from *Sesame Street*. Then I'm not. After a while, Bill saunters over.

'Hey Mike, how's the signing going?'

He knows perfectly well that I have signed just the one book: the 'fan', whose minder waits patiently in the Bryson queue, sits parked beside me slumped in his wheelchair, drool glistening in the corner of his mouth. I have wedged the book under his arm. Also, I hate being called Mike.

'Oh, you know, so-so,' I say, trying in vain to conceal the mountain of books with my arms.

'Have you heard about the new thing they have at bookshops?' Bill asks with a mischievous, Iowan twinkle. I shake my head warily.

'Yeah, like, apparently, now as you walk around the shop, there's going to be some kind of gauge under every book which shows customers how far readers have managed to get in them, or what percentage actually read them all the way through.'

Suddenly, I woke up making what Lissen described as a 'strangled yelping noise'. I had to get up anyway, it was six o'clock and the orphans were chanting.

I suspect the dream had in part been prompted by one of the more humiliating side effects of my yoga boot-camp experience, one which had manifested itself in the last couple of days (although I had also checked my Amazon rankings at an internet café the day before, so that probably had something to do with it too).

There had been several side effects of starting yoga, not all of them bad: there was the Michael-Douglas-style sex addiction, of course, but also an unprecedented but entirely natural-feeling decline in my appetite. Within four days I was subsisting on a bag of cashew nuts, some yoghurt and fruit, with perhaps a coconut from the man who sold them across the street, and nothing else. I wasn't nauseous, it wasn't that I couldn't eat, I just didn't feel the need. Yet I had plenty of energy — more than ever, actually — and, aside from the chronic muscle ache and the two hours of exhaustion immediately after my class, I felt pretty great.

'You are replacing the energy you once got from food with the energy that comes from the asanas and pranayama,' Vinay had explained. But

261

how could exercise and deep breathing create energy? It seemed paradoxical to eat less yet have more energy, but I was undeniable, living proof.

Perhaps most remarkable of all was that I had suddenly and dramatically lost all interest in alcohol. I wasn't thinking about my next drink when I woke up in the morning, and I didn't think about having one as the sun set. The craving had subsided of its own volition. The desire had gone, at least for now. It definitely helped that I was about as removed from my daily routine as it was possible to be; that there was no alcohol in the apartment; and that it was hard to come by a drink in Mysore. I hadn't seen any shops selling booze, not even Big Bazar. But like most drunks, I can be remarkably resourceful when it comes to finding a drink (I once made swift work of an entire box of my mother's liqueur chocolates, for instance, biting the tops off the tiny bottles of Cointreau and Cherry Brandy and sucking those babies dry). If I had wanted one, I probably would have found something worth drinking. But I didn't. At least, not yet.

These were the positive changes, but then there were the less welcome ones, not least the rampant acne. Within a week of starting yoga with Vinay, my shoulders, neck and almost my entire face was covered with the most chronic outbreak of pimples I have ever experienced. I reacted to this with, at first, curiosity, then mild indignation (why didn't anyone tell me I could still get spots at my age?). This was followed by self-revulsion, embarrassment, fear, Elephant

Man reclusiveness and, as the days turned into weeks, the cultivation of a desperate, Charles Manson beard. What had prompted this mass explosion of zits? Theories among the other students ranged from dirt from the shala floor being transferred from my hands to my face, to pores blocked by sweat, to diet, to — most popular of all — 'detoxing'.

At another shala closer to our apartment where we would go to access the internet, one whip-thin girl dressed head to bare feet and silver-ringed toes in tie-dyed hemp, took one look at me as I entered the garden and said, 'Wow, massive detox! Cool, cool.'

'Yah, like, it's your body's way of getting rid of all the poisons you have been inflicting on it over the years,' added a weaselly looking Canadian man with a ponytail. 'You used to eat meat, right?'

Yes, I said, trying not to make it sound like an apology.

'Your body has gone into shock from the lack of protein,' he said.

'So I should, like, go back to eating loads of meat?'

'Christ, no, man,' he said, horrified at the thought. 'That's more poison, dude. Ugh, corpses. Coconut milk is the best thing. I always eat a fresh coconut after yoga. Full of protein and vitamins.'

So, my body was in the process of expelling impurities, cleansing, renewing itself, rejuvenating and beginning afresh. Yes, well, fine, but did it have to make me look like a fourteen-year-old glue sniffer in the process? If this was detoxing, then I must be expelling every toxic substance I have ever ingested, from the first sherbet dip to the very last gin and tonic.

A day later, just to complete the gargoyle ensemble, I picked up a bulbous eye infection, the whole 'Marty Feldman in a hall of mirrors' look being compounded by the sunburn I had acquired while glaring resentfully at the yoga students at the Regalis the other day. Sympathetic to my plight, Lissen mixed up some yoghurt and lavender oil and had me lie still on the sofa for an undignified hour to let it soak in. Asger and Emil took turns to photograph the Elephant Dad in his helpless repose.

I had read in a local newspaper that every Sunday night at seven o'clock the façade of the palace of the Maharaja of Mysore was lit up with one lakh (equivalent in the Indian number system to 100,000) light bulbs. So, that night, our second Sunday in Mysore, we endured the ten-minute journey through the city centre to the palace to take a look. The moon was fat and yellow and it was already dark as we entered the palace grounds just at the very moment the lights were turned on, bathing the garden in their sulphurous glow. The façade was magnificent, like a gigantic dressing-room mirror. The crowd of a few hundred Indians and a scattering of westerners gasped as one.

There was a festival atmosphere abroad, which meant we had to be extra vigilant for middle-aged — mostly female — cheek-squeezers and hair-pawers, who, as they had been throughout the trip, were drawn to Asger and Emil like zombies. We spent a good deal of time posing for photographs, trying to imagine the future social gatherings at which these snaps would be shared with the friends and relatives of the photographers. What would they say? 'Here we are with some Europeans we have never met before and will never ever see again!' 'Look, that's me with Marty Feldman and his kids!'

Mysore Palace is one of India's more bizarre royal follies, built in a fruity Islamic-Gothic hybrid style — known as Indo-Saracenic — by the Wodeyars, Mysore's royal rulers, and designed by Henry Irwin, one of the lesser Raj architects who seems otherwise to have been restricted to a few railway stations. It reminded me of Brighton station with a little Brighton Pavilion thrown in. Inside it was a theatrical orgy of arches; Belgian stained-glass peacock windows; doors studded with mother-of-pearl inlay; and cast iron columns — the latter made in Glasgow, of all places. Though it has been owned by the government since 1947, the current maharaja — the 25th — Srikanta Datta Narasimharaja Wadiyar, still lives in some rooms to the rear of the palace and, pleasingly, according to the photos, he resembles every image of every maharaja I have ever seen, with his short, tubby frame, heavy eyelids and meticulously trimmed facial topiary.

We had expected the party mood to continue the next day with Holi, the spring festival famous for the throwing of coloured paints. Much anticipated in our house, Holi in Mysore was a bit of a washout; it turns out to be more of a northern Indian phenomenon. Lissen opted out altogether, but in the afternoon Asger, Emil and I cruised around town in an auto-rickshaw, tooled up with water pistols filled with coloured water, as well as powder bombs and bags of coloured paint. Occasionally we would catch a glimpse of a child with traces of paint on their clothing, or see a piece of brightly spattered pavement, but we saw no actual paint-hurling action.

We gave up on the auto-rickshaw and headed out into our neighbourhood on foot, finally chancing upon one unfortunate ten-year-old carrying a water pistol. Asger and Emil engaged him in a brief firefight, until the three of them decided it would be much more fun to gang up on me, drenching me with paint and water. At the end of it, we looked like evil clowns.

The next day we had been invited to eat at the home of a local family via Ling, who had previously lodged with Suraj and Devaki and their children. Hearing of my interest in food from him, they had asked him to pass on a generous invitation to lunch at their home in a posh suburb of Mysore. Together with Kim the Australian, we headed off there one Saturday morning, the idea being that I could watch the women make lunch in the kitchen, while Suraj and Devaki's kids could play with Asger and Emil.

In the small and, I am again afraid to report, absolutely filthy kitchen, I watched as our hosts made us a refreshing tomato and watermelon drink with cardamom, sugar and lime to start, then numerous aromatic vegetable and lentil dishes. Suraj's mother explained how she made home-made ghee with cow's milk (which they prefer in the south to buffalo milk for making ghee). She heated and cooled it to separate the cream and made the ghee from the butter, which was left to ferment for some days. The end result was almost inedibly ripe for my taste. I literally gagged when I tried some, and had to conceal my convulsion as a cough.

As Nita and Badri had done in Mumbai, Suraj and Devaki's family overwhelmed us with their hospitality, serving us as if they were waiters. Ram explained that, according to the principles of Hinduism, guests really are considered on a par with deities. They were a devout, Brahmin family — with a built in puja room just off their living room — thus, we all sat around the dining table while Suraj, Devaki and Suraj's mother brought us dish after dish of the best Indian home cooking, only finally agreeing to eat once we absolutely assured them that we were full. Lissen and I were still struggling to get used to this: 'I almost feel as if they are using us to build up a deposit in their karma bank,' Lissen whispered to me.

Devaki worked for Infosys, the Indian IT titan, while Suraj took care of the various family business interests, which included a sugar cane plantation.

We talked more about Hinduism — which is practised by over 80 per cent of the population — in particular the increasing tensions between

Hindus and Muslims which had boiled over into riots in Mysore in recent years. Suraj said he regretted the extremist trend and felt it misrepresented his faith. 'We have many Muslim work colleagues and friends,' he said. 'It is terrible how the politicians hijack my faith like this.'

Though Hinduism has tempered the extremes of Islam in India since the early days of Mughal rule, it is still hard to imagine two religions less suited to cohabitation. They may agree on eschewing pork, but one can only imagine the mortification with which a devout Muslim must regard Hinduism's proliferation of gaudy deities. Hindus, meanwhile, must doubtless shake their heads at Islam's lack of comforting myths, touchstones and superstitions and find its intellectualism cold and comfortless.

As always when I talk to people about their beliefs, those doctrines and rituals I usually took such pleasure in ridiculing seemed altogether more reasonable in the context of Suraj and Devaki's lives. They convinced me that Hinduism has much to commend it: it has no imams, popes, rabbis or figures of authority. There is no original sin, no big book, no set ritual by which to observe any fixed teachings, just this great, amorphous, endlessly interpretable belief system. It famously has those thirty million or so gods; but, then again, in a way thirty million are preferable to one, great omnipotent one. Instead of having an all-powerful being with a Father Christmas timeshare beard, Hindus have Brahma, a vague 'force' which seems to me less overbearing. Besides, Hindus' relationship with their gods appears to be refreshingly pragmatic — I noticed from one TV advert that they even use them to endorse toilet cleaner, something a Muslim would be unlikely to do. I think we can all agree, too, with the principles, if not the literality of karma. Though various elements of society have unilaterally exempted themselves from it (bankers, terrorists, professional footballers), wherever you encounter it, civil society is essentially held together by some sense of 'do unto others as you would have them do unto you'.

But then we got on to the subject of reincarnation, or 'transmigration' (samsara), and, I am afraid, that's where Hinduism and I part company.

'But what evidence do you have that you have lived as someone or something else, or will come back again?' I asked.

Suraj and Devaki looked at each other, puzzled. Lissen kicked me beneath the table.

'What Michael means is that he doesn't understand your beliefs properly and would like to learn more,' she said.

'Well, this is what the Vedas tell us, it is written there,' Suraj said, levelly. 'The Bhagavad Gita tells us that whatever state of consciousness we have achieved when we die, that will determine how we are born again.'

'I see,' I said. 'So, if I wanted to become a Hindu, how would I go about it?'

'Well, you can't really become a Hindu or convert in the same way you can to other religions. One is born a Hindu. Then again, you could also say that we are all Hindus, Hinduism is really just existence.'

'But what if I don't want t — '

This time the kick was sharp enough to silence me.

27

Shoving Your Head Up Your Arse, and Other Paths to Enlightenment

But the boredom. The boredom was the thing. God in a leotard, yoga is boring: boring like a local weather forecast for somewhere you're not; or cycling through a really long tunnel; or that little clock that spins when you are downloading something but it is taking far longer than it should. You stretch, you breathe, it hurts, you look at the clock and see half a minute has passed, you groan. Occasionally someone breaks wind, which momentarily relieves the tedium, but then you sweat and stretch some more. Repeat. For hours.

Early on in the second week I hit upon a trick to combat the tedium, a way to neutralise time during the asanas: I would switch to automatic pilot, following Vinay's breathing counts but leaving that hot, airless, stinking room full of lean, muscled yogis, and let my mind float around the world like a dandelion spore. For several sessions I walked around Paris, re-imagining every crack of familiar pavements: the tinkle of the bell as I entered my favourite patisserie; the aromas of the chocolateries; the rustle of the leaves in the Jardin du Luxembourg; damped footsteps taken on thick carpets in three-star restaurants.

When I had exhausted my sense-memories of

Paris, I moved on to random places I love elsewhere in the world: Shibuya at dusk when the liquid crystal begins to glow; West Wittering on a sunny afternoon when the tide drifts out for miles over the wet sand; the cobbled streets of Trastevere, sitting at a table outdoors with a bottle of Brunello; then snuffling around the bookshops of Charing Cross Road, seeing if they have any of my books and, if they have, moving them to a more prominent place just in front of Bill Bryson's; reading in the small park behind the Royal Library in Copenhagen as a gorgeous model sits beside me and asks what I am reading, and I say 'Me', and she says, 'Oh, he's my favourite author, would you like to come back to my apartment' and then we . . . drifting off into other kinds of fantasies was definitely an issue.

When the memory well finally ran dry, I panicked to find myself back in my creaking body again, and almost slumped defeated on the mat. Everything hurt. I was dizzy, thirsty, hungry, tired, embarrassed, frustrated.

I hadn't been listening to Vinay, my breathing had grown irregular and I was losing my way in the exercises, becoming more and more distracted by my physical discomfort instead of following the flow of the rhythm. As if sensing this, Vinay announced to the class in his sing-song voice, 'Your mind is like a galloping horse. You must learn to control it. If you can make every breath work with asanas, it can help you to control your body and your mind, not just while you are doing these exercises, but in life.'

272

It was true. For all the suffering they caused me, I was beginning to see how the asanas and pranayama might be able to benefit me beyond the shala, beyond India, back home in my normal life. What did all this bending and stretching, huffing and puffing have to do with my fossilised life, my all-consuming neuroses? Well, for a start, what I could now feel as I slowly began to conquer the asanas, pushing my body far beyond what I had believed it capable of, was that my physical confidence was growing. I had already had one or two exhilarating glimpses of what it must be like to feel fully, wholly in command of one's physical self, and to be master of your limbs and muscles was enormously satisfying. When your senses were telling you — screaming at you — that there is no way you can lift yourself from the floor using your hands alone (an asana called Bhujapidasana), and then you manage it anyway, your confidence soars. Several times I had laughed out loud at the audacity of my own body, at what it had been able to do: when I had finally locked my legs straight but still managed to grip my toes, for instance, or brought my forehead to rest on my knees. It had been really quite thrilling. My astonishment had usually resulted in me collapsing like a house of cards, but that was beside the point. This was an achievement of a very different kind to anything I had experienced before: not show-offy in any sense, not craving of anyone's approval, but intensely personal, surprising, and illustrative of new realms of possibility. My knackered old body was achieving things I never thought possible, things that it hadn't been able to do for literally decades.

One particular day, midway through week two, I was determined to complete as much of the sequence as I could without any humiliating interludes lying face down, resting on my mat.

I looked around the class. The Mossad hitman was attempting a Vasisthasana. He looked like a crazed starfish determined to walk for the first time, his left foot and hand planted on the mat, his right hand grasping his right foot high in the air above his pelvis. Meanwhile, the crotchety New Yorker was attempting a Supta Kurmasana — essentially shoving her head up her arse (aptly, some might say); while Kim, the Australian, was doing the splits and bending forward with her forehead on the mat — an Upavistha Konasana.

A new student had joined the class: thin, rubbery and French. She had immediately fallen in step with Vinay's commands. Annoyingly, she had been able to achieve every asana, perfectly, right from the start. She had no idea how long I had been taking the classes, and it was more than I could bear to have her see me flop, face down, on my yoga mat again.

Vinay, perhaps sensing I was on the verge of a breakthrough, was unusually effusive in his praise that day, even giving me a little applause as I managed to stand on one foot with my other leg stretched out in front of me at ninety degrees, holding its toes with both hands (Utthita Hasta Padangusthasana). I was making genuine progress. I was not only managing many of the asanas, but stretching to push my body further once I had achieved them, breathing more deeply and evenly.

Then, for some reason, Cliff Richard's 'Devil Woman' began to play in my head over and over again and, for a while, I skirted the very cusp of insanity itself. I pulled it back to thoughts of that dinner I once had at the three-star Paris restaurant Guy Savoy, which pretty much brought me to the end of the sequence.

And then, in one of the very last asanas, something quite extraordinary happened. It was a sitting position which involved crossing an arm over one folded-up knee and reaching around to link to the other hand behind my back. Previously when I had tried this, my hands had flapped around behind me, like a seal groping to find a light switch in the dark. This time, though, Vinay came up behind me and ever so gently introduced my left hand to my right, without pulling them together. They could touch! I pushed for one final stretch, fearing the crunch of spinal cartilage and a memorable ride to Accident & Emergency, but instead just managed to interlock my fingertips.

I felt like crying out in triumph: 'Look, everyone! I'm doing what you're doing. Hey! Not so crap after all!' But my lungs were squashed like discarded bubblewrap, so speech was impossible.

'You are stronger today, aren't you?' Vinay said to me as I stood in my customary spot on the balcony during the break before pranayama, gasping down lungfuls of air and ogling the juicy kokum fruit on the tree in the neighbouring yard.

I beamed. Yes, I was stronger. I could feel it.

'You know, I did think about giving up but, I don't know why . . . ' I shook my head, still puzzled by my level of commitment. 'I keep pushing myself on.'

'Well, if you didn't push yourself, there wouldn't be any point coming all the way to Mysore, would there?' said Vinay.

My pranayama routine was becoming more advanced too. This time Vinay prescribed a more complex array of breathing exercises, including the mad bicycle pump. I nearly passed out on my first attempt at that; my vision turned completely black for a moment or two, but I did it. Vinay still showed no sign of permitting me even the tiniest 'om', though.

At the end of pranayama the students would lie down for fifteen minutes or so on their backs, legs parted, the backs of their hands on the floor beside their hips, palms up. It was possibly the best part of my day, the lie-down to end all lie-downs, a sublime waking sleep. Every fibre of my body had been exhausted by the preceding four hours; my energy spent, all I could do was stare at those taunting, dormant ceiling fans. But there *had* definitely been some kind of a breakthrough today.

★　★　★

When I got home I was so dehydrated, my urine looked like single malt. Pranayama mysteriously

276

cured the raging thirst I felt after the asanas but it seemed my body still needed the fluids, so I made a note to take some water with me the next day. When that came, I could think of nothing else for pretty much the entire asana session but guzzling down my water in the changing room before pranayama began. I knew this wasn't allowed — there was even a sign forbidding drinking between sessions on the wall in the changing room. Using bat-type water radar (he never usually came into the changing room), that day Vinay caught me throwing the water down my neck in the manner of Jack Hawkins with his pint of Carlsberg in *Ice Cold in Alex*.

'No, no, Michael, stop!' he said, firmly. It was the closest I had seen him come to losing his temper. 'It will not help you at all. Drinking is not allowed fifteen minutes before you come and fifteen minutes after you leave. You will not be able to do the pranayama properly if you drink water.'

'But I am *so* thirsty,' I whined.

'Wait. Once pranayama starts you know you will not be thirsty any more. If you drown your body with water now, it will not be able to deal with it. You are too tired. It is better to let your body replenish itself: that will happen in pranayama.'

And he was right, as usual. Within a few minutes of starting the breathing exercises, my thirst disappeared. At the end of the two-hour session Vinay crouched down beside me. For one giddy moment I thought he was finally going to allow me to join in with the 'oms' but instead he gave me a new breathing exercise, even more bizarre than the bicycle pump: I was to stick out my tongue and then roll up its sides to form a kind of tongue-cannoli.

'Now, breathe in slowly through the mouth, like this,' he said, demonstrating. 'This is the only time we ever breathe through the mouth in Prana Vashya. It will cure your thirst and cool your body.' He made an alarming slurping noise, like the last of the bathwater circling the plughole and I, self-consciously, as everyone was now lying in the relaxation position, copied him, making like I was sucking up invisible spaghetti. And you know what? It didn't just cool my mouth down. I swear my body temperature dropped a notch or two as well.

'This cools your glands here,' Vinay said, pointing to his thyroid. 'They are the ones which control your body temperature.' By bathing the thyroid in air which was cooled as it passed over the saliva on the tongue, you could cool your entire body. Remarkable.

★   ★   ★

Ling had invited me to lunch at an Ayurvedic restaurant he had been wanting to show me since I told him about my, now pretty much moribund, food book project. He was telling me about his fulfilling life in Mysore.

'I was getting a massage in a four-star hotel the other week from a masseur,' he enthused. 'And we ended up having sex!'

'Oh, that's nice,' I said.

'Yeah, right, and we've become friends but, you know what? He's invited me to his wedding next week!'

Mysore was, for Ling it seemed, one giant singles bar. He had bought a jeep. 'And wherever I drive, people are waving at me and smiling. Back home I'm nothing. Here I'm so popular, it's fantastic.'

In parks, in restaurants, on the street, if Ling was to be believed he was literally fighting off advances from men all the time. 'I only have to walk through the park near the shala and I get approached. The other day I was waiting there for my boyfriend and another boy comes up, so I went off with him instead. You know, all the men are gay in India. It's the only chance for sex they get before they get married! Think of that next time they come up to you and want to shake hands.'

I was more interested in his day-trading secret. Did he really make enough money in a day to live for a month in Mysore?

'Oh sure,' he said, leaning in conspiratorially. 'What I do is this: At the end of the day I buy whatever has gone down . . . '

I waited, but the lengthy pause that followed seemed to indicate that was the full extent of Ling's strategy. He woke at 4.30 every morning before class to trade — 'The money wakes me up! I don't need an alarm clock' — and if the class ended on time, he usually had about fifteen minutes before the market closed in Sydney.

'You know, the other day, when the session went on for five minutes extra? Cost me a thousand dollars on Rio Tinto!'

Our Ayurvedic lunch was bright with flavours — unusually, for something which was so very healthy. The cooks, working on the floor of a small room just off the dining room, sent a continuous stream of vegetarian dishes — bitter gourd, carrot salad, cabbage thoren, rice, coconut relish and fresh-made chapattis — which we shared with other Western yoga students at a communal dining table.

Among the other students was a young woman with an emerald bindi. I couldn't help but ask her, feigning innocence, if she was a Hindu.

'No, what do you mean? I'm from Boston,' she said.

'Well, you're wearing a bindi, which is a Hindu tradition, so I just assumed. I mean, if I was wearing a crucifix, you'd assume I was Christian, right?'

'I believe we are all free to explore spirituality in our own ways,' she said with a slight edge.

'Yes, I suppose,' I said, returning to my tomatoes with curry leaves.

'My citta vrtti were very loud today,' a hollow-faced man with a plaited beard interrupted, addressing himself to the woman, and they talked for a while about what a nuisance that can be.

My childish bindi provocation was, in truth, more a reflection of my own discomfort with the way I was using India as a self-help supermarket. Wasn't I guilty of precisely the same kind of spiritual cherry-picking as Bindi Girl?

I asked Ling what he thought about my 'a bit

of yoga here, some breathing meditation there, perhaps some incense and carrot salad, but you can keep the gods and the chanting' approach. Surely, I was no better than those idiots who get Sanskrit tattoos without knowing what they mean, was I?

Ling shrugged.

'Well, you could say if you use the asanas and pranayama to help bring equilibrium and peace into your life, then that can't be a bad thing, can it? Even if you don't do the chanting, or shave your head, or give away all your possessions or whatever, you would still be improving yourself.' He paused. 'And, actually, I have a Maori tattoo.'

The suggestion was that by improving myself I would also, by extension, be improving the world — albeit by an infinitesimally minute factor, in the way a pebble thrown into Lake Geneva might raise the water level. At least, if I could moderate my appetites and addictions, there would be considerably more Johnnie Walker and chocolate cake for everyone else, and that would be a start, wouldn't it?

Ling seemed to come from the 'Whatever gets you through the night' school of thought, which I have a lot of time for. Over a cup of chai, he and I talked more about Vinay and his style of yoga. Ling had owned a yoga school himself and, as he had told me before, had been practising various forms of yoga for thirty years or so. 'But what Vinay does is so special,' he said, his eyes starting to well up. 'I remember, once, back in November, things just got so much for me, I actually began to cry in class, then everybody

281

else began to cry, then we all started to laugh, it was like what we were doing created waves of euphoria through us.'

I edged slightly away from him. Crying? Oh, come on, I thought. How can yoga make you cry?

28

The Rise and Fall of the Om-nivore

Then, out of remote areas of his soul, out of past times of his now weary life, a sound stirred up. It was a word, a syllable, which he, without thinking, with a slurred voice, spoke to himself, the old word which is the beginning and the end of all prayers of the Brahmans, the holy 'Om', which roughly means 'that which is perfect' or 'the completion'. And in the moment when the sound of 'Om' touched Siddhartha's ear, his dormant spirit suddenly woke up and realised the foolishness of his actions.

Hermann Hesse, *Siddhartha*.

Towards the end of the Thursday pranayama session Vinay crouched down beside me. I knew from his quiet smile that my moment had come.

'Would you like to try the 'om', Michael?''

I tried to conceal my excitement.

'Well, if you think I am ready for it.'

He told me that I was to push the tip of my tongue up to the back of the roof of my mouth, to where it turns fleshy and soft. Could I feel it? he asked. Yes, I could, I grunted. Good. Now I was to breathe in on a slow count of four ('one Mississippi River, two Mississippi River', and so on), through my nose of course, then out on a slow six count, pressing all the air from my lungs using my stomach muscles, as I had been shown before. Then in again on four and out . . . this time Vinay let rip with a deep, sonorous sound which seemed to emanate from the top of his head.

I copied him and, I have to say, my first was a very fine 'om' indeed: strong and deep to begin with, ending in a clean and dignified manner. I did a couple more. Hey, I was good at this. At last, here was something I could do straight off the bat, without any humiliating learning process. I did a couple more, relishing the buzz through my skull and inner ear. It energised me, in a pleasantly tingling, almost orgasmic way. The vibration also gave me a focus, a meditative target, obliterating all the distracting thoughts which usually crowded my mind during yoga. It was like an ultrasonic cleaner, precision blasting the crannies of my brain, reaching the parts no other toilet cleaner could reach, dislodging the decades of dirt that had encrusted there.

The beauty and purpose of the 'om' had been revealed. I was an 'om' convert. I loved the 'om', couldn't get enough of the 'om', I was an omnivore. I started to pick up on other 'om's from across the room as the rest of the class finished their pranayama exercises, and a whole new dimension of 'om'-ing opened up.

Ever since I had heard of Vinay's successes in yoga competitions, I had been troubled by the notion of competitive yoga. As I understood it, yoga was about an inner journey, the inner challenge, which is part of the reason why those

284

images we have of Californians doing yoga on the beach as the waves crash behind them are, ultimately, so bogus (ditto Sting, sitting cross-legged, upside down on a terrace overlooking his Tuscan vineyard): the environment in which you do yoga ought to be irrelevant. Part of the reason yoga has endured so powerfully in India for so many centuries, I suspect, is because it gives ordinary Indians a place to retreat to from the horrendous crowding, no matter what their surroundings, background, status or wealth. All you need is a space two metres by one. You could do it on a roundabout (as I had seen someone do in Jaipur), or in an airport terminal (Udaipur), or even on the pavement outside a busy public toilet (Mumbai). I had made a mental note to ask Vinay about competitive yoga when I got the chance. But competitive 'om'-ing, I did get. And I thrashed the lot of them, holding the 'om' longer than any of the other students, sometimes one and a half times as long.

'Good work, Michael,' Vinay said as I left that day.

'Oh, well,' I said, bashfully. 'It was nothing.'

'You held the 'om' for a really long time. I usually say people should aim for a fifteen count, but you were doing more.'

Instead of slumping into an auto-rickshaw for the short journey back to the apartment, I walked home, fizzing with energy. In celebration of my 'om' triumph, I decided to buy myself a covering mat from a nearby shala. I chose a thick cotton one in a vivid electric green; I had a notion the green might somehow give me energy

285

(you can't spend time among spiritual seekers without being influenced by this kind of woolly thinking). My new mat was quite the hit the next day at the shala.

'Ooh, where'd ya get that?' asked the New Yorker, softening slightly for the first time.

'At the shala down near the crossroads,' I said, adding with a satisfied smile: ''Fraid it was the only one they had in that colour.'

Pride, of course, tends to precede calamity, and thus it was that day, the Friday of my third week. It was unquestionably the worst session since I had started at the shala. I felt nauseous and exhausted. My new mat was soon soaked with sweat and I was drained of energy within the first twenty minutes, breathless as a tobacco company laboratory beagle. Thereafter, each asana fell further and further beyond my reach until it was all I could do merely to maintain the breathing rhythm. I had no idea why things were suddenly falling apart, but the more I tried, the more apparent it became that my body was giving up on me.

A short while into the session, I pulled an 'I can't go on' face at Vinay.

'Just stop and rest,' he said, quietly, so as not to disturb the other students.

I was feeling a bit crotchety by now, disappointed not just with myself, but resentful of the whole system, and snapped back, 'But you push us so hard!'

Vinay replied calmly, 'That's my job.' And turned away to deal with another student.

Is that all I am to you? I thought, petulantly.

286

Just a job. Is that all this means?

He made no further comment at the end of the session as I passed him on the way out. Childishly, I took this as a personal affront. It was as if all the progress I had made in recent days had simply vanished. All the effort so far counted for nothing, and if Vinay wasn't going to carry me through this dark patch, then who was? I was back to square one. What was the point? How hard did I have to work at this stuff to get even a sense of lasting progress? By the time I got home, I was in a truly foul mood. I ranted at Lissen about how sick I was of pushing my body to such extremes every day; how I didn't believe it was worth it; didn't believe yoga was any good, or that Vinay knew what he was doing or gave a damn about me. I told her that I deeply resented what she had done, undermining my book research, ruining the whole project. What right did she have to interfere in my professional life like that?

Voices escalated. Asger and Emil closed the door to their room and turned up the volume on the Hanuman cartoon they were watching on Indian TV. Things were said in the heat of the moment which should never have been said. I threatened to quit. Lissen threatened to leave, leaving the matter of who she was leaving and what nature that leaving would take, oblique. Doors slammed. I went to bed.

When I woke up, the apartment was empty. Lissen had left a note to say that she and the boys had gone to the zoo and would head from there to the cinema.

Unusually, I was ravenously hungry, so hopped in a rickshaw to the Regalis. I told myself that I deserved a treat. Sitting alone, surrounded by kebabs, curry and pillowy naans, it became glaringly evident that one couldn't *not* have a beer in such circumstances. And what would be the harm in just one? Of course, as anyone with even a passing acquaintance with a dipsomaniac could have predicted, once I had downed my first Kingfisher — ah, that sweet, cool fizz, that soothing first hit of alcohol, muzzying up my mind, buffing the sharp edges off life — I failed to see what difference it would make if I had another. I reasoned that I'd already crossed my own — all too frail — moral Maginot line. The harm had been done; more beers could hardly compound the crime, could they? And to finish things: barman! A gin and tonic ought to hit the spot. Now I'm feeling gooood. Wonder if they know how to rustle up a whisky sour? They don't? Oh well, at these prices I'd be a fool to leave without another G&T.

On my way home, my auto-rickshaw passed what seemed to be a bar, an open wooden shack which I hadn't noticed before, tucked off a main street. A nightcap! Just what I needed to round off the evening. Inside men stood in silence, downing tumblers of Indian whisky and watching a wall-mounted TV streaming footage of a fat man in orange robes sitting on a dais, chanting (which pretty much describes the majority of Indian televisual output). The small crowd parted as they saw me. I approached the bar smiling merrily. I pointed to a bottle on the shelf, grasped the soiled tumbler handed to me by the barman, and tipped the foul spirit down my throat. Emboldened, I exchanged nods with a man wearing a heavily stained vest, and what appeared to be boxer shorts, standing next to me. 'Evening!' I sang. He looked at me, bewildered, and turned slightly to face the screen. Diffident drinkers, Indians.

When I finally arrived home later that evening Lissen didn't have to ask where I had been. I went straight to bed.

I could barely wake myself to turn off my mobile phone alarm at six the next morning, although I did manage to stir enough to get out of bed. I felt like I was dragging my legs through wet sand; I was conscious, yet couldn't get up to speed with the ugly business of being awake. My bones were tired. Knitting needles probed my temples; I had a glue tongue and a deep, self-loathing grief in the pit of my stomach. Yoga was unthinkable in such a state. I went back to bed.

Lissen stirred, but said nothing.

'I can't,' I moaned. 'I just can't,' knowing full well the consequences but incapable of any other course of action, and fell like an oak back on to the mattress.

I woke two hours later, feeling horribly dehydrated and paralysed with self-pity. But I realised I could still make pranayama, so made my way, gingerly, in the sharp mid-morning sun, to the shala.

'So, how was it not to do asanas this morning?' Vinay said, only slightly pointedly, as I arrived. I explained that my body had simply refused.

'I understand,' he said kindly, but surely able to smell the booze on my breath. 'It happens to everyone at this stage. It is normal to be so tired. Your body has been through a lot, a lot it has never experienced before. And your mind too.'

Remarkably, once again pranayama revivified me but when I returned to the apartment after the session, Lissen and the boys had gone. There was a note on the kitchen table.

'Have gone to book flights.' No name, no kisses.

★   ★   ★

When they came home, and after we had put the kids to bed amid an atmosphere crackling with unspoken recrimination and contrition, Lissen and I sat down on the balcony to talk.

'I haven't bought your ticket,' she said. 'I don't know if you want to come with us or not, but I can't deal with this. It is up to you now. If you give up, and come with us . . . '

'I am not going to give up,' I said. 'I am really, really sorry about what happened. I am disgusted with myself. I just cracked. It won't happen again. I won't miss another day, I promise. Please don't go. I . . . I don't think I can finish this alone.'

Emil walked sleepily into the living room, confused by the fact that the toilet, which had been changing places on an almost nightly basis for the last two months, was still in the same place. I got up to help him, and left Lissen staring out at the church across the road.

Once Emil had relieved his bladder, still half sleeping, I tucked him back under his sheet, which he immediately kicked off because it was too warm. I stood for a while looking at him and Asger, who was sprawled out on the bed next to him and returned to the balcony.

Lissen and I talked into the night and, eventually, through a combination of pleading and promises, I convinced her to change her and the boys' tickets and stay. I finally, for the first time in my life, agreed that I had a drink problem, although I still could not concede that I was a full-blown alcoholic. In a way, that was part of the problem: if I had been a complete and utter soak, rather than a lousy part-time drunk, then the solution would have been clear (if not easy or pleasant): I would give up alcohol right now and for ever. It was just that, like many in my position, I couldn't quite bring myself to accept that label. Neither could I quite go as far as 'functioning alcoholic', although that is closer to the truth. I realise that admitting one is an alcoholic is the first step to recovery, and that without taking that first step many experts would say I was a lost cause, doomed never to take proper charge of my addiction. Equally, I cannot argue that I do not meet AA's criteria for defining an alcoholic — I very much do — but I have simply never been wholly convinced by those criteria. If you apply them strictly, I suspect that more than half the population would be alcoholics, which seems improbable, and though I know binge drinking and middle-class 'risky drinking' is on the increase, it seems to me 'alcoholic' is still too extreme a term for most people who drink in excess of the government health recommendations for alcoholic units per week. I may as well also admit here that neither do I consider alcoholism a 'disease'. It's not a disease. Without getting bogged down in semantics, can something be a disease if you can decide not to have it? What I have is a dependence, a weakness, a failure of character, a frailty, a chemical addiction: call it what you want, but it is not a disease.

I do agree, though, that a dependence on alcohol, even a relatively minor, sub-Fitzgeraldian one, lasts a lifetime; that if I was going to deal with this problem it would need to be an ongoing process requiring constant vigilance, constant application. Clearly, the previous day's reprehensible failure demonstrated that this would require a force greater than my own, feeble willpower — and more than Lissen's admonishments, this really wasn't her battle — to help keep me balanced on a day-to-day basis. Despite the previous day's rage against yoga, I already knew that there were elements of Vinay's teachings that could help with this. Even after just three weeks, the asanas had changed my body and how I felt about it. I had lost weight and a vague musculature was taking shape. I would hardly say I was addicted to yoga — besides, there seems little point in replacing one addiction with another — but I was convinced of the physical and psychological benefits of asanas. Through Vinay's instruction, I had seen what my body was capable of, which had given me confidence in myself, which in turn made me feel good about myself, which helped me push to achieve even more. This was a definite start, albeit frail and vulnerable progress towards feeling better about the world and my relation to it.

Nevertheless, I had fallen down badly. I had utterly disgraced myself, I had let down Vinay, my children, and my wife. I knew that this really was the last chance, I couldn't allow myself to screw up again. But to avoid that, I would have to get the better of a deep-seated compulsion which had been an important, even vital, element of my daily life since I had been a teenager. Alcohol had been a critical support and relaxant: my self-prescribed treatment for anxiety, angst and boredom; my off switch; my crutch; my therapist; my existential balm.

My hope now was that I would be able to use what I had learned at Vinay's shala not merely to remain dry for the rest of my time in India, but to return home with the tools to help me make a dramatic rupture in my relationship with alcohol and fill the wineglass-shaped hole in my life.

There were two options if I wanted to save my marriage and my family and, as Lissen had made starkly clear, these were what were on the line here: I could either vow never to touch another drop ever again — never taste another chilly, dry Riesling. Or feel the soothing, warm chest burn of a single malt. Never enjoy a warm sake with cool sashimi. Or the complex swirl of Château Magdelaine slowly lingering on my tongue. Would life be worth living? — or, perhaps even more of a challenge yet greatly preferable, find a lasting way to control my dependence and bring moderation and balance to my relationship with alcohol.

To do that, I had to address the reasons why I drank. There were several — to relax, for confidence, to relieve stress, out of sheer boredom, because I liked the taste, to be sociable — but prime among them was a need to switch off from my neuroses, anxieties and fears: fear of failure as a parent, writer, adult male; fear of illness; fear of disappointment and defeat; fear of life; and fear of death.

Iyengar writes,

The yogi fears none . . . Fear grips a man and paralyses him. He is afraid of the future, the unknown and the unseen. He is afraid he may lose his means of livelihood, wealth or reputation. But the greatest fear is that of death. The yogi knows that he is different from his body, which is a temporary house for his spirit . . . Though the body is subject to sickness, age, decay and death, the spirit remains unaffected. To the yogi, death is the sauce that adds zest to life.

Death as a sauce? I was quite some way from that, but the idea of achieving a sense of *equanimity* with regard to death seemed like the answer to so many of my issues, the root of many of my neuroses and preoccupations.

I was prepared to hope I might still achieve that, given time, but there remained the nagging feeling that something was still missing from the

294

salvation recipe. Asanas were one thing: I could understand how they helped make me flexible and thus more physically durable; how they massaged my internal organs and oxygenated my blood; and, as I have explained, how they helped boost my confidence and sense of well-being. But the meditative side of things was not progressing quite as well. I was finding pranayama — the breathing meditation — an ongoing struggle. I grew terribly impatient during the sessions, pretty much the opposite of what should have been happening. Of all the exercises, I only really warmed to the 'oms', not just because I was the undisputed 'om'-master, but because they, and they alone in the entire session, brought me the closest to achieving a true sense of stillness and peace. It was only during the 'oms' that I was able to clear my mind of the trivial clutter, the fear, the anxiety, the self-consciousness which cycloned in my mind. I was prepared to admit that I was missing something, or *misunderstanding* something about pranayama, but what? And if I still wasn't getting it at this stage, then when would I?

29

Launching a Kite

I vowed to leap out of bed the next day with a positive approach to my yoga practice, and did so, evacuating my bowels with gusto and striding forth in my holidaying actuary's outfit early that morning. Perhaps as a result, it was a day of genuine breakthroughs. I managed to maintain my breathing rhythm for almost the entire asana session and achieved some positions which had thus far defeated me. A couple still remained elusive, notably the killer Urdhva Dhanurasana, in which, lying on your back, you push your pelvis up into the air to form an arch with your hands facing towards your toes (I thought of it as the upside-down crab), and, of course, the headstand, Shirshasana, the grand finale of the asana session, which Vinay had not even allowed me to attempt. But when I lay down at the end of the session, I was beaming. A wave of elation washed over me and I began chuckling to myself, uncontrollably euphoric.

'Very strong today,' Vinay said to me as I left, making a strongman mime. I followed him into his office and asked if he had time to talk a little longer. There were a few things that had been puzzling me, as well as which I was eager to get to know Vinay a little better.

'You are not in as bad shape as you think,' he

said, as we sat down and I jokingly (fishingly) wondered if he had ever had as feeble a student as me. 'Your confidence was good today, you are working hard. I do have other beginners who come here like you. And, you know, yoga is not an external experience — we do not create something for others to look at, we do it only for ourselves.'

As I understood it, one of the key differences between Prana Vashya and other forms of yoga was its emphasis on constancy of breathing. When Vinay demonstrated the sequence of asanas, he often counted the breathing in and out to keep us steady. The rhythm was always the same, never deviating. Why was that so important?

'I want to give a continuous flow, to keep the energy going,' said Vinay, perching straight-backed on the edge of his chair, his face its usual solar glow of health and calm. 'Other types of yoga are more about getting you into a position, and staying there. With us, with every half-breath that you take I want you to realise your full potential, as much as you can.'

How you entered and finished each position was also important, another difference between Prana Vashya and other types of yoga, he said. It was all about maintaining a steady, meditative rhythm, a 'dynamic flow', he called it, which helped relieve the mind of the burden of monitoring your breathing.

'The basic goal of yoga is to reach a state where you experience an absence of the mind. But I am trying to find a path where we can see more than that. As you know, there are different stages — samadhi and so on — but I do not believe we can say that samadhi is the ultimate.'

'What, you think there is something beyond that?' (In everything I had read about yoga, samadhi was considered the ultimate goal, 'god-' or 'cosmic consciousness'.)

'There should be,' said Vinay, slightly bashful, as if confiding a secret ambition. 'If you look at Lord Shiva, it seems very interesting to me that he still meditates even though he has achieved samadhi.'

'Why do you think he continues?'

'That is what I want to know. I cannot say for sure, but I am very confident I can experience the best by staying on my path and working on it. I do believe in a higher power, that is God. A universal power, this power that is present in everyone. And I am not meaning religion when I say this, but the closer you can get to that energy, the more bliss you can feel.'

I told him about my reservations about spiritualism and religion, and talked a little of the different manifestations of religious observance we had seen on our travels around India, finally admitting to Vinay my atheism.

'I do think religion is a good guide and many of us need guidance in life,' Vinay said, unperturbed. 'There are many things which should be taken from Hinduism, and some which shouldn't. Whatever is good for you, whatever promotes you towards your goal. It is okay that you do not have any beliefs. You are moving towards enlightenment whether you like

298

it or not. You will definitely feel the spirit within you.'

'But I don't want to feel any spirit within me,' I protested. 'I don't believe such a spirit exists.'

'Ah, yes,' Vinay laughed. 'I understand, but you know the asanas and pranayama are good for you, right? You feel that, don't you?'

'Ye-es . . . '

'Well, that is enough for me. Whatever keeps people on a positive path.'

'This seeking of enlightenment in the Hindu manner,' I said, unsure whether to continue and risk offending him. 'I sometimes find it hard to respect. If you come from a Christian background, which is about sharing 'The Word', converting people, persuading people about a belief system, then spending so much time on introspection, on the self, can seem rather egotistical, selfish.'

'I understand, but with yoga the ego is a different concept to this. Let me explain. If you practise pranayama you will understand how to control your mind and therefore your ego. If you can come to understand yourself better, then you can understand others better and you will become a better part of society, and society will be better. Think of it like this: there are ten kites flying in the sky. You have one. Until your kite is in the air, you will focus only on it, but once it is in the air, you can focus on the other kites.'

'Like on a plane, when the oxygen masks fall down and you are told to take care of yourself before helping others?' It turned out Vinay had never been on a plane, but he got the gist, and agreed that, yes, it was similar.

I wanted to ask Vinay about the health benefits of yoga. I suppose I was testing him, trying to see if he would make any outlandish claims. 'Can it cure illnesses? I have heard some say it can reverse diabetes . . . ' (Thanks to its massive sugar and ghee intake, India is the diabetes capital of the world.)

'I do believe the asanas have the power to do that, yes,' said Vinay levelly. 'I have had students come off their insulin. It can also help arthritis. If I have a person who can breathe, I always say that I can improve them.'

What about cancer?

'It is definitely possible to prevent it. If the cancer is due to a build-up of toxins, of course it might be genetic, or it might be bad habits, but I believe yoga can at least remove the toxins.'

As we parted, I asked Vinay about his ambitions for the future, a hot topic among the other students. These days, the career options for young, charismatic yoga instructors with something new to offer are to head for the USA, make DVDs, write books and license their own brand of yoga to other instructors and make millions — Bikram Choudhury's eponymous 105 degree room method and John Friend's Anusara yoga being two cases in point. Was he hoping to snare a Hollywood star to sponsor a green card?

'No, no, I am not interested in material things, in fame or having a Mercedes,' he laughed. 'My personal development is more important to me. I am very much happy because, basically, my father's intention was to make me an engineer.'

I decided to chance a more hard-hitting question: Why were his classes apparently open only to foreigners? Wasn't that because he could charge them many times more?

'Oh, no, I do have classes for local people. I don't take them myself, my brother does. Local people don't come to this class because, for Indians, yoga is part of their life, for ever. The Indians who come to our classes do it for a very long time, not just one month. It would be difficult to integrate the two, you see.'

Finally, on a more personal note, I wanted to know why he wouldn't let me try the headstand.

'I am not letting you do the headstand yet because your strength is still not enough but when I see people practising for the first time I can judge and predict what they will be able to do after a while and I know that you will be able to do the headstand one day. I am very confident of it.'

30

La Raj aux Folles

Back at the apartment, Asger and Emil were playing with a recently acquired friend — the five-year-old girl who lived across the hall in a permanently shuttered, dark apartment, together with her grandmother. We'd made contact with them soon after arriving, as their front door was always open. According to our landlady, the girl's parents were both working in the Middle East, returning to Mysore only once every few months. The grandmother never seemed to leave the building, and lived in her nightie. She didn't speak any English, and her granddaughter had a limited vocabulary, but so happy were Asger and Emil to have a new playmate that they managed to overcome this, and were busy investigating the girl's impressive toy collection and showing her their rather less impressive one. The grandmother, meanwhile, sat passively on the floor surrounded by toys beside a playhouse which took up half of their living room.

The next day I returned to find both the girl and her grandmother in our apartment, the grandmother sitting on our floor eating her lunch. I smiled at her as I arrived in my usual unedifying sweaty and dishevelled post-yoga state, and she smiled back.

'My mummy coming home,' the little girl said,

smiling proudly. 'That's nice,' I said, although, rather heartbreakingly, she would claim this to me several times over the next couple of weeks, and I never did see either of her parents.

With Lissen at the yoga shala for her back-stretching class, afternoons were the time for me and the boys to explore Mysore. We rapidly exhausted the city's child-friendly attractions although, to be fair, they were more numerous and of a higher order than in most Indian cities. It has one of the biggest and best zoos in India, for a start, with the fattest cobra I have ever seen. Unlike every other zoo snake (which tend to be as active as draught excluders), the one in Mysore Zoo sits with its head up and its broad hood spread for lengthy periods of the day. As the three of us stood in a morbid trance staring at this monster, it suddenly struck me that, as these terrifying creatures lived naturally around Mysore, it was not unthinkable that there was a wild one within a few hundred metres of where we stood. On another of our visits, when again we found ourselves standing in awe in front of the cobra's cage, I asked a group of nearby Indians if they had ever seen one outside the zoo. A young man among them pulled his polyester trousers up above his ankles to reveal horrific scarring, apparently inflicted by a cobra which bit him while he was working in the fields just outside the city.

The cobra was, though, upstaged by the zoo's star exhibits, its white tigers, who prowled their cages in an autistic-catatonic state, driven insane by their captivity. And yet there were two other creatures who had the power to upstage even the tigers: my sons. Wherever we went in India, my job essentially became that of a secret service agent on presidential walkabout duty, fending off hands and photograph requests as firmly but politely as possible. Emil had taken to wearing a red felt bindi he had been given at a temple, which only excited even more attention, but both boys remained puzzled by the idea that complete strangers, whom they were never likely to meet again, would want to be photographed with them.

'But why do they want to take our photo?' Asger whispered to me, as a young courting couple stood woodenly behind him and Emil in front of the tiger enclosure one day, waiting for me to push the button on their camera. 'There are white tigers right there!' It was true, the other zoo guests were completely ignoring these almost mythical animals.

'Well, you are a bit different from the people they usually meet,' I said, groping for an explanation, then remembering the harmless but enduring pleasure of telling complete lies to small children. 'And, um, they think you are David Tennant.'

Ah, now everything fell into place. They thought he was David Tennant, of course. Asger is a devoted fan of Doctor Who. A week earlier, we had visited a nearby tailor, shown him a picture of Tennant dressed as the Doctor, and asked if he could knock up a similar four-button, single-breasted brown suit to the one he wore on

TV. Since collecting it a few days earlier, Asger had insisted on wearing the suit and a matching tie he found in Big Bazar, everywhere, despite the searing heat. To be mistaken for Tennant was, then, enormously gratifying for Asger, and from then on he was more than happy to accommodate anyone who wanted a photo, and even tried to press autographs on some.

The only place he agreed to lose the suit was at the city's water park, which was ironic given that the locals kept all their clothes on even when frolicking in the wave pool and on the water slides. Every single one of the visitors kept virtually every square inch of flesh covered. Thankfully, none of the pools were deeper than thigh height, otherwise countless waterlogged jeans and saris would have been responsible for a good few drownings, I'd imagine.

While visiting the city's vibrant, hundred-year-old Devaraja market — where, we finally figured out, everyone else did their food shopping — we had got to know one of the stallholders, Aariz. His stall had attracted the attention of Asger and Emil in the run-up to Holi because of its row of primary-coloured, conical mounds of powder paint, but Aariz also sold essential oils, perfumed with sandalwood, jasmine, orange blossom and dozens of other rare and costly aromas, as well as home-made joss sticks. We ended up spending a good hour sniffing through his stock that first day as Aariz sent his assistant to fetch us cups of hot, sweet chai (the start of an addiction for Emil, who is perhaps the last person on earth in need of a caffeine kick), and we always popped by whenever we were on one of our afternoon exploring missions in the centre of town.

One day, while Aariz and I were chatting about iPhones (his greatest dream was to own one), and sipping tea, I felt a stiff poke in my kidneys. I looked round to see a portly, middle-aged woman, caked in make-up, holding out a podgy, bejewelled hand.

'Give twenty rupees,' she said, in a deep voice as she towered over me. I shrugged. She clearly didn't need the money, so I wasn't about to give her a rupee.

'I think you should give her something,' hissed Aariz, clearly uneasy. 'If you don't there'll be many of them within minutes, all screaming. Really, please.'

I took another look at her. 'She' was, quite clearly, a 'he': a eunuch. I had read that eunuchs earned a living by threatening to create scenes in public, at parties and other gatherings where they could bring maximum social embarrassment. Part of me was tempted to stand back and let the full Raj aux Folles unfold. But there was no telling the lengths she might go to and she might well have friends nearby. Besides, I wasn't sure I was up to the intensive question-and-answer session I knew would ensue from Asger and Emil. In the end I gave her a note and she tottered away, stopping at each stall on her procession through the market.

Aariz invited us to dinner at his place one evening during our second week in Mysore. It turned out that he lived with his wife and two children, plus his unmarried sister, his brother and his brother's wife and three children, as well as his mother, in a three-room (plus tiny kitchen and a rudimentary toilet/bathroom), third-floor apartment in a rundown part of western Mysore. Aariz's family were Muslim, ranging in devoutness from Aariz, who wore loud Hawaiian shirts and was clean-shaven (though did not drink alcohol, he was keen to stress), to his brother, Arif, a gem dealer, who sported a large black beard, a shaven head and wore a kurta to down below his knees. 'We are like night and day,' Aariz grinned as he introduced us to Arif, who didn't speak English.

On the wall were devotional sayings and posters. One depicted 'miracles of Islam' — the word 'Allah' in Arabic had appeared, variously, on a tomato, on a fish's scales and in the shape of a baby's ear, and all were pictured, albeit fuzzily and with the telltale signs of Photoshop. I guessed the posters had been put up by Arif rather than Aariz.

The families welcomed us shyly and we sat on mats on the floor to eat, with our (right) hands, what turned out to be some of the most delicious food I tasted in all our time in India. The lavish spread had clearly cost Aariz's family a fair chunk of their weekly food bill. There was a spinach dish, a coconut curry, two pilaus, piles of chapattis and, most costly of all, a beef dish. Aariz joined us on the carpet, but his brother and the women of the family did not eat with us, watching instead through the window from the rooftop courtyard.

Aariz told us about the recent anti-Muslim

feeling in Mysore which had culminated in riots. 'Someone cut the head off a pig and threw it into our mosque,' he said, shaking his head. 'A nine-year-old boy died in the riots and in the end they imposed a curfew on Muslims. We couldn't go out in the evenings.' For a while he had had to close his stall completely.

'It's all political,' he continued. 'There's no bad feeling between Hindus and Muslims in Mysore, or India. My customers are mostly Hindu. All the other traders on Banana Street [the row of stalls in the market where he trades] are Hindu. There's no problem between us, it's all created by politicians.'

Lissen asked about Aariz's sister, and whether they were looking for a husband for her. 'Oh, we've been trying to marry her off for ages,' he said, rolling his eyes. 'But they all want these big dowries, a hundred thousand rupees one family asked for, plus motorbikes and all this, plus the wedding will be for three to five hundred people.'

I could not conceive how a family living eleven to a room could ever afford such an event. And I suspected that Aariz' shy, beautiful sister would remain single for some time yet.

31

Vinay's Story

I had another chance to talk to Vinay at the start of my last week on his course. This time his mother, Premalatha, sat in on the chat, a benign, silent, smiling presence. I wanted to hear how he had first become interested in yoga and he explained that it had happened when he was just seven. Vinay had seen a brochure his mother had brought home about a local class. This was at the time of the Barcelona Olympics.

'Basically my intention was to practise gymnastics,' he told me. 'I had seen the Olympics and that was my aim. There was no spiritual aspect for me. It was completely physical at that time.' To the seven-year-old Vinay, yoga looked like gymnastics, so he went along to the class, which was run by a man called Jalendra Kumar.

'Within six months I became a totally dedicated practitioner,' he said. 'Jalendra could see something in me, and helped and supported me. He is a very good man. He took me all over India from my first competition in the north when I was eight.'

The whole notion of competitive yoga was still confusing to me. How could you take something that was supposed to be an internal, meditative activity, and turn it into a competition?

'Yes, I understand what you are saying,' said Vinay. 'But yoga competitions are as much about publicising yoga and telling people about it as they are about the competition. There are parades and demonstrations, and it's a way to get young people interested. It is true, it could have become an ego thing for me, but I had good people around me.'

Eventually, Vinay gave up the competitions. 'I had won most of them,' he said, not boastfully but simply as a matter of fact. 'When I was eleven Jalendra introduced me to pranayama, and then I could really understand what yoga was. By the age of fourteen, I was taking my own classes. I wanted to develop my practice so that it would be a challenge not just to the body but for the mind as well.'

People saw Vinay practising his new form of yoga, and started to ask him to teach it to them. 'The changes I saw in those students was amazing, and that made me more confident about it and assured me that it would definitely help a lot of people. A few people did not really see it as a proper practice, they thought I was amusing or annoying and when my students used to give demonstrations many people said, 'How can you do this? This is not right.' I just used to smile. We were always able to show its benefits, which would always reassure me. I am not against Ashtanga at all but our vinyasas [a sequence of poses bookended by the Sun Salutation, and, for me, the most excruciatingly challenging element of the Prana Vashya cycle] are quite different and very new. In Ashtanga

310

there is more utilisation of one part of the body, like the arms, individual elements, but my focus was to work on the entire nervous system so that awareness should extend to every part of the body in movement, in every position from head to toes. I did not want energy to be focused and retained in one specific area. I wanted consciousness to flow around the body.'

I pressed Vinay to help me understand how the asanas could help me mentally, how they could help me change who I was and how I faced up to the world.

'It is really an approach to the mind as much as the body. Usually, when we get into situations of anxiety or stress the body tends to react; you breathe differently. So, my system is programming you right from the beginning, programming your mind so that you can control your breathing and then experience the same level of breath control to keep yourself level and in control whatever duress the body is going through.'

So, it was as much about building self-confidence and self-control as getting fit or strong?

'Precisely. How many times have you thought to yourself that you would have done better in a situation if only you had kept calm? If you had a bit of patience of mind, but you stressed yourself. Prana Vashya helps the mind to maintain its calm and balance at all times and through this to realise its full potential. What we do is to try to create a trend, not in the muscles, but in the nerves, so that it is instilled into you not to give up, that you can do it, you can perform these positions and hold them, while

311

breathing slowly, regularly. We are trying to increase your confidence levels at a nerve level. You are programming your body to be strong so that any new thing that it will face, you are prepared for it, you will have the confidence in your body to do it. If you can stay in these positions and breathe slowly five times, that builds confidence.'

'How is that different from being able to swim twenty lengths, or win a tough game of tennis?' I asked. 'Doesn't that also make you confident?'

'Yes, but in those cases you are using the body to work on something external: that is a different kind of work. With yoga it is completely within the self. You don't need any extra materials, any equipment, any external goal. It is working purely with the body to understand its capacity.'

I told Vinay that there had been a couple of moments in his class when I had experienced some kind of high. I hesitated to call it spiritual, it was as much physiological as anything mental, but I just felt, well, zingy, zesty, fizzy, chuckly. Happy, I guess.

'That is very nice to know,' he said. 'You know, there is no requirement for a leap of faith or anything religious here. What I want you to do is to have that feeling and try to enhance it and it will naturally bring the belief in you. It is a matter of acting it, then experiencing it. What happens usually, Michael, is our mind is constantly introducing distractions, we call them 'citta vrtti', that part of your mind which is constantly talking and thinking, so I will be talking to you, and you will be thinking about something else and that will be the citta vrtti. Citta vrtti can be helpful — it makes associations, helps you interpret what you are experiencing, helps creativity — but it is unhelpful if you are seeking awareness. So, what we try to do with the pranayamas and asanas is to try to reduce the citta vrtti. There are many layers in the mind and the citta vrtti is one. If you reduce the citta vrtti, this space cannot stay a vacuum, so it will be filled with awareness, another of the layers. Likewise, when there are thoughts, your awareness is reduced.

'You know, Michael, the mind is like how a cow eats. It swallows first, then, when required, it brings its food back to chew it, and again takes it back. The mind, ideally, should take a topic and try to analyse it later, but what happens for most of us most of the time is that it starts to digest instantly in the wrong way. Through yoga, you can digest things properly the first time, because you are present, you are clear, you are focused — you have fewer distractions.'

'But when we are doing asanas and pranayama, there is nothing to take in. We are achieving this state of clarity, but isn't it a waste?' I asked.

'No, it is preparation. You are being programmed. Your mind drifts, of course, while you are doing yoga, but it can't drift for too long otherwise you lose the breath. The way of breathing with Prana Vashya forces you to concentrate, it trains your mind to concentrate.'

'Like cleaning a dirty window?'

'It is more that, in pranayama for instance, we are giving you a grip to climb higher, like building a muscle. My basic goal before your time with me ends is for you to be able to focus clearly on what you are doing so you are less influenced and interrupted by the citta vrtti. The citta vrtti are the primary reason for experiencing stress. If you know how your mind is operating, then you have the capacity to control it. If your awareness is always outside, then you will forever be adjusting to the world. If your awareness is within, then you are in control. Pranayama helps you know how your mind works. If you can understand it, then the mind will become the basic supporter of your actions.'

'But I think I know my own mind by now. I should do at thirty-nine.'

'The mind you know is a different mind. That is your conscious mind, that's the one you have been working with. The unconscious mind has so much more potential.'

We talked some more, mostly about Vinay's childhood, with his mother still sitting smiling in the corner of the room. I knew from the other students that Vinay's father was ill. He told me that, when he was fifteen, his father suffered a major stroke, leaving him unable to work. Overnight, the family lost their only source of income.

'He was everything for our family,' said Vinay. 'My mother had not even been shopping alone. We had a money crisis. It was a great deal of stress and I could not understand it at that age. We had to work very hard.'

The father recovered — and these days is much improved — but for a while there was pressure on Vinay to become an engineer. It was Jalendra, his yoga teacher, who came to the rescue.

'He kept me going. He never doubted me. He is an amazing person. He used to take care of me, feed me.'

I actually got to meet Jalendra later on and, though his English was not good, I did manage to talk a little to him about what he remembered of Vinay in the early days.

'After three months I could see he was different. He properly observed the asanas,' Jalendra, a diffident but clearly warm-natured man in his late forties said. Jalendra had helped support Vinay's yoga career, taking him to the All-India Champion of Champions event in Ranchi where he competed against six thousand students of all ages, and won.

That was one important turning point for Vinay, Jalendra explained. But there was another: a controversy which I had already heard rumour of from several yoga students in Mysore, and which continued to reverberate throughout the city's yoga community. It was at a Mysore Rotary yoga event which had taken place six years before. Jalendra was to receive an award for his voluntary work teaching yoga to the poor of the city. 'But I am quite a quiet man,' Jalendra told me. 'I had never given a speech or had an award. I was nervous, and didn't really know what to say.'

Instead, he thought it would be nice to ask Vinay to give a display. 'His display would say everything I could not about my yoga,' Jalendra

315

said. The problem was, there was another guest of honour at that Rotary event. None other than the legendary yoga master, guru to Madonna, Sting and Gwyneth Paltrow among others, Pattabhi Jois, who was accompanied by his grandson, the heir to Jois' yoga empire.

For reasons still not quite understood by either Jalendra or Vinay, Jois took great umbrage when Jalendra invited Vinay to give a demonstration. Their guess is that Jois — who, though he preached the relinquishment of all possessions and attachments, cruised Mysore in a limousine and lived in some comfort — took it as an affront to his status. Who were these upstarts to try to teach the great Pattabhi Jois about yoga?

Jois stormed out, trailing his grandson behind him and never spoke to either Jalendra or Vinay again. Jois died in 2009, but Jalendra and Vinay were not invited to the funeral, and have not since spoken a word to his grandson, who continues to keep the Pattabhi Jois flame alight at his world famous Ashtanga Yoga Research Institute in Mysore.

'It was in the newspapers. It was a bit controversial. They were really angry,' says Vinay. 'All Jalendra wanted was to show his achievements through his students.'

For some reason I wanted to confess everything to Vinay. I had already, in his classes, exposed myself, and shed so very much of my dignity. I wanted to tell him about my drinking, and ask him how yoga might help curb my helpless appetites.

He listened in silence to this foreign man with

his alien weaknesses, weaknesses which he — a teetotal, vegetarian, highly disciplined yoga guru — couldn't possibly relate to or recognise.

'Becoming aware is the best thing, the best way to leave this behind,' he said. 'You are aware of the ill effects of your lifestyle. You are learning the importance of the body now that you have started your yoga practice. You know what your body is capable of. Now I want you, when you go home, to continue your practice — asanas and pranayama. Find an hour, two hours, every day . . .

'What? There's no way . . . I have work, I have kids . . . '

'If you do this, you will do everything else quicker, more efficiently. You will have freshness. You will be giving up the negative and preparing yourself to be more positive. You will get strength from your yoga practice. Haven't you noticed how your appetite has diminished since you started with me?'

I told him that some days I was living on nuts and yoghurt and feeling better than I had ever done.

'The energy you get from class replaces the energy you need from food. You only really need to eat once in a day, it is just a matter of keeping that internal system strong. Whenever you feel like alcohol, use that time to do pranayama, just half an hour to start with. It will expand on its own. You won't want to drink. Trust in me, trust in yourself.'

Trust wasn't an issue, it was more that the time Vinay was suggesting I spend every day on

317

asanas and pranayama seemed to me completely unrealistic. I couldn't set an hour and a half or two hours a day aside for introspection and self-improvement. Again I became despondent. If that was what it was really going to take to turn my life around, I truly was doomed after all.

32

Enlightening-up

While waiting for Vinay to open the shala for class one morning, I overheard Kim, the simple-minded Australian, talking with the crotchety New Yorker about a Transcendental Meditation course the latter was thinking of taking.

'It's, like, that California cult with the flying yogis, right?' said Kim.

'No, it's not a cult, it's just a really great meditation technique,' said the American, whose name was Emily. 'There's a whole town in America where they did it and crime rates dropped. It can cure depression, tension, stress and anxiety and help you concentrate better.'

My ears pricked up.

' . . . and Clint Eastwood has been doing it for years.'

I was sold.

'Hi, I couldn't help overhearing you talking. When is the course?'

'Well, I've been trying to reach the guy for a week,' Emily said. 'They say he is, like, amazing, and that he was one of the original disciples of the Maharishi [Mahesh Yogi, friend of the Beatles and inventor of Transcendental Meditation]. But I can never get him on the phone. They say he's in Bangalore, then they say he's teaching, then they say he doesn't exist on the number I have. If you want to try, here . . . ' she gave me a phone number on a scrunched-up piece of paper.

Over the next week I tried ringing the number ten or so times, each time getting a different person, each with a differently impenetrable Indian accent (it was their prerogative to speak with an impenetrable Indian accent, of course, this being India and all, but it was still frustrating). It didn't help that I had no name to ask for. Eventually, I was told that 'he' would be in the next day at five o'clock.

I rang at five. No answer. I rang again ten minutes after that, and every ten minutes for the next hour. Why I didn't just give up, as I would have done in ninety-nine out of a hundred similar situations (trying to get through to a human at my bank, for instance), I don't really know. I was intrigued, particularly by the claims I had subsequently been reading online that TM could 'still' the mind, not just during meditation itself, but in your everyday life.

The idea of meditation has always appealed to me in a 'reading about it and thinking 'Yes, I might like to try that. When I'm retired'' kind of a way. On the one occasion I had tried it, when Lissen bought me some very expensive meditation CDs (one of her earlier attempts to curb my drinking, I now realise), all they had succeeded in doing was to send me very expensively to sleep. Still, everything I had read about the effects of meditation seemed to chime with my own situation.

I rang the number again and, just as I was about to hang up, a quavering voice answered,

'Anantha Research Foundation.'

I explained that I had heard someone on the number offered Transcendental Meditation courses, and that I and some friends would like to sign up. We were to come the next day at four o'clock, the man said brusquely, spelling out an address in the centre of the city. Well, that was simple. So, the next day Kim, Emily (whom I had begun to warm to, now realising her prickliness was merely a form of conventional human discourse in New York) and I squeezed into an auto-rickshaw for the ride across town to a shabby, narrow street in the centre of Mysore.

'I heard that the Dalai Lama's right-hand man has to wear a weighted hat to keep himself from levitating away,' Kim said excitedly, as the auto-rickshaw crashed into a pothole, hurling all three of us up in the air.

We then spent some time walking up and down the street looking for anything which might resemble an Anantha Research Foundation, asking nonplussed passers-by for directions. At last we spotted a small, scratchy, handwritten sign outside an equally unprepossessing house. We poked our noses tentatively around the front door to find a glassed-in porch where an elderly man sat gazing out into space, with an elderly woman lurking in a corner in a similarly catatonic state. Was this some kind of retirement home? Or were they TM experiments gone wrong? We enquired about the Research Foundation, and the man tilted his head ever so slightly towards an unlit corridor at the rear of the building.

There, in a dark, book-lined room we found

321

Mandayam A. Narasimhan, Professor of Sanskrit and director of this, the (one-room) Anantha Research Foundation. He was a short man in his early sixties, dressed in a white cotton vest, with a dhoti wrapped around his plump belly, a shock of thinning, wiry, white hair and a thin red stripe — a Brahminical caste sign — bisecting his forehead. He smiled at us, his eyes crinkling in an amused twinkle, and welcomed us in a voice which bubbled with a chuckling undercurrent.

Three other students were already there in the low-ceilinged study: an almost unbearably sexy, young Portuguese couple — he in a dhoti, she in ethnic woven-wear — and an older Swedish woman of a similar tofu-and-tie-dye persuasion, with henna-ed hair, silver toe-rings and a nose piercing. They sat on the floor; Kim, Emily and I chose three wicker chairs at the back of the room. As we sat, I scanned the titles of the books which surrounded us. *Quietude of the Mind* was one of them. Next to it was *The Tao of Physics*. Next to that, a Bill Bryson. There were also piles of ancient brown Sanskrit texts scattered like autumn leaves over every surface.

'Is it okay to sit on chairs?' asked Kim nervously.

'The yogis advise that you do not sit on hard ground as it drains energy,' Narasimhan said, gesturing that we should sit.

Ha! I thought, looking at the pious floor-squatters.

Narasimhan sat on a slightly raised dais in front of us beneath a becalmed ceiling fan, a shrine to his left decorated with offerings of flowers and fruit. He folded himself up with his left foot placed to the right of his right knee and his right foot beneath his left thigh. One day, I thought, India will get around to connecting all those fans to an electricity supply.

'Welcome to the Transcendental Meditation Workshop,' he continued. 'This technique comes from Vedic times, it is very, very ancient but it was developed in the 1950s by the Maharishi Mahesh Yogi to improve health of individuals and promote world peace. It is a meditation technique which you practise twice a day for twenty minutes in order to eventually pass through seven states of consciousness.'

The first three states are waking, sleeping and dreaming, he explained. The fourth is transcendence, and then come 'cosmic consciousness', 'god consciousness' and something simply called 'unity'. Here we go again, I thought. If it hadn't been such an intimate gathering, I might well have snuck out.

Narasimhan continued. The Maharishi devised TM specifically to fit in with the lives of modern westerners. It did not involve any asanas, I was relieved to hear; instead we would use a mantra, spoken silently to ourselves, in order to descend, or 'transcend', into an ocean of pure consciousness. As I understood it, this ocean was rather like a cosmic National Grid; TM-ers prefer to claim it is just another name for the unified field with which quantum physics is so preoccupied. He was going to give us a mantra, he said solemnly.

'What is a mantra, exactly?' asked Kim.

His answer was refreshingly frank: 'In a way, it

is a nonsense. It has no meaning, but it has a very great purpose. It is a vehicle for silencing thought. With it you can dive deep down into your unconsciousness using the mantra as a weight. Modern society produces more and more tension in us. In the external world, the faster you are, the more you achieve, but in the internal world you must go slow: the slower you are, the more success.'

'Can't you just take a nap?' I asked.

'Sleep is not enough to take care of that imbalance, of that stress and tension and speed, but if you can meditate with a mantra for twenty minutes twice a day it relaxes the mind so that it can discharge and recharge. It is equal to five hours of deep sleep. The mantra is like an ultrasonic washing machine,' he continued, echoing my own experience with 'om'-ing. 'It cleanses the whole system. In twenty minutes you can dive down to the source of thought, which brings you to the site of least excitation. It is *not* sleep, because you are aware of things around you. It is fine to scratch and move during meditation, but as you go deeper you will breathe less, you will move less, over time you won't notice mosquitoes or itches, or whatever.

'Anxiety and stress are nothing but a lack of quietude. Every action produces anxiety of one level or another. The anxiety state is the energy produced to tackle any given circumstance, like the fight or flight response, for example, but it can also be on a much lower level. If you are already in an anxiety state, then you have to use even more energy to tackle the problem and you might not have any more energy, which is when stress is produced. What we are saying with TM is that, when you get into a more orderly state by becoming quieter, those old anxieties which have become stresses get smaller and your state of quietude is gradually restored. Most stresses are from anxieties which you cannot remove, past anxieties which you cannot get rid of and, as we age, these abnormalities increase because of certain emotional blocks which we create in ourselves. Children are flexible physically and mentally, but as you grow older you get stiff, locked up. You can relax with sleep but the sleep of today is not enough to remove those stresses. We have created a world of anxiety, all the phantoms in our mind. How do you tackle these phantoms? Yes, you can use tranquillisers or alcohol, but that can only exacerbate stress in the long term. They themselves become stresses, so you need a more natural process which is side-effect free, which can work for anyone, has no risks, no dangers, is a simple, quiet, slow process, not drastic.'

I persisted: 'But I can relax in my bath and solve a problem, or look out of a train window.'

'Right, right, but you cannot overcome all the mental noise of modern life that way. I always give this example: you are standing on one side of a busy street trying to talk to a friend on the other side. You have to shout to be heard above the traffic, but if there is no traffic, he can hear you even if you whisper. The more noise, the more difficult it is to concentrate. Yes, you can sit and think about a problem, but most people only come up with the same, or temporary solutions. TM helps you find another more creative path. Possibilities become apparent if your mind goes into a quieter state.'

The mantra (*man* is Sanskrit for 'mind', *tra* means 'control' — mantra is actually the plural for the singular *mantram*), replaces your thoughts, he said and, because it is a mumbo-jumbo word with no rational or emotional association it has the effect of wiping clean or silencing your mind. As you meditate, your body enters a deeply relaxed state with body function levels similar to those of deep sleep. 'Think of it as a teacher entering a class,' said Narasimhan. 'Everyone goes quiet.'

'Why do we all have to have a different mantra?' asked the Portuguese girl.

'It is like medicine. It is different for different people. I will select a mantra for each of you. I have been doing this for forty years and seen perhaps 30,000 people. I assess people instinctively.' We all made suitably impressed noises. 'In my everyday life I must turn off this instinct otherwise I become like a garbage bin for everyone's thoughts.'

'Do you mean to say you can read minds?' I asked. Narasimhan made a gesture as if to say, 'All in good time', adding enigmatically: 'If people knew what I can see and know about people, they would be too scared to come here.'

He told us all to stand up, then placed a flower in each of our hands, before performing a brief puja at the shrine in the corner of the room, placing a banana and coconut in front of a hazy black-and-white photograph of a man (I later learned this was Brahmananda Saraswati, or 'Guru Dev', the Maharishi's guru), lighting a lamp, and wafting it gently while singing a quiet prayer. Having taken back the flowers from us, he sent us out of the room, before calling us individually to receive our mantra.

Outside, there was palpable excitement about the whole mantra business.

'I know a lady whose tenant went to do meditation in Sri Lanka. She came back insane!' said Kim, frowning.

I wondered aloud about how Narasimhan chose our mantras. The Portuguese man said with some authority that the mantra-giver allocated them according to the person's age, height and marital status, all of which we had revealed on a form we filled in early on in the session. The Portuguese girl came out, having been given her mantra, looking suitably serene. Then it was my turn.

The room was even darker now. Narasimhan was sitting on his dais. He beckoned me to sit on the floor in front of him and then told me my mantra (they call this 'passing the mantra') in a low voice, and asked me to repeat it twice to check that I had heard it and could pronounce it correctly.

Mantras are supposed to be secret. You must never utter your mantra out loud. When meditating you are only supposed to say it inside your head, and you must never share it with anyone else. This is not because anyone believes it has any magical or mystical powers in itself;

more that if you enter into a dialogue with someone about it they may bring some amusing or unpleasant association to bear which could diminish the mantra's efficacy. Such as: 'Ha, that sounds like my boyfriend's nickname for my vagina,' or 'What? Your mantra rhymes with Bury St Edmunds?' and so on; consequently, you will forever think of that person's genitals or home town every time you attempt to meditate — genitalia and East Anglian market towns being precisely the kinds of things you are trying not to think about.

That was all fine as far as I was concerned. Quite logical. In fact, I was already beginning to buy completely into the whole principle and practice of Transcendental Meditation. Clear your mind, wipe the slate clean and find a calm centre within for twenty minutes, two times a day? It sounded precisely what I was looking for. I could easily imagine it helping with stress, concentration, focus and anxiety, and I was willing to introduce it into my life forthwith. That wasn't the problem.

The problem was my mantra. I hated it. It was an endless, strangled, vowelly moan — roughly approximating to: 'Aayieeenggh'. (Incidentally, if that *is* your nickname for your vagina, this may be the root of those relationship problems you are probably experiencing.)

So, there I was in the midst of this quasi-sacred, potentially life-changing moment, and all I could think of was, 'I bet he gave the Portuguese girl a much better mantra than that.' I looked at him, having repeated the mantra softly out loud twice to his satisfaction.

'Any questions?'

'Well, erm, what if I don't, you know, *like* my mantra? What if I really, really do *not* like it?'

'Time. Give it time,' he said, chuckling. 'It's fine that you don't like it. I have chosen it for you. Don't forget, it is best not to meditate after a meal or you will probably fall asleep, or before sleep because it will give you energy and you won't be able to sleep.'

And that was that. I left the room, holding the door for the Swedish woman to receive her, doubtless, really cool, exotically Indian-sounding mantra. When everyone had received their mantras, we all filed back in to try them out.

'Close your eyes, and try to clear your mind. Do not say your mantra out loud and do not actively decide to say your mantra even in your head, just wait for it to come. You can wait a couple of minutes if you have to, don't worry,' he said. 'It is important not to strain to retain the mantra. It is like waiting for a bus. Watch the traffic pass, watch your thoughts pass. Don't worry if you only get to say it a few times.'

We sat in silence, and repeated our mantras to ourselves for a few minutes. Mine didn't improve with repetition, indeed, I found that I could not repeat it, even silently, without my tongue spasming in sympathy with its tortured syllables. Mosquitoes buzzed and tickled my legs. I had an itch on the side of my head. Then one on the back of my hand. I adjusted to ease a thigh cramp. Soon I began to get all cross, which even I could see wasn't the point of meditation.

Narasimhan brought us gently round after just a few minutes, with some more words of advice.

'It is not important to pronounce the mantra properly, and don't worry if your mind wanders. Let it wander, watch it wander, then allow it to return.'

We tried again, this time for fifteen minutes. Ordinarily, when you practise Transcendental Meditation alone, you are not allowed to use a timer to tell you when the twenty minutes are up, or get anyone to disturb you; nor are you supposed to meditate for longer than twenty minutes. You are meant to gradually gauge the time internally (something I struggle with to this day: twenty minutes can seem an absolute eternity when you are sitting with your eyes shut). This time, though, Mr Narasimhan led the session, bringing us round after fifteen minutes by gently suggesting we stop repeating the mantras to ourselves, pause in silence for a couple of minutes, then massage our eyes awake.

So, were there white lights and searing insights? Well, no, not really. My hands went curiously numb, as if they were no longer there, and I felt a strange, headachy tension deep at the front of my brain, which then receded, but the most striking thing was how intensely difficult it was to maintain the mantra. It was like a big, new bar of Lux soap, slipping constantly from my grasp as other empty, air-headed thoughts elbowed it aside. It felt odd, then frustrating, then calming and, every so often, briefly, something else: for a couple of moments I did experience a slightly exciting, slightly alarming, plummeting sensation, akin to the one you sometimes get just as you are falling asleep, except this didn't culminate in sleep, nor did it seem to be heading in that direction. I was plummeting towards another place altogether. Curious . . . But, crucially, TM was not nearly as boring as pranayama. And, against all the odds, my mind seemed, potentially, to be an interesting, enjoyable haven to retreat to.

This is how David Lynch, a prominent advocate of TM, describes his first ever meditation:

> It was as if I were in an elevator and the cable had been cut. Boom! I fell into bliss — pure bliss. And I was just in there. Then the teacher said, 'It's time to come out; it's been twenty minutes.' And I said, 'IT'S ALREADY BEEN TWENTY MINUTES?!' . . . It seemed so familiar, but also so new and powerful . . . It takes you to an ocean of pure consciousness, pure knowingness. But it's familiar, it's you. And right away a sense of happiness emerges — not a goofball happiness, but a thick beauty.

I can kind of see what he means. I certainly experienced the elevator sensation, but the twenty minutes seemed an absolute eternity to me, albeit an enjoyable, at times scary, but mostly relaxing one. Lynch also talks in his book, *Catching the Big Fish*, about the creative benefits of TM; only once has an actual, concrete idea come to him during meditation, but it does bring him a clarity which helps him 'catch ideas' during his conscious life.

'So, your homework for tomorrow is to meditate two more times for twenty minutes at home. Don't forget, no alarm clocks, you need to train yourself to know when to stop after twenty minutes. I do need to assess you before you go,' Narasimhan said in conclusion. 'If someone is having a history of drug or alcohol use it can go very wrong indeed, so I need to monitor.' Did I imagine it, or did he look specifically at me when he said this?

Perhaps the effect of my TM introduction kicked in sooner than I expected. As I walked home that evening through the patchily lit streets of central Mysore I felt almost as if I was seeing India for the first time, and with more tolerant, less fearful eyes. In fact, I would go as far as to say that I fell in love with India during that twenty-minute stroll home. Front doors were opened and lives spilled out on to the dusty roads as kids played and elders sat chatting on plastic garden chairs. The day's work having been accounted for, the people of Mysore were now getting down to the important stuff of life: food, conviviality, a smoke, a chew, a spit and a gossip.

Before we had left home, people had told me that it would take a good two weeks to adjust to life in India but, in truth, until now I had held it at arm's length. I had been afraid of India, afraid of sickness, of theft, of injury, of guilt, but also of what it might do to me, with its surfeit of spirituality, its cacophony of ritual and belief; and afraid of how it might change me, for better or worse. I had locked the doors and windows to it all, but now I wasn't so fearful or intimidated.

A blizzard of stars pricked the pitch black sky. I looked up at the crescent moon, felt a warm gust of evening air and listened to the rip of two-stroke engines as children scurried beneath the yellow lights. For the first time, this whole glorious, shouting mess of a country felt like a place I wanted to return to, over and over, for the rest of my life.

33

A Message to Michael

Asger and Emil had not had their hair cut since landing in Delhi almost two and a half months earlier. They were beginning to look like they were auditioning for an am-dram *Jesus Christ Superstar* — in stark contrast to the short, neatly trimmed, and often heavily oiled hair of most Indian boys. So, one afternoon, I took them out to try to find a barber. After they had vetoed a couple of barbershops on the grounds of their lengthy queues and being 'a bit stinky', we finally found a suitable-looking place on a parade of shops near us: it was scruffy and dark but, crucially, it was empty apart from the two chubby, unshaven men who worked there and were mooching around waiting for custom.

I sat Asger first, then Emil, down in one of the barber's chairs for 'a bit of a trim, not too much off, but still quite short'. Chubby Bloke One (clearly the senior partner), did a fine job. I'd go as far as to say they were the best haircuts they had ever had, and cost just thirty pence each. So, naturally, when I needed a trim myself, I popped back to Chubs and Co.

'Sorry, sir, we are having power cut,' Chubby Bloke Two, alone in the shop that afternoon, told me. This was a problem as I wanted my hair cut close all over with electric clippers. I was about to leave when he grabbed my elbow.

'Sir, sir, please be waiting. Electricity come again soon. Five minutes.'

I didn't have much else to do, so I put my bag on the counter and sat and read some Bollywood magazines. Chubby Bloke Two sat and watched me expectantly. After a while, he stood up abruptly and said, 'Like face massage? Very nice. Very relax.'

Well, I thought, I've never had one of those. Might as well. It's hardly likely to cost much. So I sat as he slathered aggressively perfumed pink almond cream over my face and began to rub. Did he really need to use so much cream? I wondered as he smeared my eyes shut. Had he mistaken me for a cross-Channel swimmer? After a few minutes kneading my cheeks, he stopped for a moment. I could still hear his fatty breathing and, then, a rustling of clothing as someone else scuffled into the shop behind us. I grew suspicious and managed to prise one eye open and peer through the pink haze just in time to catch sight of the hairdresser's sausage fingers making their way into my bag which — foolishly, I admit — I had left open on the counter with a few rupee notes clearly visible.

'Wha — . Whoah there!' I said, sitting up and catching a glimpse of myself looking uncannily like a startled Barbara Cartland in the mirror. 'What are you doing?' I looked around to see a pair of heels scampering out of the shop.

'Just pushing money in, sir,' the man said, backing off. 'Didn't want it to fall out. I wasn't stealing it. No, no, no. No problem sir, no worry.'

'Well, it looked like you were taking it, I don't . . . ' I paused. He hadn't stolen any money. I knew I had three 100-rupee notes, and they were all still there. Plus, the electricity had just come back on, and I did need that haircut. I could kick up a fuss and get the police involved but, really, I would have done precisely the same in his position. A couple of hundred rupees is probably a day or two's wages for him. What was it for me? A couple of glasses of wine?

So I wiped the rest of the almond cream off, he cut my hair and, afterwards, seeming to have entirely forgotten his attempted larceny, charged me twice as much as he had for the kids.

From the barber's, I had to get across town for another lesson with Mr Narasimhan. I walked for a while, thinking I knew the way through Mysore's relatively straightforward grid of streets, but soon got lost. I asked directions from a man who was just climbing on to his motorbike. He started to explain the way I should go, but it seemed I was further from the Anantha Research Foundation than I'd thought. Seeing my dismay, the man said, 'Look, why don't you climb on, and I'll take you?'

'What, on the bike?' I said.

I am extremely scared of motorbikes. Possibly more than I am of spiders or nuns.

'Yes, it is no problem. I can go that way with you. I have time.'

I couldn't really refuse and I felt that, following directly on from my unfortunate experience at the barber's, it was almost as if India was trying to send a message, to make amends. So, I agreed. The motorcycle Samaritan — whose name was Rajiv — took me, safely, right to the door of the Research Foundation, dropped me off without asking for anything for his trouble, and we parted with a handshake.

The other students were already waiting in reverential silence in Narasimhan's vespertine study. Emily and Kim had moved down on to mats on the floor. I sat where I had before, on a wicker chair at the back of the room. Our second session started with questions and comments on our experiences meditating at home.

'My lips went funny,' the Portuguese girl complained.

'I drank coffee, but didn't like it. Why?' asked her boyfriend.

Narasimhan, in the same dhoti and white vest as before, nodded to himself as if giving all this great thought, ignored them, and began to talk instead about the scientific research into TM which showed that it decreased blood pressure, and then about how it changed the energy patterns in the brain. People who have meditated for some years develop larger frontal lobes, he said. This is the area of the brain considered to be where your memory resides (or at least, the better your frontal lobes function, the better your memory; I checked up on this and it has been confirmed in research by a Dr Andrew Newberg of the University of Pennsylvania). Meditation has also been proven to strengthen your prefrontal cortex, the part of the brain which is most damaged by the distractions of the modern age, like the internet, endlessly flicking TV channels, or checking every five minutes to see how many people haven't visited your blog. Meditation calms the prefrontal cortex and this, the theory goes, improves one's ability to concentrate.

The Swedish woman, who had been growing more and more restless during all this, interrupted to confess that she had fallen asleep while trying to do the homework meditation the night before.

'Do not worry! Go to sleep!' Narasimhan laughed. 'After sleep, do ten minutes' meditation. And if you get disturbed, open your eyes, stare at a distant point, close your eyes and start again. Out of twenty minutes, you will only be properly meditating for five to eight minutes, usually, but that's okay.'

'Can you use meditation to deal with bad stuff in your head?' asked Emily.

'Not exactly. You can't use it to catharticise bad memories. You can't say, 'I'm going to sit down and think about a dead friend,' but after perhaps three years you will be able to use the mantra to meditate on certain issues, to solve problems.'

'My mantra goes to the back of my mind,' interrupted the Portuguese girl.

'What is at the foreground?'

'Thoughts.'

'So, switch it around. Sometimes your thoughts will be in the foreground, sometimes in the background. Don't worry.' He flapped his hand. 'I am not asking you to throw thought out and hold on to the mantra, it will come back of its own accord, don't worry.'

'So, when I try to use my mantra to drive away thoughts, like some kind of psychic machine gun, that's wrong, is it?' I asked.

'If you actively use the mantra to block thoughts you will get pain in your temples. I know it seems foolish to the rational mind to repeat something that has no meaning. If you prefer, I know a teacher in Bombay who tells their students to concentrate on a vision of a blue egg . . . In a sense it doesn't really matter — whatever works — but the rational mind is your biggest block. Beyond that, beyond the sensory realm, is an ocean of consciousness. Have faith in your mind.'

Now there was a challenging concept. I had all but lost faith in my mind — in its ability to concentrate, to create, to function beyond the hummingbird caprice of my voracious, pleasure-seeking synapses.

'Anyway,' he continued. 'What thoughts are you trying to drive out?'

'Anxious ones, I suppose. Fears.'

'We are all anxious about the future, about survival. If you can get rid of that, then you are a yogi. Many of our fears are linked to our attachments, to things and people. So why not get rid of your possessions, renounce the world, renounce the system? Get rid of your car,' he chuckled. 'There will always be someone to take you where you want to go. Ultimately, you won't even want to speak.'

I was about to ask him whether he was serious about this when Emily asked a question.

'I feel I get really angry when I meditate,' she said.

'If stressed during or after meditation . . . we prescribe ice cream,' he laughed. 'Eat ice cream! The anger will go. In the morning your meditation will give you energy. At the end of the day, it will calm you.'

Narasimhan led us in another meditation practice, after which we filled in another questionnaire ('Did you notice improvement in relations with others?' 'Did your thoughts disturb you?'), and the session ended.

I lingered, waiting for the Portuguese girl's inane questions about what clothes to wear while meditating and whether it was safe to drive afterwards, and asked if Narasimhan had time to talk. He responded as if he had been expecting this, and showed me into a smaller room, his home, across the corridor.

34

Things More Pleasurable than Hair Transplants

Here, we sat in the half-light, me on a rattan chair, he on a small divan. I looked around the room. It was no more than five metres square with peeling paint, electrical wires hanging from wounds in the walls and no natural light. Narasimhan's worldly possessions amounted to a small fridge, a kettle, a wardrobe and a small desk. He smelled of cloves and cardamom. I asked how he first discovered Transcendental Meditation.

'I was among the first disciples of the Maharishi in the 1970s. I came from a family of teachers of philosophy going back eight hundred years. My father, grandfather, uncles, all were on a devotional path. My father decided that there were no clear yoga fields which were for ordinary people — to do it you had to be a monk and go to the Himalayas to practise — so when the Maharishi came on the scene, he said, This is it! And they signed me up for it. There is an Indian belief that if one son in a family becomes a yogi, then one hundred generations before and after will be purified, so they said, Let's send him and all our sins will be washed!

'The Maharishi adapted ancient techniques in a modern way and caught the imagination of the youth. Here was a man who could show us we were transcending with a machine! So it was very captivating. I had the privilege of conducting many courses. I became very close to him. In those days we all slept in a big room together.'

Naturally, I wanted to hear the inside story on the scandals which dogged the movement and the Maharishi right up until he died, while living in great luxury in the Netherlands in 2008. The Maharishi was fond of women; some, including Mia Farrow who had first-hand experience of fending off his advances, say he was a bit of a sex pest; also he became phenomenally wealthy, which would seem to be at odds with the Vedic teaching in which his technique had its roots. Others have said his organisation took on the air of a cult.

'By the 1980s the organisation became very big and, you know, as it becomes more popular the leader loses his contact with the masses. I used to talk to the Maharishi about what was happening and he just said we are all at different levels of evolution, there are contradictions in everyone. He was very forgiving. He was aware people were taking advantage of him, but he would never punish them. There was a classic example once: he asked me to bring the beggars from the banks of the Ganges to the ashram, give them soap and toothpaste, provide them with all their basic necessities. And we did. For fifteen days everything was fine, but then the beggars started fighting among themselves over the free things. I went to the Maharishi and said, 'Why should we treat these beggars like this, they are of no use', and he said simply, 'These people ran away from their homes because they could not cope with society, but if they practise yoga they will become great. If only one takes something out of this, then I am happy'. In fact ten stayed and ninety left.'

Narasimhan returned to Mysore in the early 1980s; the Maharishi's ashram was reclaimed by the forest, the government having terminated its lease amid public disapproval of the sexual chicanery which allegedly went on there (although Narasimhan says that the government was implementing a reforestation programme, and this was always planned). Since then he has dedicated himself to translating and preserving thousands of ancient Vedic texts written on rapidly disintegrating palm leaves — there is a whole building full of them in Mysore, apparently, and another in Calcutta. He believes they may contain valuable wisdom on subjects ranging from medicine and health to astrology which could be of use to us today.

'You talked earlier about not having a car,' I said. 'And how there will always be someone prepared to give you a lift, but if everyone checked out of society like that, then it wouldn't function. Someone has to own the car. Provide the food . . . '

'There is always another generation coming through. I am not talking about the young giving away everything they own but, as you know, in the West there are many people with a car who are so old they cannot drive. It is those people who should let go because there is no need for them to keep up with this race, to try and stay young. They are stuck in their youth but their body is old, and that produces a pressure. You should shift your activities according to your age and what you want and expect from life.'

'But when I get to sixty-five or whatever, I like to think I will have deserved that big car, the holidays in the West Indies, the hair transplant,' I said.

'But we in India think that there are things that are much more pleasurable than hair transplants,' he laughed. 'And, you know, one day you will get too old to properly enjoy these things. You will be too old to travel on holiday to Rome, and what I am telling you is that I have a method by which you can sit wherever you are and be happy. You can travel anywhere you want to go within your mind. So what I am trying to prepare you for — and the earlier you start, the better — is to be strong enough to play in the world as you like, but also to get ready for when your body is weak and not to get stuck in any age — that is like being mentally retarded. So while old people in the West are struggling to look after themselves, and the cosmetic companies are enjoying the profit, what you must understand is that these trappings, ultimately, bind you and you must know that one day you will have to release yourself.

'When you are younger you are interested in specific questions — how will I make money, how will I become successful, how will I marry and have children? When you are older it is usually a more broadly negative reflection — the

344

country is going to the dogs, the younger generation are doing things wrong, and so on. With Transcendental Meditation and yoga we always try to prepare you for a more positive view so that you won't feel miserable. I may still think that the world is going to the dogs, but here in my room, why should I worry, why should I suffer? It is about reaching that kind of equanimity, of accepting negative or positive.'

'So you are saying, essentially, once you get to fifty you should give up on life, give up on the world?'

'No, no. Before fifty you are over-eager to change the world and you think you can transform it, and then you fail — and that, I'm afraid, is inevitable — and you will be frustrated. But I want to teach people to accept their failures, to take them with a pinch of salt. Wouldn't that be wonderful? So you won't have all those aggressively sad feelings of frustration you had when you were thirty. There comes a smoothing out of ambitions and activities as you age. That is how it should be, and with yoga you don't get stuck in the negative, you learn always to be positive and contented, whatever happens. You do whatever you have to do but do not worry about the effectiveness of the results so much.'

'Is this what you meant when the other day you said that we should give to beggars and not worry about how that beggar will use the money?' I asked. This had been troubling me because of our own experiences.

'Yes, absolutely. Know your limitations. Know

345

your duties and how much you can do, and stop at that. I have never married, never had children. I am a bachelor throughout my life. I have relinquished everything. I do not miss possessions. I welcome them if they come, but I don't feel I have to possess things. A car? That is a vehicle to transport me with least physical effort to some other place, so any car or horse-drawn thing will do. My room is modest, as you can see, but I don't need anything. I know I am getting older physically — I am sixty-six — I am not worried. I am not worried by how much people pay for my course — we say students should make a donation.[1] I have desires and ambitions to see projects through, as with the ancient texts I work with, but these things are not an essential part of my life. This is where the yoga system helps you to modify yourself. It teaches you to make your attachment to the most permanent, enjoyable entity, which is yourself. That is the trick. That is what spiritualism is, not all these temples and chanting: these are only external aids, guides to put you on the track of self-realisation.'

'So why all the silly rituals? Why have you got twice as many temples as schools in this country? Yesterday on the TV I saw that a girl was married

---

[1] In the West, trained TM instructors charge hundreds of pounds for the four-day introduction course, which the Maharishi used to defend, very cleverly, on the grounds that, the more people paid for something, the more seriously they took it.

off to a dog because an astrologer said it would be a judicious thing to do. What does that have to do with enlightenment?'

'Ritual helps people to enter into spiritualism on one level. You bring flowers to your lover at the beginning to attract her. Later on you bring flowers to her in gratitude. It is the same with religion. At the start, we go to the temple because we think we can get something out of it. Later on, we go in gratitude because it has given that something to us. When you go in gratitude, you have become spiritual.'

'But I rejected all the window dressing long ago. Why haven't you?'

'I enjoy the window dressing and, for the poor, for the uneducated, all of this is a means for them to enter spirituality. You do accept, don't you, that people have different levels of intellectual ability?'

'We-ell . . . '

'Come on. Around the world, how many people are actually really rational? The majority are caught at some level or other by distractions, but to bring them back I use those very distractions so that they come towards me. You rationalists are as bad as the religious because you are trying to impose an intellectual analysis which the ordinary human being is incapable of taking.'

'You are talking about blind faith, but when is anything blind good?'

'Yes, there is no evidence of God, but it makes your life easier if you believe. You have faith in other areas of your life, why not this one? You believe your employer will pay you at the end of the week, and he believes you will do your job. In a restaurant, you believe the food will be served. You believe that we are made up of electrons, neutrons, protons, but you cannot see them, right?'

'Oh come on, scientific knowledge is available to all. It is properly proven.'

'Yes, but how many avail themselves of that evidence? I have not personally carried out Newton's experiments, but I accept them. People are generally prepared to accept certain things this way.'

'But . . . ' I was about to point out that it is possible for him to test the theories, if he wants to.

'You will tell me that it is at least possible for me to test these theories, if I have the equipment and so on. I will come to that — although, has anyone proven the Theory of Relativity? But I accept these theories because the intellectual society or a group which I admire and trust has accepted them. This is faith, what I call faith. If I believe in a statement without doubt in my mind or the need to verify it by myself, that, in India, is faith. Blind faith is just something that cannot be rationally proved, cannot be experienced.'

I opened my mouth to point out that this was just another definition of blind faith, but he continued.

'And you will say, 'Aha! That is blind faith,' but in India we have yoga and other techniques by which the scriptural authorities which have come to us can be verified at a rational and experiential level. Yoga practice will tell you what is true and what is not true. It is all in the practice of asana, pranayama, meditation.'

'But how — '

'It will happen by itself. You will see. Trust me. You will know when you get there, as with love, when you start witnessing your own mind. Things will happen in three to six months. You will be scared, that is why you like to be in your own cocoon, but why stick in these three dimensions, Michael, why not go for the fourth, or the eighth dimension? Why stick to three? Your anxiety will always be there when you voyage into the unknown. Think of Columbus with his ancient equipment. You think that yours is a single life,' he said and smiled broadly, shaking his head ruefully, wagging a finger in mock admonishment. 'But mine is a multiple life. In this life I might only get as far as the window dressing, but some day, some life, I might reach the core.'

'Why not encourage everyone to get to the heart of the matter in this life instead of being mired in all that ridiculous, impenetrable ritual?'

'Because there is not always the intellectual capability. That is not patronising. That is a fact. Hinduism might appear ridiculous and impen-etrable to you but it is a religion which has been designed to suit the masses at all levels of intellect. It is not impenetrable because of a dictum on impenetrability, there is always penetrability — you just have to know how. It is fluid, it is not black and white, but grey and, to an outsider, very confusing because it tries to give every individual his own religion: nobody is left out. But for nobody to be left out, it necessarily has to be amorphous. Rationalism grew out of a stark disappointment in Europe — that God had let you all down in World War I and World War II. Think: people went to their places of worship to get relief, but many were shot in those places of worship, whereas in the East we didn't have such calamity.'

'Well, you may not have had a holocaust but I look around me here in India and see the most godforsaken place on earth.'

'Yes, because we left everything to God! That is what has gone wrong. Whereas, in the West, everything was left to the individual, and that is why individuals suffer mentally so much today. You feel, you rationalists, that the failures of society are your personal failures. This is why duty and responsibility should go hand in hand — in India we place responsibility on God. Our scriptures say that humans have been given the capability of managing themselves and should call on God only if a problem arises that is beyond our capability. But Indians, oh, we call God every time for *all* problems! This philosophy that God will take care of everything only came in the last two hundred years because we were dominated by a foreign power which we did not know how to overthrow. So we started accepting this God, the psychology of the people was defeated, we lost the will to protest, until Gandhi came along. The British drained our economy and also tried to impose their culture on us through education but I say they could do this only because we were vulnerable to it. We could have protested, but we took an escapist philosophy rather than a confrontation philosophy. Look, I know you like to think of yourself as rational, as thinking things through, but pursuing the rational path blows your ego up into the universal ego.'

'Because you think you can learn everything, know and understand it all?'

'Yes. You can do anything. But there comes a point when your rational ego leaves you because you get old, your physical capabilities desert you. That is when you get the phenomenon of devotional rationalism — when old people go back to religion to compensate for the pain of not being rational. Of course, if you remain totally, brilliantly rational, when you become physically weak you just take poison.'

'You mean euthanasia. Martin Amis says we should have euthanasia booths on every street corner . . . '

'Well, as long as you are satisfied with your life, yes, you should be able to choose to end it, but you should not take away your life out of desperation. Self-surrender is different: that is saying, 'I have done everything that can be done, I am satisfied with all the things that have happened to me, I don't want to be a burden on society.' That is total detachment. In Indian philosophy, this is the ultimate. As long as you do not do it with regret, I have no objection to suicide.'

'I know exactly how this next question is going to make me sound, but how long will it take before I see an improvement?'

'Oh, there are too many factors for me to judge that. Whether you are an extrovert or introvert for instance, but internally you will know when you cross the Rubicon.'

'What an annoying answer.'

'Yes! Okay, look, if I knew about your whole life I might be able to tell. Emotional people just jump in even if they haven't understood it. Rational people analyse it too much. The best is a balanced person, they achieve faster. There has to be the balance between the left and right hemispheres of the brain. You will get there. I have complete confidence in you.'

By now we were sitting in virtual darkness. I could see only the gleam in his eyes from reflected light. 'I have taken up too much of your time,' I said. 'I should go. Thank you.'

'No, no, I can open the door, then you can see me. It is a pleasure to talk, it clarifies my mind when you ask these questions. If you just agreed with me, I would just be a tape recorder saying the same thing, but when you ask why, how, and say you don't agree, then I have to think and reassess whether I am wrong, or whether you are wrong. Usually, it is you!'

'I envy your certainty.'

'If you don't have a sheet anchor, if your faith is not there at any level, you go mad. Your sheet anchor is your rationalism, you believe that by questioning you are capable of analysing all the knowledge of the world by yourself. The rational mind pays a heavy price emotionally because it has to live with all these imperfect situations all around, and the rational mind sees that solutions simply cannot be imposed at all times and all places. Sometimes there are no rational solutions.'

There was still one question I hadn't quite had the nerve to ask, about yogic flying. Up until now I had been in thrall to Narasimhan's wisdom, tolerance and common sense. What if he turned out to believe in yogic flying?

'Well, it's not really levitation,' he explained. 'It's a six-metre jump. Any gymnast can do it, but the difference is, a gymnast will get tired. A yogi's heart and breathing will be consistent, he won't get tired. That is the magic of it.'

How about mind reading? He had implied that he could read minds at our first session . . .

'I have learned that you should never tell people that you have powers. You will never do anything else but show them!'

This seemed a bit of a cop-out but I settled for it and got up to thank him again for his time and patience. Then something odd happened. As I was leaving, while I was shaking his hand, Narasimhan said, 'About those business cards you are having made. Where are you getting them done? I need some new ones and . . . '

'I, erm . . . ' How did he know I was getting some business cards made? I hadn't mentioned it to him, had I? I was quite sure I had not. But it was true. It had been on my mind to pick up the cards I had ordered from a friend of Aariz's at the market.

'Someone just outside the market,' I finally said, my mind whirring. 'I'll give you the address at tomorrow's class.'

35

Fitter, Stronger, More Reproductive

We were reaching the end of our time, not just in Mysore, but in India. We had been away for more than three months and Asger and Emil were struggling to recall details of our home and their rooms, Emil in particular. Surprisingly, though, they were far from desperate to return.

'But we are coming back next week, aren't we?' Emil asked me two nights before we left. I explained that it would be some time before that happened. Probably a little longer than next week. He was distraught.

'But I never found my monkey. What about Visala?' — the little girl across the hall.

I explained that we wouldn't be seeing her for a while. Emil fell silent. Asger was deeply put out that going home would entail a return to schoolwork which he had successfully side-stepped for much of the last fortnight, and quickly drew up a list of things he had to buy before going home (jewel-encrusted Sikh dagger; auto-rickshaw; a dozen Indian Kinder Eggs). Meanwhile, Lissen was already talking of returning to Mysore with a group of female friends for more yoga with Vinay and spent a day touring the city saying goodbye to her new network of friends.

I finished my TM introduction course during

our last few days in Mysore. I now had a technique which could accompany me anywhere in the world, and which I could use throughout my life to switch off, put the world on pause for a few minutes a day and settle my jumping-bean mind.

My yoga practice was not so straightforward. Though by the end of my fourth and last week of Prana Vashya yoga I was, to misquote Radiohead, 'Fitter, stronger, more reproductive', Vinay's asana sessions remained agony right up until the end. The temperature had been rising steadily during our month in Mysore and on the penultimate day I had literally begged Vinay to open a window. 'After,' he said, smiling his beatific smile.

I finished that second-to-last session in a zombified state, lobotomised by fatigue, merely pulling shapes, an asana mime. Vinay, noticing my plight, asked me, 'Do you feel any pain here?' pointing across his chest. Presumably he thought I was having cardiac arrest. If I had said yes, I might have been allowed a lie-down but for some reason I found I was incapable of lying to Vinay so I shook my head, and he pushed me on. Miraculously, I summoned the reserves to continue and forced my weary carcass up into the air for the penultimate asana, the 'upside-down crab'. This was the first — and, it will come as little surprise to you to hear, the last — time I achieved this. It stands to this day as the pinnacle of my modest yoga achievements. The headstand would, of course, have been a more satisfying denouement but that remains my great white whale, my nemesis, my Waterloo and . . . I'm not all that fussed, to tell you the truth. As Vinay said, yoga is not a competition and even if it is, you are only competing with yourself, right? That, as far as I am concerned, is the ultimate win-win.

At the end of the session, as I was lying on my back wrestling my heartbeat back to something close to normal, Vinay approached, bent down, lifted my head up slowly and slipped a rolled-up towel beneath it.

'Is your heart beating in your head?' he asked me quietly, as he gently placed my head back down on the towel. I nodded. It was such a tender gesture that I am afraid I began to cry. That may sound embarrassingly sentimental — and sentiment is the crippled cousin of emotion — but I was beyond embarrassment. I did at least manage to keep a lid on the heaving sobs which had mustered in my chest like steam beneath a kettle lid, but still the tears mingled with my sweat and ran in salty rivulets down my cheeks. When I got home, I bolted for the bathroom, locked the door and wept convulsively. But it was a good cry, a cathartic cry, a cry of satisfaction from having hauled my creaking body and my even more enfeebled psyche to the end of a course which, at one point, I genuinely feared might kill me.

The next day, when I left the shala after my last ever session, there was no ceremonial farewell, just a handshake with Vinay and garbled thanks on my part. I have a photograph from that moment (taken by Kim, so there is a bit of thumb obscuring one side of the shot) of me wearing just my old swimming shorts, standing in the changing room, drenched in sweat, beside Vinay. I look like death, frankly, as I always did at the end of a session, but Vinay's energy glows like a young sun. If I were prone to such New Age fancies, I'd almost say it was cosmic.

36

Release of the Rescue Animal

> Men seek retreat for themselves: houses in the country, at the seashore, in the mountains . . . But it is in our power, whenever we choose, to retreat into ourselves. For nowhere either with more quiet or freedom do we retreat than into our own minds . . . Tranquillity is nothing other than the proper ordering of the mind.
>
> Marcus Aurelius

Going to India to 'find yourself' is the oldest cliché in the book (though not this book obviously; you'll doubtless find loads more older clichés than that here). In my defence, I originally travelled to India with the more noble intention of finding a really great sarson ka saag recipe, but took a detour: a wrong turning which turned out right.

What I did find in India were some simple tools which have helped me to bring a little more balance, stillness, clarity and discipline to my life. (I also got the saag recipe but, naturally, now I am home, I am unable to source half the ingredients I need to make it.)

So, the nitty-gritty. I'll come to the point because if I were in your position I would want a really straight answer to this question: how, exactly, do a few stretches and sitting still for a bit make one feel more positive about one's life, curtail one's more harmful habits and make one a happier, better person?

Let's take the exercise bit first.

Definitions of what yoga practice actually is range from the purely devotional — praying, chanting — to the purely physical, such as those faddish yoga systems, like Bikram, which emerge every once in a while, usually in California, claiming to be the next big thing in fitness training, and invariably championed by a man with a ponytail and a publicist. In the midst of the devotional-physical spectrum there is Ashtanga and its derivatives (including Vinay's Prana Vashya), which instruct us that, by focusing on a physical regime of asanas we will, in time, also attain some form of spiritual awakening, enlightenment or transcendence, whether we seek it or not.

Personally, I am not actively seeking these things, nor, indeed, am I entirely convinced of their existence. Certainly, I am not seeking to connect with any universal energy fields or supernatural force. Mr Narasimhan was able to rationalise some of Hinduism's eclectic ritual, practice and belief for me, but as wise and eloquent as he is, he still did not convince me to make that all-important leap of blind faith towards having my own belief. And that's fine. I remain stubbornly, proudly, a resolutely unspiritual being and, in fact, I am more at ease with that position than I ever have been.

So why is it that, every day, after the kids have

left for school, before I have breakfast and get ready to face the day, I do twenty to thirty minutes of Vinay-style Prana Vashya yoga? Why, if not in the hope of one day attaining the dream of every yogi: moksha?

Though I can't say I especially enjoy it, and frequent oaths and curses can be heard coming from Emil's bedroom (much to his irritation, his is the only really suitable yoga room in our house, being both warm enough and carpeted) while I am working my way diligently through my asanas, my yoga has many tangible benefits which negate the need for that extra carrot of transcendent enlightenment. Firstly, it keeps me supple and flexible, at least more supple and flexible than I might otherwise be, and I believe that if I keep myself that bit more bendy I will be that bit more physically resilient as the years take their relentless toll. I no longer emit involuntary grunts when rising from squashy sofas, for instance. I no longer have to take a deep breath before putting my socks on every morning. During my short but relatively intense morning programme I build up a sweat which is satisfying; the deep breathing oxygenates my blood; and I am also willing to accept that these asanas help my nervous system function more effectively, keep my metabolism ticking over and massage my internal organs, though I have no scientific or medical data to support this. My own personal experience is simply that I feel fitter, springier and stronger.

And I have witnessed another interesting effect at work with these asanas. I have told myself that, for the rest of my life, these twenty to thirty minutes of exercise are the bare minimum that I must do, every day if possible; and they usually are possible, wherever I am in the world, even without a yoga mat, or the extra incentive of Emil standing, scowling with his arms folded in the doorway. I have done a deal with myself; actually, it's more than just a bargain: I have *convinced* myself that these daily exercises are essential for my continued healthy existence.

Part of the deal is that, if I do this every day, I need never feel guilty about the almost complete lack of any other physical activity in my life. That's not to say I have discarded all notions of other exercise (I do swim, walk and play tennis — real, not Wii — from time to time), just that the guilt has no purchase on my conscience here. As we saw in the early part of this story, self-discipline had never been one of my strong points but by demonstrating to myself that I have been able to keep this agreement, by doing my twenty minutes of proper, Vinay-approved stretches every single morning, I have proven to myself that I have discipline. My discipline has then become a self-fulfilling prophecy, if you like. By showing myself I possess the discipline, I possess the discipline. And by having the discipline, by demonstrating this solid, unwavering commitment, I am able to maintain that same discipline, not just in my morning's physical jerks but, crucially, in other areas of my life. I am now, demonstrably, A Disciplined Person.

That's the first element of how my experiences

in India have altered my life for the better. The second element is what I grandly call 'My Meditation Practice', which is nothing more than simply sitting still for twenty minutes once a day (twice, if possible), with my eyes closed, repeating a — still aggravating, but these days slightly more acceptable — mantra over and over to myself.

I am not naturally predisposed to evangelism but I do believe that meditation is something that could help almost everyone, believer and atheist alike. I am not necessarily advocating Transcendental Meditation; there are of course hundreds of different types of meditation, some of which I have since had a chance to experience.

A short while after we returned home, a magazine commissioned me to return to India to go on a six-day silent retreat at a kind of spiritual resort just outside Bangalore. The thought of not speaking for six days was both terrifying and intriguing, like the sex lives of Tory politicians. At my induction on arrival, the resort's head of research, Krishna Prakash, was at pains to warn me that my vow of silence might bring me to difficult places: 'When you are silent, all the sleeping demons come,' he said. 'Some people can't do it. They have too much to sort out.'

In fact, I found the experience to be complete bliss. Silence turned out to be the ultimate self-indulgence, turning those six days into a refreshing retreat from the world (needless to say, no TV nor alcohol were allowed at the resort). It was reassuring, too, that I was able to cope with living within my head for almost a week and that it didn't, as I had feared it might, lead to a breakdown. Indeed, so acclimatised did I become to contemplative muteness that when it was time to leave I felt like a rescue animal being released after a long period of convalescence. If I hadn't missed my family as much as I did, I don't think I would ever have wanted to leave my cage.

While at the retreat, as well as a rigorous twice-daily, two-hour Ashtanga asana practice, I tried out various other types of meditation, like sound meditation and candle meditation, the latter involving staring cross-eyed at a flickering candle for an hour until my retinas screamed for mercy. Neither were really for me, but I also tried Yoga Nidra, or 'sleep yoga', to which I became an instant, wholehearted convert. Aside from the obvious plus that you do it lying down, Yoga Nidra took me closer to what you might term 'transcendence' or, at least, another state of consciousness, neither sleeping nor awake — than any other form of meditation I have tried. It is like a psychic roller coaster — they call it a 'hypnagogic state' — from which I would venture back and forth, or up and down, or whatever the correct directional descriptor is, from sleep to being awake, never quite properly falling unconscious yet still from time to time completely closing off from what the instructor was saying. They say this is alpha brainwave-generated 'conscious dreaming', or 'super-consciousness'; I have no idea whether that is true, or what it really means, but I do know that Yoga Nidra is a deeply rewarding, reinvigorating form of meditation which, in an ideal world, I would practise a couple of times a day.

Sadly though, Yoga Nidra is simply not practical for me. I could never realistically bring myself to take two hours out of my day to lie down to gambol amid various states of being. It's just not going to happen. Apart from anything, I don't have the patience. Transcendental Meditation's bite-sized pauses from life, and the brief but meaningful moments of clarity they bring are, on the other hand, more manageable: twenty minutes I can do, particularly if I can do it while waiting for Asger and Emil to finish their karate class, or on the train, or sitting in a quiet corner of Heathrow Terminal 4, instead of heading for Garfunkel's and downing a dark goblet of Grenache.

An awful lot of what has been written about TM, the claims made for it by the Maharishi and his followers, the entertaining antics of the members of the Natural Law Party and so on, are to me largely beside the point. The profundity of the mantra selection, or 'passing', seems rather overstated (though clearly lucrative), for instance. In a few minutes online you ought to be able to rustle up a mantra that works for you. That said, I am a feeble-minded snob, so the fact that I received my mantra from a close disciple of the Maharishi in a small, dark room filled with Vedic scripts in a side street in Mysore has made me cherish it that bit more (and is surely the only reason I have persisted with the damn thing for so long).

For all I know — or care — the Maharishi

may have been a free-range charlatan; he may have been a venal sex pest who ran a masterful PR campaign over the course of his forty-year career to amass tremendous wealth and power (back in the sixties, he used to announce a new level of consciousness every year or so, like the Beatles launching an LP), or he may have been a pure and blameless astronaut of human consciousness. I don't think it matters terribly much, as long as TM works for you. And if it doesn't, then there is almost certainly another type of meditation that will, some with no fruitcakery whatsoever.

Critics say that TM is just a beginner's form of meditation, the quick and dirty way to transcend. This is also probably true, but there is independent scientific evidence — from un-biased sources — that TM reduces hypertension, depression, anger, anxiety issues and neuroses, while increasing levels of concentration and helping people conquer addiction. And what I do know for sure is that my TM practice works for me. It is convenient, easy and effective; I don't need to go to a special class to do it, I don't need to put on a CD, or light a joss stick, or spend an hour focusing on different parts of my body in turn. I can do it anywhere and at any time, as long as I am not operating heavy plant machinery.

So, if we set aside talk of transcendence, yogic flying and Universal Fields of Pure Being, my meditation does nothing much more than relax me. I switch off, turn within, recharge. It makes me feel calm yet energised; I am relaxed, but aware. Have you ever opened a computer file to find that the font size is, for some reason, massively too large, with all the letters elbowing in front of each other like an angry crowd? For me, meditation turns my world back into 12 point, frees up white space around the text and makes life that bit more clear and manageable. Sometimes during meditation I skirt the realm of dreams. I have had powerful, if brief, waking dreams while meditating, or seen striking images and scenes; occasionally, too, my head begins to loll towards sleep proper, but the mantra always pulls me back to awareness and I find it quietly thrilling to be able to toy with, or control, my consciousness like this. Am I transcending? Who knows? Am I seeking 'God consciousness' or 'unity consciousness'? No, because I don't believe for a minute that they exist (although that doesn't stop me sometimes trying to reach for them in the midst of my meditation in much the same way that I tried to use The Force as an eight-year-old after seeing *Star Wars*; then again, I am easily led when it comes to superstitious mumbo-jumbo, as we saw with the curse of the ritzy-turbaned fortune teller).

So, my asana practice makes me feel disciplined, therefore I am disciplined. It also keeps me flexible, moderately fitter than I might otherwise have been, and has helped me keep the weight off since India. Meanwhile, meditation is like Listerine for my mind. It freshens and relaxes me, brings clarity. But do yoga and meditation make me happy in the grander scheme of things?

I have come to the conclusion that there is no point in looking for happiness; certainly there is no point in dragging your family to the other side of the world to search for it in a bunch of temples and churches. That way lie disappointment and regrettable clothing decisions, many of them tie-dyed. Happiness is transient, ephemeral, ungraspable. You can't will it into your life, capture it, or make it manifest by prayer, despite what the self-help books tell us. And, of course, you cannot be happy without being unhappy for some of the time. It's the law.

A while ago, the *New York Times*, the planet's newspaper of record, set out to quantify the essential criteria for happiness. These were, the journalist concluded, the following:

Be in possession of the basics — food, shelter, good health, safety.
Get enough sleep.
Have relationships that matter to you.
Take compassionate care of others and of yourself
Have work or an interest that engages you.

Now, far be it from me to argue with such an august institution as the *New York Times*, with its battalion of fact checkers and patrician insistence on the use of honorifics, but I think that these are just some of the fundamental elements you need in your life in order merely to *prepare* for the *possible* eventuality of *fleeting* happiness.

J.D. Salinger once famously described happiness as being something solid, compared to joy which he said was a liquid and more difficult to keep hold of. I'm not sure that's true for me. I see joy as a gas; joy truly is fleeting and ephemeral. Happiness is the liquid — you can hold on to it, but not for long. So what, then, are the solids of life? Equanimity, peace, clarity, awareness, equilibrium — these are the foundations which I believe you *can* consciously create in your life and develop so that, when happiness does come rivering by, you'll have your bucket ready.

Part of that preparedness has, for me, involved confronting several of my less edifying habits — primarily the drinking, because it holds the key to many of the others: the neuroses, the temper, the relentlessly negative outlook, and so on. In truth, since that dark and shit-faced night in Mysore, I haven't done all that much confronting of alcohol. Through the lack of any other quantifiable explanation for what has happened, I am afraid I am forced to stray into quasi-mystical territory here: but my craving for alcohol has simply subsided. I can now squeak a cork back into a still half-full bottle of wine; I can stop after a couple of glasses; I no longer feel the overpowering compulsion to drink myself into oblivion every single evening; and I drink fewer units of alcohol each week than the number judged safe by my government. This is something of a miracle, or would be if I believed in miracles. Part of the explanation, I think, is the self-fulfilling discipline I spoke of earlier; I have managed to turn myself into a disciplined person, and disciplined people can stop at three glasses of wine. But the truth is, that deep craving to escape has mostly vanished. I still drink, and I still enjoy drinking (these days strictly wine only), but I no longer drink to numb myself. Blotto is no longer my goal, and that has a great deal to do with the equanimity which my yoga and meditation practice have brought me. Magically, for that is the only word I can think of, I don't feel quite so anxious, quite so fearful as I once did, and the only real explanation I have for this is the techniques I learned in India and their continued implementation in and impact on my daily life.

My new-found equanimity — a very Indian word, equanimity; it is one of the 'four immeasureables', or virtues, of Buddhism, together with joy, love and compassion and plays a central role in the teachings of the Bhagavad Gita and Patanjali — appears to have infiltrated and neutralised several problematic areas of my life. By equanimity, I don't mean simply not giving a damn about anything or withdrawing from life, but a mild stoicism in which you try to remain immune to external forces, to protect yourself from those slings and arrows, while never relinquishing control or responsibility for your life. Actually, it is Asger and Emil's admirably even-keeled response to their experiences in India that have provided me with my equanimity role models. They seemed able to soak up everything that country could throw at them: engaged and alert to it all but admirably unfazed at the same time. I think I am more positive and accepting now, less taut and fretful. My concentration is vastly improved (I have banished Twitter links from my Bookmarks folder, which also helped); I'm not quite as neurotic as I used to be; and my temper has calmed. I don't get so upset if someone cuts me up in traffic, to give one particularly mundane example: at last I have come to properly understand that such incidents are not personal. And I now realise that my printer does not hate me and is not trying to push me to the brink of a breakdown. In other words, I have come — belatedly, I realise — to the conclusion that *it's not all about me*: some drivers are imbeciles, and mine is a shit printer. This, of course, is as much to do with ego as with acceptance of the world or the adoption of any ancient Greek philosophy. Paradoxically, by withdrawing during meditation, by directing my focus within, I seem to have reined in my rampant ego. By focusing on my self, that self has become less strident and shouty.

And finally, to India. As I have said, it is not necessary — nor even desirable — to travel to India to sort out your problems. Lord knows, they have enough of their own without a bunch of messed-up foreigners adding to the pile. But, the one thing India can do is to put things into perspective. As Sathnam Sanghera writes in his book, *The Boy with the Topknot*: 'In India, you need only glance out of your window to feel grateful for your lot.'

I defy anyone to spend any time in India and not return home considerably more grateful to have running water, a roof over their head and broadly adhered-to traffic regulations. And if India doesn't make you appreciate these things then, frankly, you don't deserve them.

I used to spend a disproportionate amount of my time dwelling on the 5 or so per cent of the human primate population who were wealthier, more successful and more acclaimed, than me — I was always 'comparing-up', if you like, when it would have been far more helpful, not to mention more representative of reality, to appreciate what I had compared to the other 95 per cent of the world who have less. A.C. Grayling once wrote, 'One route to happiness is to stop peering over the fence at the Joneses.' Take a look over the fence, instead, at how the Guptas, the Kumars and the Patels are living, at their houses made from fruit packaging, their open sewers and their littered gardens. And when you have seen children working on building sites, or virtually naked, living up to their ankles in filth, or pushing an ice-cream cart past your house every day trying to earn a few rupees; and when you have witnessed all this together with your own children, the sense of relief that you don't have to watch them endure something similar is unbounded.

With the Western economy having disappeared into an abyss of debt, many of us are now waking up to the fact that we did have enough of everything after all; that we don't need a 3D TV, a 4G iPhone, or a rhinestone-studded Dolce and Gabbana jumpsuit to make our lives complete; that simply having sufficient of everything will do fine. Rather than always stretching towards greater excess, many of us are having to learn to make do and to find our fulfilment without a credit card in our hand. This, in turn, leads us to that beloved 'mindfulness' trope that we must all learn 'to appreciate the small things'. Well, it may be a cliché, but I genuinely find that these days I have a whole new appreciation of how great a really nice cup of tea can be, or of the fact that our bathroom is warm in the morning, or of those increasingly rare moments — soon, tragically, I suspect gone for ever — when one of my sons silently reaches for my hand while we are out walking, and I squeeze it tightly, and he squeezes back, and my heart nearly bursts.

I still wouldn't *mind* having a Maserati or a second home in Provence, and there is no question that I would look peachy in that jumpsuit, it's just that now I can probably live with the thought that these things might not feature in my life.

Paul Brunton wrote, 'The white tourist who 'does' the chief cities and historical sights and then steams away with disgust at the backward civilization of India is doubtless justified in his deprecation of it. Yet a wiser kind of tourist shall one day arise who will seek out, not the crumbling ruins of useless temples, nor the marbled palaces of dissipated kings long dead, but the living sages who can reveal a wisdom untaught by our universities.'

I don't claim to be that 'wiser kind of tourist' — and I am certainly guilty of a good deal of steaming disgust at India, not all of it unjustified — but I was fortunate to have a wife who was, and who nudged me towards asking a few pertinent questions about my behaviour, my beliefs and my life.

Thank you very much . . .

To Vinay Kumar, whose spiritual strength, compassion and wisdom I greatly envy, and who quite possibly saved my life or at the very least helped me make some significant adjustments to its trajectory. He doesn't claim to be in the life saving business, of course, he is far too modest for that but he does run a ship-shape yoga shala about which you can read here: www.pranavashya.com

To Mr M.A. Narasimhan, a great scholar with whom I consider it one of the great privileges of my life to have spent time. He doesn't have a website, or any reliable contact details, I'm afraid. He's like the A-Team — if you have a problem, if no one else can help, and if you can find him, maybe he'll talk to you.

To my publisher Dan Franklin at Jonathan Cape, whose support I hope one day to repay with actual book sales, and to Tom Avery, also at Cape, for all his help with this book and previous ones.

To my previous agent, Camilla Hornby, and my current one, Kirsty McLachlan at David Godwin Associates, for their advice and encouragement.

The cover of this book was designed by the very patient and tolerant Matt Broughton at Random House, from an original idea by the genius that is Peter Stenbæk.

And thank you to our good friend Dorte Juul without whom Lissen would never have heard about Vinay, and to Suzy 'The Big Leap' Greaves, the only self-help guru worth a dime whose friendship and wisdom I value more than I sometimes let on.

To Asger and Emil: I realise you didn't really know what you were getting into with all this India business, but hope you don't judge me too harshly if you ever get around to reading this. It was the greatest of joys having you two along for the ride.

And, of course, to Lissen. You do tend to be right about almost everything in the end. As always, thanks.

Other thanks

Although we did end up paying for pretty much all of the trip (not for want of trying on my part, I can assure you), we did have some help with arranging some of the logistics of the first couple of months and in the shameless blagging of some nights' accommodation which we might otherwise never even have had a sniff of being able to afford. For this I must thank Cox and Kings, in particular Roop Kumar (www.coxandkings.com); and Yasin Zargar at Indus Tours (www.indus.co.uk). Both are excellent companies if you are planning a trip to the subcontinent, I might add.

If you are looking for a Keralan idyl, we can thoroughly recommend Philipkutty (www.philip-kuttysfarm.com) — thank you to Anu and her very special family for their kind hospitality

— or, if it is a resort you are after, the Lalit Bekal (www.thelalit.com) is lovely too, although there are probably a few more people there these days.

In Delhi, the Park Hotel is nice (www.the-parkhotel.com — they have a few around India), and, of course, if you have the money — and I am not saying you don't — there is simply no more splendid way to see India than to stay at the many Taj hotels dotted about the place (www.tajhotels.com). In particular special thanks go to the extraordinary Umaid Bhawan Palace and its impeccable staff, among them J.S. Bhatnagar, the incomparable executive chef. Thank you also of course to chef Hemant Oberoi.

A good travel company for Kochi (Cochin) is Marvel Tours who you can contact at gopucok@marveltour.net.

If you are looking for a long term place to stay in Mysore, I suggest you contact www.mulberrybay.in.

The silent retreat place I visited was Shreyas (www.shreyasretreat.com). Frankly, I can't think of anyone who wouldn't benefit from spending time there.

I would like to thank my fellow students at the yoga shala — and apologise for the disruption I must have caused with all my histrionics — and finally, say thank you to all the Indians who we met along the way and who made our trip so enjoyable and memorable — most notably to Vinod Kumar and our various guides and drivers; to Rahul Verma, Sourish Battacharya and Bakshish Dean; and to Nita and Badri, Suraj and Devaki.

We do hope that you have enjoyed reading
this large print book.

Did you know that all of our titles
are available for purchase?

We publish a wide range of high quality
large print books including:
Romances, Mysteries, Classics
General Fiction
Non Fiction and Westerns

Special interest titles available in
large print are:
The Little Oxford Dictionary
Music Book
Song Book
Hymn Book
Service Book

Also available from us courtesy of
Oxford University Press:
Young Readers' Dictionary
(large print edition)
Young Readers' Thesaurus
(large print edition)

For further information or a free
brochure, please contact us at:
Ulverscroft Large Print Books Ltd.,
The Green, Bradgate Road, Anstey,
Leicester, LE7 7FU, England.
Tel: (00 44) **0116 236 4325**
Fax: (00 44) **0116 234 0205**

Other titles published by
The House of Ulverscroft:

ALL TEACHERS GREAT AND SMALL

Andy Seed

Twenty-five years ago, newly qualified teacher Andy Seed and his wife Barbara moved to a remote village in the picturesque Yorkshire Dales. There, they anticipated a daily round of gentle simplicity in the countryside. However, whilst Andy fell in love with teaching and living in a village, life as a primary school teacher was anything but simple . . . *All Teachers Great and Small* tells the true story of Andy's first year at Cragthwaite Primary School — how he bravely negotiated the vagaries of the local dialect, made disastrous bids to provide a family home, naively and hilariously tried out newfangled ideas in a school stuck in a 1950s time warp, and ultimately discovered a little part of England he was proud to call home.

ENGAGE

Paul Kimmage

On a cold Tuesday morning in March 2005, the cream of young English rugby gathered in Northampton. Matt Hampson was one of them. He had dreamt of playing rugby for England ever since he had picked up a rugby ball. He was playing in an England Under 21 team that included James Haskell and Toby Flood. But during the training session that morning, as the forwards engaged, the scrum collapsed and Matt took the full force of the blow. He woke up in an intensive care unit, paralysed from the neck down and dependent on a ventilator to breathe. In *Engage*, award-winning journalist Paul Kimmage combines with Matt to tell this uplifting true story about one man's strength and determination to overcome the odds.

LOST IN SHANGRI-LA

Mitchell Zuckoff

Just before the end of the Second World War, a US Army transport plane flying over New Guinea's hidden Baliem valley crashed into uncharted mountains. Somehow, three of the twenty-four passengers and crew survived the crash: Lt. John McCollom, Sgt. Kenneth Decker, and Cpl. Margaret Hastings. Hurt, and afraid, they prayed for deliverance — from their wounds and from the spear-carrying Dani tribesmen who roamed the mountains, a people untouched by the modern world. For seven weeks they experienced many adventures in this isolated paradise, relying on each other's courage and the kindness of the world's most remote tribes. Until their rescue came in an incredible glider mission.

MADELEINE

Kate McCann

'The decision to publish this book has been very difficult, and taken with heavy hearts . . . My reason for writing it is simple: to give an account of the truth . . . Writing this memoir has entailed recording some very personal, intimate and emotional aspects of our lives. As with every action we have taken over the last four years, it ultimately boils down to whether what we are doing could help us to find Madeleine. When the answer to that question is yes, or even possibly, our family can cope with anything . . . What follows is an intensely personal account, and I make no apology for that . . . Nothing is more important to us than finding our little girl.'

OUR QUEEN

Robert Hardman

She has travelled further and lived longer than any of her predecessors. She has known more historic figures than anyone alive — from Churchill to Mandela, de Gaulle to Obama. Queen Elizabeth II is one of the most popular public figures on Earth. In Robert Hardman's portrayal of our Queen he travels around the world with her and meets her family, as she marks sixty years on the throne. Elizabeth II has reigned through Britain's transformation from an imperial power to a multicultural, multimedia nation. Our Queen sits at the head of an ancient institution, which remains — simultaneously — popular, regal, inclusive and relevant. This is purely down to the shrewd judgement of a thoroughly modern monarch with no small assistance from the longest-serving consort in history.

MY BOY BUTCH

Jenni Murray

As a much-loved and respected presenter of BBC's *Woman's Hour*, Jenni Murray has been a source of comfort and inspiration for generations of women. But when Jenni was diagnosed with breast cancer, her world fell apart. She survived surgery, but the gruelling chemotherapy took its toll, leaving Jenni with a crippling bone disease. In constant pain and bound by a prison of disability, it was her Chihuahua, Butch, who gave Jenni the strength to rebuild herself. Jenni recounts the formation of this extraordinary bond. Butch became Jenni's 'little shadow', her closest companion, constantly devoted to her, making her life worth living again. Jenni describes how a life can be changed by love, and how Chihuahuas, the smallest of dogs, have the biggest of hearts.